BUILDINGS REBORN: new uses, old places

BUILDINGS REBORN

Barbaralee Diamonstein

Preface by Congressman JOHN BRADEMAS

new uses, old places

HARPER & ROW, Publishers

New York   Hagerstown   San Francisco   London

FIRST EDITION

ISBN: 0-06-011068-6
LIBRARY OF CONGRESS CATALOG CARD NUMBER 78-2134

78 79 80 81 82 10 9 8 7 6 5 4 3 2 1

for Pamela, Peter, Tommy, and Tim

CONTENTS

Preface: JOHN BRADEMAS

"IN ITS LAND and in its history," President Carter told Congress, in a May 23, 1977, message on protection of the environment, "a nation finds the things which give it continuity. By preserving places that have special natural, historic, and scientific value, we can insure that our children and grandchildren have a chance to know something of the America that we—and our ancestors—simply took for granted." Eight months later, the president announced the establishment of a "National Heritage Program" that represents a watershed in the historic preservation movement in the United States.

The new program is no isolated phenomenon. In 1976 the National Advisory Council on Historic Preservation prepared, for the Senate Committee on Interior and Insular Affairs, a report, *The National Historic Preservation Program Today*, which foreshadowed much of the analysis and policies contained in the president's National Heritage Program. Late in 1977 representatives of a number of nonfederal organizations met under the auspices of the Conservation Foundation to review the national heritage proposal and gave their recommendations to the president. And the principal purpose of the 1978 annual meeting of the National Trust for Historic Preservation was the first major evaluation by the trust of the historic preservation movement. All these developments mark a turning point in the preservation movement in this country and make the appearance of Barbaralee Diamonstein's book most timely.

The title of Ms. Diamonstein's book, *Buildings Reborn*, catches the redemptive quality associated with a religious commitment and translates that quality into an attitude that she believes crucial to what we do, or fail to do, about our built environment. For the sites and structures of earlier times are incarnations, often irreplaceable, of the American heritage. They teach us of our traditions. They embody the continuity of our culture. When we thoughtlessly obliterate the buildings and places of our past, we demonstrate an insensitivity to what we were, a disdain for what we in part still are. By saving—and adapting to re-use—the best of our old buildings, we link the communities of today to the foundations of our culture.

As our towns and cities grow and our commercial, industrial, and residential areas expand, the task of safeguarding our national heritage becomes more difficult. We often meet the demands for more living and working space by tearing down existing structures, frequently erecting new ones on the same site. But we need not always, in responding to the requirements of the present and future, destroy the old. Wise preservation can renew the integrity and utility of a structure and re-establish a place for it in the life of a community.

Examples of this regenerative process are many and are multiplying. Faneuil Hall, the meeting place of revolutionaries in Colonial Boston, and the adjacent 19th-century Quincy Market are now the center of a thriving commercial area. The Union Depot in Duluth, Minnesota, built in 1892, was one of the finest American examples of Norman architecture. It fell into disuse as a railroad station and was scheduled to be demolished, but now houses a museum, a theater, and business offices for performing arts organizations. Ghirardelli Square in San Francisco, once a chocolate factory, now teems with visitors to its shops and restaurants. Boston's Chickering Piano Factory today provides studios and housing for artists and craftsmen. In downtown Richmond, Virginia, the 19th-century Blues Armory has been renovated as a 750-seat theater with commercial facilities. One could cite a long list of fine old structures being saved, not solely as ornaments, but as spaces that retain their original scale and beauty while being adapted to modern use.

As a legislator, I must note that the interest of Congress in protecting and preserving places of historic importance reaches back to the start of the century, a considerable time in the life of a nation so young. The Antiquities Act of 1906 authorized the president to proclaim as national monuments buildings and landmarks on federal property. With the creation of the National Park Service in 1916, the secretary of the interior was authorized to provide for the preservation and restoration of historic properties of national significance. It was not, however, until 1949 that Congress chartered the National Trust for Historic Preservation, a nongovernmental organization devoted to the preservation of such properties, both public and private.

Nearly a generation later, in 1966, Congress passed the National Historic Preservation Act, landmark legislation that significantly expanded the federal commitment in this area. The law established the National Advisory Council on Historic Preservation to encourage a more vigorous national program for saving our heritage of structures and sites. The legislation requires the secretary of the interior to maintain a register of historic properties and provides federal matching grants to the states to assist their preservation efforts.

More recently, congressional concern with historic preservation was reflected in the approval in just one year—1976—of three important measures. The 1976 amendments to the Land and Water Conservation Fund Act expand the scope of the National Historic Preservation Act to include a historic preservation fund. With monies derived from offshore oil revenues, the fund can now provide greater federal assistance to states and communities for preservation activities. The Tax Reform Act of 1976 includes provisions designed to remove the tax code bias against historic preservation. One new feature prohibits taking a tax deduction for the cost of demolishing historic structures, thereby removing an important stumbling block in the way of preservation efforts. The same law also permits a faster tax writeoff of expenses incurred in restoring commercial property of historic worth. A third measure, the Public Buildings Cooperative Act, requires that before constructing new federal facilities, federal agencies consider the adaptive use of space in historic buildings.

Members of Congress have introduced scores of bills of interest to preservationists. These proposals range from acquisition of the Susan B. Anthony house in Adams, Massachusetts, as a national historic site to a bill extending the time within which tax deductions may be taken for the value of buildings donated for historic preservation. Congressman Frank Thompson of New Jersey has sponsored a measure to help communities convert architecturally significant but abandoned railroad depots into theaters, museums, libraries, or other cultural centers. Legislation was recently introduced to adapt the famous old Pension Building in Washington, D.C.—the scene, in its grand court, of seven presidential inaugural balls—for use as a national museum of the building arts.

Responding to President Carter's Environmental Message of 1977, Secretary of the Interior Cecil Andrus and a task force developed a proposal that embodies the principal features of the National Heritage Program. The program would provide for the first time a focal point for efforts to protect the cultural and natural legacy of the nation. A single agency within the department of the interior will coordinate all federal programs that affect national heritage sites and will encourage preservation efforts at state and local levels. The new agency, working closely with the states, will undertake a comprehensive inventory of heritage resources of national significance and develop criteria by which state agencies can document important regional resources. The resources listed, both national and regional, will be protected through laws and regulations aimed at minimizing destruction or impairment and through policies designed to promote their preservation and adaptive re-use.

So Barbaralee Diamonstein's book, to repeat, could not have come at a more propitious time. Ms. Diamonstein, moreover, is splendidly qualified to write such a study. Her interests, experience, and education are extraordinarily diverse, encompassing the arts, politics, journalism, and social reform, and her illuminating analysis reflects her remarkable range of concerns. This book, I am confident, will inspire many Americans to adapt the best in the buildings of our past to the service of our needs of today and of tomorrow.

A CENTURY AGO John Ruskin said of architecture: "We may live without her, and worship without her, but we cannot remember without her." Our built environment is the most tangible record we possess, the most palpable proof of civilization's continuous evolution. That, surely, helps explain the enormous impact of the concept of historic preservation the last 15 years or so.

As recently as the early 1960s, preservation was an esoteric concern, the subject of low-key letter-writing campaigns, polite protest meetings, and little more. Today this mild-mannered movement, this gentle ocean swell is more like a *tsunami*, a scale-7 earthquake rather than a soft subterranean tremor. Scarcely a major city in the United States has not been touched—in some cases almost completely transformed—by the preservation movement. In countless smaller cities and towns and villages as well, the impulse to save the gabled old house on Main Street from deterioration or the Beaux-Arts rail terminal from the wrecker's ball is manifest. The point of the effort is nothing less than to preserve our past, to provide an anchor for our collective memory. As the architect Giorgio Cavaglieri writes: "Buildings and their grouping and assemblage are more than the shelter of our activities; they represent us beyond our life, they interpret us to posterity and they illustrate our past to us. It is in this context that the preservation of examples from the past acquires enormous importance in a culture."

Preservation does not, and emphatically should not, mean merely restoration. Probably the single most important aspect of the preservation movement is the recycling of old buildings—adapting them to uses different from the ones for which they were originally intended. This phenomenon goes under myriad names, not all of them entirely apt: renovation, rehabilitation, remodeling, recycling, retrofitting, environmental retrieval, extended use, adaptive re-use (possibly the most precise term of all, though not exactly euphonious). Successful revitalization demonstrates that the forms and materials devised in the past are still valid when properly adapted to the functions of today's life. Interest in preservation has increased nationally in large measure by way of recycling—a practical means of preservation availa-ble to the smallest town, the most modest commercial enterprise. The approach, moreover, may involve the conversion of a girdle factory into an early education center, as has been done in Pittsburgh; a Federal-period house into an Off-Track Betting parlor, as in New York City; a torpedo factory into an arts center, as in Alexandria, Virginia; a tannery into a 284-unit apartment complex, as in Peabody, Massachusetts; a grammar school into senior citizens' housing, as in Boston.

Its impact can and often does reach far beyond the individual building or complex of buildings involved, to affect a neighborhood, a district, an entire city. Ada Louise Huxtable, the architecture critic of *The New York Times*, writes in her *Classic New York*: "A city, in its most real sense, is its buildings. Whatever the life, spirit, activity, or achievements of the city may be, they are expressed in the mass of asphalt, brick, stone, marble, steel, and glass that has accumulated during the city's existence."

By continually recycling this accumulation of masonry and metal, we do more than keep hard-hats occupied and preservationists happy. The New York Landmarks Preservation Commission, then in its tenth year, issued a statement on the occasion of National Preservation Week in 1975, putting it this way: "Creative adaptation provides pride in our heritage, a link with the past, respect for the aesthetics and craftsmanship of another time, insights into our development, ample creative opportunity for architectural innovation and problem-solving, enhancement of the urban fabric, greater security, stability and beauty, while conserving basic materials and meeting modern needs." The projects described in this book provide examples of how structures from other eras have been rescued from destruction and put to uses never contemplated by their original architects or designers. Some buildings have had extensive design changes, others minor ones. Some are brilliant representatives of their styles and periods; others are quite ordinary. I've tried to include examples of each, for, as Michael Middleton, director of Britain's Civic Trust, observes: "A town is more than a collection of important buildings. Preserving a limited number of outstanding buildings, while failing to retain and enhance the more modest streets and

Metalwork detail, Boston. Photo: © Robert Perron.

14 space that form their proper setting, has been likened to keeping the cherries out of the cake and throwing the cake away."

This book is only in part about lintels and mullions. It is surely not about old homes that have been nicely preserved as museums or as stops on the Wednesday house tour. It is about buildings that have been kept alive by consciously changing their roles.

From Seattle to Savannah, from Mobile to Minneapolis, from Biloxi to Brooklyn, I have gone to look at such buildings—most, though not all, of the ones included here. Equally important, I have talked to people—city officials, shopkeepers, housewives, citizens concerned about their communities. Regardless of the size of the city, "adaptive re-use" proved widespread. What does all this mean? It represents a new wave in architecture, yes. But, further, it is a significant social phenomenon in its own right, one that reveals a great deal about our country and about our attitude toward our resources and ourselves. It is a part of, rather than a symptom of, a more widespread social revolution occurring in the United States.

From an original list of thousands of projects (all of them in the United States), I chose what I considered to be the 207 best examples. Next I winnowed that list down to the final 95 that you see here. Making the final selection was no easy task. Among the quite literally thousands of examples and photographs to choose among, hundreds would be considered first-rate. Some outstanding projects were omitted: the New London, Connecticut, Railroad Station; the Chickering Piano Factory in Boston; the Cannery in San Francisco. A number—perhaps a third of the total—are projects that have been well-publicized elsewhere, like San Francisco's Ghirardelli Square, Butler Square in Minneapolis, the Jefferson Market Library in New York City. Why repeat them? Because they are *so* outstanding, because they have stood the test of time, because they are such important illustrations of various facets of the movement.

What were my general criteria for the final 95? One yardstick, of course, was the quality of the architecture. Another was whether the adaption was sympathetic to the original building, to its new use, and to the community of buildings around it. I also tried to include a diversity of categories—places to live in, work in, shop in, play in; some of the projects combined all those uses. In the end, though, such a choice must be somewhat arbitrary, for this book is designed to be representative, not definitive. As for the photographs included, they were contributed by the architects, designers, and developers of the projects shown here. Some were "homemade," taken by the proud inhabitant of a newly recycled landmark.

Some were made by the best architectural photographers in the business. Many of the "before" shots, taken prior to the renovation work, are, like the buildings they show, very old. All, I think, were taken with the special feeling that people sometimes develop for the buildings in which they spend their lives.

We are no longer a young country; the Bicentennial made that clear to us. Nor are we a naïve or innocent country any longer; Viet Nam and Watergate convinced us of that. We are, rather, a country that is moving uneasily—kicking and squirming, sometimes—toward a more reflective and perhaps more graceful way of life in our middle age than we had in our rebellious infancy and riproaring youth. This has led us to a number of new approaches: an appreciation of the conservation ethic, a respect for the handmade object, an awareness of our historic past, a realization that new need not mean better. All of this, together with our susceptibility to nostalgia, has gone into the making of the recycling phenomenon.

John Morris Dixon, editor of *Progressive Architecture* magazine, remarks: "This re-use and reworking of architecture is historically normal; failing to do so was aberrant." Yet what makes the whole phenomenon so fascinating is that it represents a veritable revolution in American attitudes, a reversal of the pioneer ethos, what Walt Whitman called "the pull-down-and-build-over-again spirit," of the United States. Change meant progress, progress meant newness, and newness meant throwing out what was old—including the built world. The frontier had much to do with this. Out West, a Main Street would be built between breakfast and dinner and a whole town would sprout overnight at the sites of the great gold and silver and copper strikes, and what could go up in practically no time could come down just as quickly.

This attitude was also a product both of 20th-century technology and of the reductionist philosophy of modern architecture founded on the notion that old forms must be swept away to accommodate new functions. Yet today, says urban designer Jonathan Barnett, "adaptive re-use of old buildings is also a form of architectural criticism; people reject many of the new buildings they see, preferring what they have to what they expect to get instead." In the same vein, one rarely hears any more of a "remodeled" apartment or house. Why? Because the word connotes the junking of the old. More and more, people seem to prefer what the past had to offer in the way of handcrafts, custom design of hardware and moldings, attention to details (newness still prevails, though, when it comes to choosing appliances). Ornamentation, decreed a crime by modernists, is no longer taboo but desirable, a relief from the glass-and-steel grid that epitomizes modernism. If you doubt the significance of this trend, if you question whether people really do feel this need for embellishment in their surroundings, talk to a rental agent. They tell me that the reference to a "landmark building" in an ad is the ultimate lure.

Villard Houses, detail. Photo: Steven Zane, courtesy H.A.B.S., Library of Congress

In Europe, of course, this attitude has prevailed for some time. Pierre Schneider, the Parisian art critic, cites Rome as the supreme example of a city where this ongoing process of renewal by conversion has succeeded. "The whole city is—or rather was until a very recent date—the scene of a permanent and ubiquitous process of architectural and urbanistic readjustments, adjunctions, subtractions which, while causing the despair of the archeological purists, have been the prime factor in keeping the city present, in endowing it with a magic one never encounters in the mummified historical monument." As early as 1630, Sweden's King Gustavus Adolphus, the fabled "Lion of the North," appointed a director of antiquities to inventory and protect the country's cultural and architectural patrimony, and France's King Louis Philippe did the same two centuries later. One of the Frenchmen who held the post created by Louis, Eugène Emmanuel Viollet-le-Duc, became perhaps the most famous restorer of all time, returning to their early glory the cathedrals of Amiens, Laon, Notre Dame, the walled city of Carcassonne, the Chateau de Pierrefonds.

Many of the Continent's great cities were very nearly destroyed in World War II, yet, when the time came to rebuild, there was seldom thought of starting from scratch. Instead, the historic cores of London, Warsaw, Prague, and Leningrad were restored or rebuilt pretty much as they had been.

This was not done out of any simplistic reverence for the old but, as Professor James Marston Fitch of Columbia University, the "father" of professional training in historic preservation, concludes, out of a realization that familiarity makes for livability and comfort, that too concentrated a dose of the new may leave people feeling uprooted and disoriented, that a proper balance must be struck between conservation and new development. New solutions have often resulted in unanticipated problems, whereas traditional solutions have been adapted and perfected over centuries. In *New Uses for Old Buildings*, Sherban Cantacuzino, executive editor of the English magazine *Architectural Review*, notes: "Because their structure tends to outlive their function, buildings have continuously been adapted to new uses—a fact which has enabled generation after generation to derive a sense of continuity and stability from their physical surroundings." These new uses, he points out, "tended to 'happen' quite casually. The Victorian Gothic cotton exchange at Preston, for example, is now a cinema, while the corn exchange at Banbury conceals a public house behind its grandiose Neoclassical facade."

Plainly, Europe has had what Yale art historian Vincent Scully calls a sense of "urban architecture as representing communication across generations over time." It took a while for a similar sense to ripen in the United States. Philadelphia's Independence Hall, cradle of the nation, narrowly escaped demolition in 1813. In 1850, when New York State purchased Hasbrouck House in Newburgh, site of George Washington's headquarters for the last two years of the War of Independence, Governor Hamilton Fish had to head off criticism for his rash extravagance saying, "There are associations connected with this venerable edifice which rise above the consideration of dollars and cents."

Much of what remains of our architectural heritage, however, is not the result of careful planning but of accident. According to Grady Clay, editor of *Landscape Architecture* magazine, the great impulses for preserving our patrimony were "poverty, plutocracy, and privacy." Poverty figured strongly in places like Savannah, Georgia, and Charleston and Beaufort, South Carolina, where nobody had the money after the Civil War either to fix up the buildings that survived or to tear them down. Plutocracy built the great "cottages" of Newport, Rhode Island, Bar Harbor, Maine, Tuxedo Park, New York, and other gilded playgrounds. Perhaps the greatest factor was privacy—in the sense that whole neighborhoods, villages, and towns were isolated from, or bypassed by, the steamroller of industrialization and modernization. These places, writes Clay, "are everywhere: the great clusters of stone house-barn-outbuildings-fences scattered along the U.S. 40 axis of central Kansas; the gingerbread carpenter's Gothic of bypassed Victorian districts from San Francisco to Macon, Georgia; the slowly disintegrating mountain villages of ancient Mexican and Indian cultures within a day's drive of Santa Fe, New Mexico; the towering and echoing blocks of semi-abandoned commercial buildings in Lower Manhattan."

This has left a residue of old buildings in towns and cities all over the country, some worthy and some not. There is a certain homogeneity to the built environment in the United States—partly a result of generic problems that occur in widely scattered localities and are dealt with in similar ways; partly a result of our penchant for standardization; partly as a result of our chain-store economy. Thus, practically every community has not only its MacDonald's, its Pizza Hut, and its adult book store but also its newly designated historic district filled with recycling projects. And practically every community has its share of redundant buildings often with no policy for dealing with them.

The first official federal recognition that, even in so raw and new a land as the United States, there was much more worth saving, came with the Antiquities Act of 1906. In 1916 the National Park Service was created and intended especially to preserve prehistoric sites and artifacts in the West. Congress proclaimed "a national policy to preserve for public use historic sites, buildings, and objects of national significance." Unfortunately, while that was the national policy, it was by no means the national practice.

Aware that its earlier efforts had been insufficient, Congress in 1949 established the private, nonprofit National Trust for Historic Preservation. For years the trust languished, attracting mostly antiquarians, dilettantes, and activists who had little grasp of the necessary arts of economics, politics, and publicity. Moreover, the time was not yet right for their efforts. As late as the mid-1950s, the trust's total membership was 4,500. Today it totals more than 125,000, and is still growing fast. What is more, it can count on sympathy and active support from many times that number. "A few years ago," says its president James Biddle, "when we went to a community, we were lucky if we saw the garden club. Now it's mandatory for the mayor and the city council to come to lunch and meet the Trust." As Ada Louise Huxtable puts it, preservation has become "a true public coalition from grass roots to *grandes dames,* recognized from Congress to City Hall." The most astonishing growth in the preservation movement has occurred during the last decade, when interest in preservation has become a fundamental element in city planning.

What happened to give the movement such an enormous push? A number of political, economic, social, and philosophical trends converged:

Urban renewal, the panacea for America's troubled cities in the 1950s and 1960s, has had its evident failures, bulldozing entire neighborhoods and replacing, in all too many cases, old but serviceable houses with forbidding, multiple-unit monoliths that lacked humanity, scale, and any sense of community or architectural distinction. In the face of this juggernaut, as Carole Rifkind writes in *Main Street: The Face of Urban America,* "time-honored landmarks, at the heart of the town, were sacrificed as obsolete—the courthouse, city hall, hotel and railroad station. Cleared away, too, were those elements that had added texture to the town fabric: the dwellings of the poor, small shops, surviving factories. . . . Homogeneity replaced diversity. Order obliterated vitality. Space succeeded place."

In city after city, such projects rapidly became breeding grounds for crime and alienation, accelerating the decay of downtown districts and the flight to the suburbs of those who could afford to get out, aggravating the despair of those who could not. For many Americans, the enduring symbol of urban renewal's shortcomings is St. Louis's Pruitt-Igoe housing for low-income families, opened with great fanfare and razed with explosives only a few years later. With no sense of neighborhood, no mix of little shops and restaurants, no intermingling of economic groups as is found in areas that have grown more naturally, Pruitt-Igoe had become a lower-income ghetto, crime-plagued and ultimately uninhabitable.

An activist spirit flowered in the 1960s, producing a feisty, "show-me" mood among citizens toward all institutions—and especially their local, state, and federal governments. Decisions to level landmark buildings or whole districts were no longer silently accepted, nor were they protested just by a few women chaining themselves to bulldozers. They were challenged by growing numbers of men and women who had taken the trouble to learn about building codes and who knew how to apply political pressure.

This activism had also spawned a vigorous environmentalist movement, whose partisans soon realized that environmental recycling and architectural recycling were intimately linked. In the words of James Marston Fitch: "Except for isolated country churches or a castle here or there, any monument worthy of preservation can only be preserved in its context. . . . The issue is fundamentally an environmental one. This, of course, explains the new kind of unity that exists between conservationists—the people who are dedicated to the protection of the natural or god-made environment—and architects and historians who are interested in protection of the man-made environment. It is now understood that these are two sides to the same coin."

A new sophistication was evident, spurred by rising levels of education, wider travel, and the far-reaching effects of television and other forms of modern communication. Peter Drucker, the management expert, predicts that, as the end of the century approaches, more than half of America's working population will hold jobs connected with one or another phase of communications and education. This "knowledge society" is virtually upon us, and its members have a new awareness of values and of history. That can only give further impetus to the preservation movement.

A skittish economy took us on a roller-coaster ride from the boom of the mid-1960s to one of the worst recessions in the nation's history in the early 1970s, and thence to a baffling, seemingly incurable round of "stagflation." At the very moment when public awareness of the importance of historic preservation

was growing, the economy's tailspin brought the bulldozers to a virtual halt; construction was one of the hardest hit industries in the country. And with unemployment running at high levels, preservationists were quick to make the point that renovating buildings is more labor-intensive than new construction: every million dollars of renovation work generates 107 jobs, versus 68 for a new building.

The energy crisis brought a belated and stunning realization of the finitude of our resources—and of how little time we have to save them. There was a powerful case to be made for adaptive re-use as an energy saver. Describing the conversion of Minneapolis's massive old Butler Brothers warehouse into a dramatically redesigned complex of offices, shops, and restaurants, architecture critic William Marlin of the *Christian Science Monitor* wrote: "Buildings like this—they encrust the back blocks of most every city and town—are a kind of stored up energy: the energy it took to make those materials, to ship them, to put them together as a complete work, to operate and maintain over the years. And when they are refitted, instead of ripped down, one can think of taking the energy which would have been needed to build a brand new 500,000-square-foot structure as having been saved for other efforts."

The decline of modernism, with its impersonal and often brutal Minimalism, brought the beginnings of a more eclectic, less didactic postmodernist era. While many spare, unadorned modern structures continue to be built, some of excellent design, ornament is no longer considered a crime. This change in attitude can only help those buildings once condemned by architects (even before they were condemned by zoning boards) largely because they were not sufficiently functional. This does not necessarily mean that we will soon be seeing new buildings with gargoyles and gingerbread, fretwork and corbels, spirals and turrets; it is just that such wild flowerings of the designer's imagination will no longer be dismissed out of hand.

To all these elements add another: the philosophical, if you will, or simply a reviving spirit in the wake of the Viet Nam–Watergate years. This spirit burned brightly during our Bicentennial year and shows no sign of dimming. In *The Unsettling of America*, Kentucky poet-novelist Wendell Berry writes: "The modern urban-industrial society is based on a series of radical disconnections between body and soul, husband and wife, marriage and community, community and the earth. . . . Only by restoring the broken connections can we be healed." Never did the disconnections seem so pronounced as during the period

Actors Theatre, Louisville. Photo: Steve Grubman.

from the mid-1960s to the early 1970s. Yet one might, without being labeled a foolish optimist, find signs that a healing process is well underway. In New York, as one glass-and-steel tower after another rose along Manhattan's major arteries, the city was losing some of its finest structures. Pennsylvania Station went, with its massive arches, trusses, and cathedral-like spaces; so did the elegant Savoy-Plaza Hotel, and the Metropolitan Opera House. With a building binge threatening to wipe out whatever old and good remained, New Yorkers formed the Landmarks Preservation Commission, which in less than 14 years managed to win landmark designation for more than 500 individual structures as well as 31 historic districts embracing an additional 14,000 buildings. The commission rightly took pride in the fact that it "has not wanted to make museums of all its historic treasures," but has vigorously promoted the recycling of designated buildings instead: the Astor Library, still in use as the New York Shakespeare Festival; the Jefferson Market Courthouse, now a branch library; a bank converted into the Bouwerie Lane Theatre; another refitted as the First Ukranian Assembly of God.

New Yorkers had been able to draw on the experience of preservationists in earlier times, and in other parts of the country. Following on early movements to preserve individual monuments—such as the successful campaign to save Mount Vernon, led by Ann Pamela Cunningham in the 1850s—had been broader preventive measures pioneered by Charleston and New Orleans in the 1920s and 1930s. The first local preservation society in the United States was founded in Charleston in the 1920s, and its efforts were sanctioned in 1931 by the passage of the country's first historic district zoning ordinance. Charleston's initiative was followed by New Orleans in 1936 with legal protection for the Vieux Carré. In 1940–41, the Carolina Art Association conducted the first architectural survey in the United States, cataloguing 1,168 buildings and ornamental iron gates and fences. In 1947, Historic Charleston Foundation was chartered to educate the public on the subject and to buy and rehabilitate buildings and neighborhoods.

In the past decade, New York has become a pacesetter in local preservation work. By one estimate, it has succeeded in designating three times as many landmarks and four times as many historic districts as 14 major cities whose combined population is twice New York's. In a long-term effort, Savannah, Georgia, has carried forward such sophisticated techniques as the revolving fund, and is one of the few cities to have attempted to renovate depressed neighborhoods without displacing their residents. In recent years Philadelphia has carried out the early

pledge to historic preservation manifest in the city's 1813 purchase of Independence Hall as a historic monument. Historic districts have now been designated from Mobile, Alabama, St. Louis, Santa Fe, Providence, Rhode Island, to Cape May, New Jersey, Seattle, Minneapolis, Cincinnati, and Boston. What is more, no fewer than 500 cities have adopted preservation ordinances—a fivefold increase in a decade.

Across the continent on the West Coast, meanwhile, a well-to-do San Francisco businessman named William Roth was trying to bring new life to a square-block cluster of red-brick buildings, dominated by the old Ghirardelli Chocolate Factory not far from Fisherman's Wharf. He had a vision that materialized with an impact felt nationwide. Ghirardelli Square, begun in 1963 and completed in 1968 at a cost of $11 million, became an exemplar of adaptive re-use: a vital, attractive complex of shops and restaurants characterized by airy spaces and interiors that do not violate the buildings' original design. Nearby, the old Del Monte Cannery was converted into the multistoried Cannery, giving the area another extremely appealing and successful magnet.

Both projects are, in a sense, patterned after the European shopping arcade and the Oriental *suq*, or bazaar, but they are also something more: places where people can stroll, shop, stop for a meal, sun in the interior courtyards, browse, talk. Ghirardelli and the Cannery not only rescued a moribund district, they are now the leading tourist attraction in one of the nation's favorite tourist cities.

As the preservation movement gathered impetus, similar squares began to sprout all over the country, some brand-new, others ingenious adaptations of old factories, rail depots, trolley barns, warehouses: Larimer Square in Denver, Trolley Square in Salt Lake City, Canal Square in Washington, Quaker Square in Akron, Pioneer Square in Seattle, Gas Light Square in St. Louis, Jackson Square in New Orleans, Wooster Square in New Haven.

According to a study on "Adaptive Use Facilities" prepared for the National Endowment for the Arts, "tied for glory with the square is the roundhouse, the sheds, the depot, the tracks—anything having to do with railroad stations, the superstars of the recycling galaxy." By one estimate, 40,000 railroad stations were built in the United States from 1830 on, and roughly half have been destroyed or have deteriorated beyond rescue. But 20,000 remain, many not being used, and many of these are ideal for re-use.

That has not escaped the notice of recyclers. Old terminals are now centers of community activity in Baltimore; Waterbury and New London, Connecticut; Ann Arbor, Michigan; North Easton, Massachusetts; Duluth and Minneapolis; Natchez, Mis-

20 sissippi. Los Angeles's Union Station, built in 1934, is being remodeled to accommodate not only a railroad museum but also shops, restaurants, and a meeting center for civic and cultural groups. In Spencer, North Carolina, the huge Southern Railway locomotive repair shops are being studied for refitting as a regional shopping center. The copper-domed, 67-year-old Grand Central Station in Tacoma, Washington, is getting two glass arcades for shops. In Pittsburgh, an abandoned 40-acre railroad yard will become Station Square, a shopping-office-amusement complex. In Dallas, shops, restaurants, and transportation offices are being installed in Union Station. St. Louis's Romanesque Union Station, built in 1894 and patterned after the French walled city of Carcassonne, is being redone as Union Center, with hotel, offices, shops, and eating places. Perhaps best known of all is the Chattanooga Station (home of "The Chattanooga Choo-choo"), which has been converted into a multi-use complex of restaurants, shops, gardens, and a hotel with pullman car suites (one of them being the original Wabash Cannonball club car).

There are other potential stars of the recycling movement: schools, many of which stand empty because of changing demographic patterns; unused police stations, firehouses, and city halls; abandoned military forts, barracks, and arsenals; churches, libraries, empty factories, mills, and warehouses.

Already, many such structures have been recycled into places to live in. The earliest wave of the preservation movement, however, affected mostly blue-chip residential areas and involved less recycling than renovating: Washington's Georgetown, Philadelphia's Society Hill, brownstones on the upper East and West Sides of Manhattan, Brooklyn's Park Slope, New Orleans's French Quarter. Then began a second wave that does not yet seem to have crested. Urban affairs expert Neal R. Peirce writes: "Now the upswing is spreading to hundreds of less fabled neighborhoods—often because of their architectural distinction or premier locations." And no longer are townhouses alone involved. Now, the recyclers are expanding into old warehouses, factories, wharfs, and tenement buildings, all the urban residue of the industrial revolution. The studio lofts of Manhattan's

Old Federal Courts Building, St. Paul, detail. Photo: Cheryle Walsh, courtesy Minnesota Landmarks.

SoHo district pioneered this trend; now one finds it in such places as Seattle's Pike Place Market and the Faneuil Hall–Quincy Market area beside Boston's waterfront.

Preservationists, recyclers, developers, all seem to be taking heed of what Thomas Babington Macaulay wrote in 1835: "The best way to save an ancient building is to make it a pleasant residence for a modern family." In Manhattan, superb cast-iron buildings from the late 19th century that seemed fated for destruction because they had outlived their original functions as factories, warehouses, or department stores are now housing tens of thousands of people. In Jersey City, a bank was converted into luxury condominiums, with a sauna in the old bank vault. Houses have been fashioned from ice houses, water towers, gasoline stations, sausage and piano factories, cabooses, churches, schoolhouses.

The National Council for Urban Development noted in a report: "All over America, homebuyers are calculating that they can buy and fix up the old cheaper than they can build new. Or they like the old better anyway. Or they're tired of commuting, or it costs too much. Or the emerging city offers more amenities than they knew, and they'll bring in more. Or city living is again safe. Or they'll be safe in an energy crunch."

The upshot, plainly, is a tremendous boost for America's cities, what *New York Times* architecture critic Paul Goldberger calls "the keystone of a new urban movement that may be for the late 1970s what the brownstone revival was for the early part of the decade—a method of channeling investment back into the center city and propping up what had been until recently an altogether depressed real-estate market in many cities." Indeed, the recycling of older buildings often seems to accomplish what some glittering new construction cannot.

Particularly striking during the second stage of the recycling phenomenon is the emphasis on converting more modest structures. "We're going to see a lot more adaptive uses of everyday buildings," says architect Hugh Hardy of Hardy Holzman Pfeiffer Associates, "because after all, they are what give a community its character. If we limited adaptive uses to great buildings, we would rapidly lose the scale and sense of community that ordinary buildings provide." The National Trust agrees. "The last frontier," reads a trust report, "is the large warehouses and eccentric office buildings of the early 1900s that are difficult to preserve because townspeople have not yet come to consider them quaint and interesting and because it can be difficult to find adaptive uses for them."

Nonetheless, this frontier is already being ex-

plored. In a report submitted to the Senate Committee on Interior and Insular Affairs in 1976, the Advisory Council on Historic Preservation notes: "Since 1966, a portentous shift has occurred from an accent on the preservation of single monumental properties of national significance to concern for the preservation of humbler properties as well—those sites that reflect the ordinary life of America. A restoration project is today as likely to be a 1915 vaudeville theater as a colonial mansion." Describing the conversion of a less than distinguished gasworks into a stylish office building with atrium, *Washington Post* architecture critic Wolf von Eckhardt commented: "What is so interesting about all this is that the concept of recycling existing buildings works as well for mediocre 20th-century buildings as for glamorous Victorian mansions or colonial warehouses."

In the two years between 1976 and 1978, Congress, the courts, and the president acted in various ways to give preservation a boost. In 1978, although the fiscal 1979 budget recommended only $45 million in matching federal funds for the Preservation Fund, a total of $100 million was authorized; by 1980 the authorization will rise to $150 million. By contrast, in 1975, the states asked for $200 million, the Ford Administration proposed giving $10 million, and Congress compromised by making available the grand total of $17.5 million—roughly the cost of four miles of interstate highway.

In addition to such major congressional bills as the 1976 amendment to the Land and Water Conservation Act, the Tax Reform Act of 1976, and the Public Buildings Cooperative Use Act of 1976, other laws likely to have significance are: a Public Works Act aimed at high unemployment areas and emphasizing projects designed to restore historic properties; and a Park Mining Act calling for a two-year study to determine what steps can be taken to protect both natural and historic landmarks from the effects of activities like surface mining. On a smaller scale, federal monies for homeowners' improvements and renovations are available. Maintenance is as much a part of preservation as renovation. The "sweat equity" program addresses the issue of how preservation and recycling affect the poor.

Perhaps most important of all for preservation may be a new law that permits the General Services Administration to transfer architecturally and/or historically worthy buildings to a locality for $1 in return for assurances of successful preservation and re-use. Under this law, the old Federal Courts Building in St. Paul, a grand Romanesque Revival structure, was turned over to the city to be converted into a cultural-community center with an art museum, concert hall, restaurants, shops, and offices. Other recyclings of federal buildings are anticipated. Just how important this law may prove in the future can be grasped from these statistics: The GSA is one of the world's biggest rental agents, managing 200 million square feet in 2,000 federally owned and 7,000 federally leased buildings.

As for the courts, their most notable role may lie in the future, for preservation efforts are so relatively new that the laws involved are still being tested. Virtually every building presents a special case, and there is no predicting on the basis of precedent how a particular decision will go. Even so, there have been some major victories in recent times. A Federal Appeals Court prevented the destruction of a Victorian cottage in New Orleans's French Quarter. Maryland's highest court prohibited demolition of a Gothic Revival church in Annapolis. The Connecticut Supreme Court barred the destruction of a landmark building in Norwich to make way for a parking lot.

Most heartening, perhaps, was the decision by New York State's highest judicial body, the Court of Appeals, upholding the designation of New York City's Grand Central Terminal as a landmark. A lower court had upheld the owners' argument that the designation would mean a significant reduction in profits; the Court of Appeals ruled that a fair profit does not necessarily mean the maximum possible profit, especially not when the building's historic value is taken into account. The decision was appealed to the U.S. Supreme Court, which, in June 1978, upheld the concept that landmark buildings have intrinsic value and that society's interest in them takes precedence over maximizing profit. The preservation movement won a truly significant victory.

In the executive branch, President Carter indicated a genuine commitment to the goal of preservation when he said in 1977: "We must make conservation of our cultural heritage a priority in our nation, a goal to be shared with other nations as well. . . . We must offer federal support and leadership in this effort, both here and abroad," and followed this with a concrete proposal that a Heritage Conservation and Recreation Service be established to protect America's cultural and natural resources. The president also called for creation of an Endangered Buildings Revolving Fund and examination of the feasibility of a National Bank for Historic Preservation. Whatever the long-range fate of these proposals, the fact that President Carter made them is surely encouraging, particularly since, as governor of Georgia, he created a similar Georgia heritage program and gave it his active support.

For all of this imposing support, however, the preservation movement cannot look forward to clear sailing. Since the National Register of Historic Proper-

ties was created in 1966, it has designated about 15,000 landmarks. Some 3,000 of these have already been destroyed, often by developers who, anticipating objections, move swiftly to wreck buildings before court orders can enjoin them from doing so.

The old waterfront in New Bedford, Massachusetts, redolent of the whaling days, is gone. Only five years ago, Louis Sullivan's Chicago Stock Exchange was demolished (only the columned Trading Room with its brilliantly intricate stenciling was preserved and moved to the Art Institute of Chicago) to make way for a commercial office tower, which is already in financial straits. Last year, Cincinnati's Albee Theater was leveled, despite its listing in the National Register. St. Louis recently saved a number of buildings, but only by an eyelash. One was Union Station; the other was Sullivan's 84-year-old Wainwright Building, one of the country's first skyscrapers.

Many buildings are on the endangered list: the Pension Building (proposed to house a new museum of the building arts) at Judiciary Square in Washington, D.C.; the old Buffalo, N.Y., Guaranty Building, now the Prudential, built by Sullivan & Adler in 1895; the 133-year-old Greek Revival Florida State Capitol in Tallahassee; the 82-year-old City of Paris department store in San Francisco with its soaring central atrium and exquisite glass roof; Cincinnati's echoing Union Terminal; the Los Angeles Central Library, at age 52 a veritable ancient in a city where almost everything seems to have been born yesterday; Frank Lloyd Wright's Taliesin East in Spring Green, Wisconsin, built in 1925.

Beyond such immediate dangers are other, longer-range ones. Even some of the most ardent defenders of preservation are concerned with what one critic has called the "boutiquefication" phenomenon—the cheapening of restoration and recycling work with excessive chic. "It's obvious that there will be fuzzy edges," concedes James Marston Fitch. "Kitsch is being perpetrated around the perimeter." There are those who argue that it is already penetrating much deeper than that. The National Trust's James Biddle, for example, reports that "we have to fight constantly against the desire to make a lovely 1890s town look like a 17th-century New England village." Architect Charles Peterson, an eminent restorer, warns of "the boutique-guitar-and-drippy-candle boom. There's nothing too wrong about that but it's a fad that next year might quickly turn into a craze for parachute jumping, Chihuahua dogs, and Polynesian nose flutes."

A more worrisome problem is "gentrification," a word coined in England but applicable here on a far wider scale. It refers to the forcing out of established

Aerial view of Faneuil Hall area. Photo: courtesy Faneuil Hall Marketplace, Inc.

residents, often the poor, the elderly, the racial minorities, from neighborhoods that have been rediscovered and revitalized. The result is often rising property values and taxes that put the old neighborhood beyond the reach of those who have lived there the longest. In a sense, gentrification is the reverse side of the blockbusting phenomenon. It has proved to be good for cities by increasing tax revenues, encouraging retail shopping, and improving the physical fabric, but bad for the existing tenants, often small businesses or people with few alternative places to live or work.

Preservationists were particularly stung when such criticisms reached a wider, more general public with Calvin Trillin's biting *New Yorker* magazine piece, "Thoughts Brought on By Prolonged Exposure to Exposed Brick." Wrote Trillin: "When old warehouses and abandoned factories all over the country started being scrubbed up into boutiques several years ago, we travelling people accepted them more or less the way we had accepted the advent of Holiday Inns—at

first marvelling at their presence, and then grumbling that they all looked alike. The brick exposed in Ghirardelli Square in San Francisco tended to look like the brick exposed in Pioneer Square in Seattle, which had some similarity to the brick exposed in Old Town, Chicago, or Underground Atlanta or the River Quay in Kansas City or Larimer Square in Denver or Gas Light Square in St. Louis." Trillin's indisputable conclusion: "Some of the historic renovations are chic and some of them are tacky."

Trillin and other critics have been focusing particularly on Boston's Faneuil Hall–Quincy Market renovation. Some argue that the adaptation not only has turned the building into a merchandising shrine but also has eviscerated its original architectural and market character. It has been recycled, says Trillin, into "a slick, controlled atmosphere for the affluent and sophisticated. The truly sophisticated in Boston, of course, now treat Quincy Market the way they might treat a large and overcrowded cocktail party —explaining to anyone they happen to meet there that they just dropped in for a minute and really despise large gatherings and just wanted to show a friend from out of town what all the talk was about. They say they can't wait to walk across the street to shop in the raucous stalls in Haymarket Square and the family-run stores of the North End."

Fair? Up to a point, certainly. There *is* an excess of cute candle shops and macramé plant-holders and checkered tablecloths and bentwood chairs in many of the new complexes. There *is* an undeniable danger of sameness, and the prime offender, as Trillin shrewdly realized, is all that exposed brick (which, by the way, is less an authentic touch than a designer's fancy; brick walls have long been covered with plaster or other material to provide thermal and acoustic insulation). What is more, redevelopments like Faneuil Hall Marketplace do look shinier and more orderly now than when they were first built.

Some of the criticism may well stem from the fact that Faneuil Hall Marketplace and like re-uses are proving a roaring commercial success, at least so far, and that arouses hostility in some. It has also drawn throngs, and that, of course, irritates the true elitists. It has not driven out the poor, who never lived in the old granite-faced warehouses that were recycled, but it may push up real-estate values in the vicinity enough to displace some of them, and that is a real problem.

One solution would have been to restore Faneuil Hall–Quincy Market as it was two centuries ago, thereby preserving it as a museum. But that would have done little for Boston's vitality or, more specifically, for the vitality of the district that surrounds it and has won a new lease on life. Such museums at times have their places as preserves and reminders of the past, but museums do "mummify" things, and if buildings and neighborhoods are to go on functioning, they are not the answer.

In his foreword to *Presence of the Past* by Charles B. Hosmer, Jr., the late scholar Walter Muir Whitehill

wrote: "We cannot crystallize or pickle the past, nor can we, where there is vigorous life in a community, turn back the clock as it was possible to do, through a combination of hardly-to-be-repeated circumstances, in Williamsburg. But we can and should, through imaginative adaptation, preserve, in large segments, not only isolated historic sites but whatever architectural and natural features will give continued grace and variety to our cities, towns and countryside."

A parallel to the danger of "museumization" is overpreserving or overrecycling. "The time may come," says James Marston Fitch, "when too many old buildings are being saved—but that time is not yet foreseeable." We need a national policy on redundant buildings so that salvation is not ad hoc, nor is it simply local. Schools, churches, police and fire stations, libraries, city halls, railway terminals, hospitals, mills, barns, industrial and commercial buildings, stately old houses are the victims of incremental decay all over the country. Not all can, or should, be saved. The list of meritorious buildings is finite; and exhaustive inventory is possible. So is an architectural and economic rescue and revitalization procedure.

Obviously, some legislative gains have already been made, but continued success is contingent upon continued militancy among preservationists. Preservation Action, true to its name, has led the national lobby for increased funding, calling for such reforms as full $100-million funding for the fiscal year 1979 National Historic Preservation Fund, implementation of 70 percent federal/30 percent local funding for surveys and planning in the states, and redefinition of program formulas in HUD, the Economic Development Administration, and Public Works to allow more preservation projects to qualify for funding.

Preservationists eventually must face the question: Do we, a generation from now, save the moldering burger stand because it is an artifact, a reminder of how we once lived? There is movement toward appreciation of contemporary vernacular along with turn-of-the-century vernacular as a means of studying ourselves and our culture. MacDonald's has already been twice "museumized," once at the Renwick Gallery in Washington and once at the Cooper-Hewitt Museum in New York. The issue is selectivity as well as reflection of the past simply because it happened. What do we want now that we are aware of what we had and have?

Where the built environment is concerned, change is both essential and inevitable. If everything were a designated landmark, the result would be stagnation, petrification, death. Weary though we may be of glass boxes and golden arches and suburban "ranches,"

they do at least indicate a certain vitality. Describing Britain's volunteer conservation groups, Peter Melvin writes in *Progressive Architecture:* "They wield considerable power and influence over environmental matters—to the extent that sometimes even a proposal to demolish an indifferent building or cut down a spindly group of trees is met with howls of protest."

Some preservationists unwisely pooh-pooh the issue of costs. That does the movement no good and could cause it some harm. Architect Arthur Cotton Moore, in his foreword to *The Historic Buildings of Washington, D.C.,* speaks of "the dreamlike quality of some preservation efforts." Says Moore: "Buildings, all buildings, are economic vessels. No buildings—not churches, post offices, mints, factories, houses—are without functional purposes with some sort of economic justification." His inescapable conclusion: "If preservationists want to save as much as possible and do not want to be labeled as merely anti-new, anti-development, or anti-everything, we should be finding new economic uses for buildings."

Aware of this, most preservationists argue that recycling does, in fact, make very good commercial sense, that it is cheaper to adapt an old building than to tear it down and put up a new one in its place. With the data available, however, it is possible to support not only this argument but also the opposite one. Dr. Richard Steidl of Minneapolis, who bought the former Pillsbury Library there and converted it into a complex of doctors' offices and laboratories, wrote in a letter, "The individual who recycles buildings is generally doing it out of a feeling for history, tradition and beauty, rather than financial considerations." Dr. Steidl continued, "The cost of renovation exceeded the new cost by a factor of five." Yet, when New York University recently recycled the old Central Plaza Building into a school for the arts, its experience was precisely the opposite. Refitting the old catering emporium cost $5 million; a new arts school would have cost $25 million.

Nor do other examples clear up the confusion. In converting a 100-year-old grammar school in Gloucester, Massachusetts, into apartments for the elderly, the Boston firm of Anderson, Notter Finegold completed the job for $18,500 per unit; a block away, a similar apartment complex, started from scratch, cost $26,500 per unit. Faneuil Hall Marketplace cost nearly double the estimated $75 per square foot of similar new construction. Yet annual sales at the complex are running close to $300 per square foot, more than double the national average for shopping centers.

In the end, the relative economy or expense of renovation depends on the specific situation. If the new use is not compatible with the characteristics of

Reconstruction of Benjamin Franklin's house,
Philadelphia, by Robert Venturi. Photo: Mark Cohn, 1976.

the old building, the cost of adaptation runs high. Sometimes the sales value of novelty—as in the case of costly plans at Quaker Square in Akron to recycle grain silos into apartments—or the cultural value of history preserved may offset the extra expense, but in most cases, recycling must be considered a social and environmental issue: Uses must complement and not destroy their natural and built surroundings.

Recycling means big savings in re-used materials, and savings of another kind as well, because new buildings generally employ large amounts of materials like glass, steel, and aluminum, which are energy-intensive—that is, they consume inordinate amounts of energy to produce. True enough. But adapting a building usually means installing modern heating, cooling, electrical, plumbing, and fire prevention systems, all of which are apt to eat up the savings realized elsewhere.

Says Giorgio Cavaglieri, the noted recycler (and probable coiner of the phrase "adaptive re-use"), who adapted the Astor Library for the New York Shakespeare Theater and the Jefferson Market Courthouse for the public library system: "The real reason that preservation has become popular is because people believe, often wrongly, that it is cheaper to re-use what there is than to build anew. To do it well

is not cheaper." George Notter of Anderson, Notter Finegold makes the same point. "The plus factor," he says, "is achieved by developing the potential assets into a final project of greater amenity—one having the right location, more space in either height or volume, more area or more character, materials of a special quality or a potential for time savings in construction." But the total cost, he concedes, is often the same in the end.

Is there any economic rationale, then, for recycling? The Federal Tax Reform Act of 1976 is already providing recyclers with very tangible benefits—speeding up depreciation for rehabilitated buildings, for example—and various local statutes like New York's J-51 program offer further tax breaks. Beyond such hard-headed, dollars-and-cents considerations, however, there is another factor to be weighed. It is what Sherban Cantacuzino calls "the unquantifiable value of age and character."

That may be a difficult argument to sell to a developer who is anxious to flatten that row of Victorian gingerbread or the cast-iron shopfront. Yet the next wave of preservation may well depend on just such intangibles as age and character: on the quest for quality, the newly awakened sense of history (linked with the waves of nostalgia that regularly wash over us), the environmentalists' campaign against waste, the desire to slow down the pace of technology and cushion ourselves against future shock. In any event, more and more people, better-educated and better-traveled than ever, are accepting such arguments."In recent years," says writer and urban activist Brendan Gill, who is also chairman of the board of the New York Landmarks Conservancy, "we have come to see that the preservation and gradual re-weaving of the fabric of the city is much to be preferred to a gross ripping up and hasty re-stitching of that fabric. We deplore today the ritual disembowelment of cities in the name of urban renewal that only a short while ago was being practiced by federal, state and city governments. No city, and no neighborhood inside a city, can survive being 'improved' by radical surgery. On the contrary, we know that it is likely to die of it. Plainly, the way to improve a city is to save as much as one can of its past and by a sympathetic adaptive use of that past, create for it a healthy, nourishing future."

Architects, along with developers, construction men, and real-estate packagers, once formed a virtually solid front against the preservation movement. That was not too difficult to understand. The architect's training and temperament sharpen his desire to put his signature on a building of his own, not to add a curlicue or dot an "i" on somebody else's signature. If Michelangelo had had the time and the resources, he might have leveled Rome and Florence and rebuilt them to his specifications. Inigo Jones might have done the same with London, and so, a few years later, might Christopher Wren. And don't forget Le Corbusier's plan to replace much of Paris with a city of unembellished skyscrapers. All were great builders, to be sure, but who would want a world with nothing but their buildings—even Michelangelo's?

Architects resisted adaptive re-use because, says architect Harry Weese, who converted a Louisville bank into the new Actors Theatre, it is, pure and

simple, "a threat to the system. It may keep architects from building new structures, developers from doing the same, and governments from satisfying their edifice complexes." It was only recently, concurs Hugh Hardy, that "you could re-use a building without losing your standing in the profession." And, adds architect Robert Stern, "We have to change architectural education and go beyond the whole narrowness of the modern movement and recognize that the things architects are interested in are not necessarily the things users are interested in. We need to develop restoration technology, to add new buildings to old ones in sympathetic ways, and to build new buildings in constraining ways." Even now, says James Marston Fitch, "the society is ahead of the profession. All the spectacular instances of individual buildings or whole towns being conserved are done by laymen."

Yet today, recycling is the salvation of many an architectural firm. In 1975, such firms derived 20 percent of their total income from remodeling work; this year the total will reach 33 percent, and no fewer than 87.6 percent of all private architectural firms in the United States will handle at least some conversion jobs. Says Fitch: "The architectural profession, if it has any future at all, must go back to the retrieval and recycling of the built world."

This is easier said than done, however, for recycling can be devilishly difficult to handle. As Boston architect Roger Lang of Perry, Dean, Stahl and Rogers notes: "The *Bauhaus* taught architects to shape space to fit the function— 'form follows function.' That's an inductive process. But recycling is a deductive process. First you look at space and then deduce what kind of functions it will accept." The fact is that many, if not most, architects do not yet know how to modify an old building without compromising or even destroying its design. Citing the problem of working "in a historical context," Peter Melvin says, "the new use frequently requires an extension, or at least a major rehabilitation, and in these circumstances the designer's skill is fully tapped. As opposed to preservation, where painstaking restoration is the order of the day, adaptive use conservation requires good modern design which does not devalue the existing buildings." The fact that so few are able to handle such work gracefully may well be at least partly a legacy of the modernist movement with its de-emphasis of his-

tory and its limited vocabulary for dealing with buildings. Plainly, these shortcomings must be remedied.

Some buildings, of course, should be left alone— or restored to their original glory and maintained in that state. "If Michelangelo did a building," says Giorgio Cavaglieri, "you'd want to keep it that way, but most buildings are not of such artistic value. So it is good to adapt them." Otherwise, our built environment would become one vast museum. As Tony Wrenn and Elizabeth Mulloy write in *America's Forgotten Architecture*: "The 'historic' part of preservation is being sidestepped in favor of an approach that is geared to conserving the resources of the built environment in ways that make them consistent with contemporary needs and demands." This implies a certain amount of broad planning, and the fact is that, more and more, adaptation has moved from a haphazard thing—recycling a loft here or a train depot there—to become a superb planning tool. It is no longer just a matter of restoring a mansard roof or a Neoclassical colonnade, but of looking at entire neighborhoods or districts. Ada Louise Huxtable says that the interpretation of zoning and landmark law and the methods and rationale of control and compensation in the light of today's public and community values are considerations well worth review. In the 1950s and early 1960s, when a mayor wanted to give his city's decaying downtown a new lease on life, he would marshall the bulldozers, the real-estate assemblers, and the shopping mall designers, level a few acres, and start from scratch. Today, if he is smart, he is just as apt to summon the landmarks commission together with the planning commission, a few preservation-minded architects, and perhaps the architecture critic from the local newspaper to see whether that cluster of abandoned but still sound warehouses, that empty turn-of-the-century office building, that unused schoolhouse could be recycled into a whole complex of offices, shops, residences, restaurants, and playgrounds to serve as urban connective tissue between neighboring streets and structures.

Architecture is called the "inescapable art," but many of our proudest old buildings escape from us every year, making way for routine office buildings or rectilinear condominiums or, worst, parking lots. That doesn't *have* to happen. Here are 95 examples to prove it.

BUILDINGS REBORN: new uses, old places

Quaker Square

From: mill, silos
To: shops, restaurants, offices, model train yard

"It peddles nostalgia," says one Akron businessman, trying to explain the roaring success of Akron's specialty shopping complex, Quaker Square. Initially, Akron financiers were distinctly cool to the idea of converting the old home of Quaker Oats, despite the obvious sentimental appeal of the idea and the demonstrable profitability of predecessors like San Francisco's Ghirardelli Square. Thanks to the ingenuity of five local real-estate and design specialists, however, the idea became reality.

Quaker Oats was invented in a hand-operated mill built in 1854 by German immigrant Ferdinand Schumacher in his Akron grocery store. That launched the American breakfast cereal industry, and by 1885 Schumacher was the country's "oatmeal king." A fire leveled the central block of uninsured company buildings in 1886, and only through mergers was Schumacher able to re-establish the business and rebuild the factory to the current 6 brick buildings and a cluster of 102-foot-high grain silos with 21-inch-thick reinforced concrete walls. Ultimately, however, he lost the company in a proxy fight and died penniless.

The factories ceased operation in 1970 and stood vacant for several years adjacent to the University of Akron to the east and the swiftly declining central business district to the west. In 1973 Quaker Square Associates bought the land and buildings, complete with abandoned equipment, at a fire-sale price: $325,000. Financing the renovation of the complex was another matter, given the resistance of Akron bankers to touching the eyesore with the silos. As president of QSA, the partners appointed an experienced developer, Jay Nusbaum, who raised some $200,000 in seed money by selling the machinery to Canadian milling companies no longer able to find replacement parts for their turn-of-the-century equipment. With the money, they began sanding floors and cleaning brick for the 1975 opening of the first four retail shops and a branch of a beloved local ice cream parlor and hamburger emporium whose name drew customers. After this initial phase, they convinced the First Federal Savings and Loan Association of Akron to invest $1.1 million, later increased to $2 million. Preservation, adaptation, and new construction proceeded around existing enterprises, lending an anticipatory excitement to the project. The architects, Curtis-Rasmussen, are among the original QSA partners.

Much of the old complex was preserved, due in part to the low budget: highly varnished old floors, studded wooden doors in keystone brick arches, old stairways with ornate railings, parts of the mill equipment, including the conveyor belt gears, sorting equipment, and the "man belts" that carried workers between floors. Stained glass and other nonindustrial niceties were salvaged from buildings slated for demolition elsewhere. The stone basement, the oldest part of the building (it survived the 1886 fire), now accommodates a restaurant in the area where guns once puffed rice and wheat. Within the mill buildings 50 businesses are now housed, including a leather worker, a scarf seller, a photographer, and a cookie baker. The top two floors include office space for a few lawyers and small businesses; these are reached by an inconspicuous modern glass elevator.

The adjacent Railway Express building and the Quaker Oats railway siding have joined the complex, the railway loading dock providing one of the greatest attractions to the annual 3.5 million visitors. Two "depot" restaurants opened in that area, supplemented by parked dining cars that can be rented for parties and conferences. Carrying the railroad theme further, the complex became the showplace of the world's largest model train collection, 400 locomotives and 1,100 passenger and freight cars over a mile of miniature track, all gathered by Akronite Mac Lowry. Authenticity is enhanced by the life-sized trains passing frequently along the main Akron tracks bordering the square on the west, and by the arrivals and departures of a historic steam train run by the Cuyahoga Valley National Park, which lies between Cleveland and Quaker Square.

To date, $2 million has been spent on the project, and Nusbaum foresees 25 more businesses in as yet undeveloped space, a 300-room hotel and apartments in the grain silos, and a convention center. Already, Quaker Square has helped revive Akron's decayed downtown section. Greenery has sprouted on Main Street, a jazz night club has opened in an abandoned bank, a theater has been renovated, and up to 90 percent of the closed stores have been reopened. Day and night, strollers come to the square's shops and restaurants from the university's E. J. Thomas Performing Arts Center across the tracks, and from the reawakened business district. And local businessmen are no longer so cool to the idea of Quaker Square.

TOP: aerial view. Photo: Samaras Photography, Akron.

MIDDLE: after, interior, shop.

BOTTOM: after, interior, office

The New York State Bar Center

From: row of 19th-century townhouses
To: headquarters for the New York State Bar Association

When the New York State Bar Association announced plans in 1968 to demolish a row of three 19th-century townhouses to make way for its new headquarters in Albany, the group ran into unexpected community opposition. The Albany Historic Sites Commission, the Hudson River Valley Commission, newspapers, and politicians all voiced concern over the prospective destruction of what was perhaps the last remaining "wall" of 19th-century facades in the state capital. The row harmonized with the adjacent New York State Capitol and courts buildings; a modern office building would not.

The architectural firm of James Stewart Polshek and Associates hit upon a solution that saved not only the townhouse facades but much of the structure behind them, to a depth of 30 feet. The preserved buildings were linked at the rear, by means of enclosed multi-story corridors and a courtyard, to a new structure consisting of three skylighted, stepped building elements. Though the new building is spare, almost austere, its scale and design neither clash with nor overwhelm the older buildings. The center, dedicated on September 29, 1971, won a 1972 AIA National Honor Award.

James Polshek, now dean of the Graduate School of Architecture and Planning at Columbia University, was then a relatively unknown architect who had completed two award-winning research laboratories in Japan. He rehabilitated the old houses for reception and conference rooms and designed the new structures for day-to-day operations, with the intervening courtyard serving as a focus of the complex, with greenery and stone paving.

One problem for the architect was to convey a sense of legal tradition in a building employing contemporary concepts and materials. Polshek's solution was to base the design on that of an English inn of court. The Great Hall, 40 by 66 feet and 40 feet high, recalls the Great Hall in the Middle Temple in London. To accentuate the almost Medieval feeling of the hall, it was hung with eight brilliantly colored appliquéd banners representing the evolution of the seal of New York State. A larger banner, 28 feet long and 6 feet wide, portrays the world's legal systems and bears the words from George Washington's letter to Edmund Randolph, asking him to become the first attorney general of the new nation: "The due administration of justice is the firmest pillar of good government." The banners, using heavy fabrics and modern motifs, were created by Norman Laliberté of Amherst, Massachusetts. The entire building centers around the Great Hall, which is flanked by the Hinman Library and an office block comprising four levels of office and clerical space.

The center is not a big structure, with 30,000 square feet, but the abundance of windows and skylights gives a sense of spaciousness. The construction was not inexpensive for that time: It cost $1,626,616. Foundation changes caused by poor soil conditions and careful rehabilitation of the townhouses added significantly to the overall price. But the result is a prize-winning complex that emphasizes tradition and continuity and exists amicably with its distinguished neighbors.

LEFT: before, exteriors. Photo: courtesy James S. Polshek Assoc.

ABOVE: after, exteriors. Photo: George Cserna.

LEFT: view across Lafayette Park. Photo: courtesy James S. Polshek Assoc.

BELOW: after, facade. Photo: George Cserna.

RIGHT: after, interior. Photo: George Cserna.

University Plaza, State University of New York

From: railroad station, newspaper building, federal office building
To: university's central administrative offices

Since its birth in 1948, the State University of New York has mushroomed to include 72 campuses. Its central administrative offices in Albany have changed addresses three times in an effort to keep pace with the university's growth and are currently spread over five separate Albany locations. By late 1979, however, some 800 employees of SUNY's central administration and two affiliated agencies, the State University Research Foundation and the State University Construction Fund, will work in the new State University Plaza complex at the foot of Capitol Hill on lower Broadway.

The complex consists of the Delaware and Hudson Railroad Building, the contiguous Albany Times–Journal Building to the south, and the Old Federal Building that anchors the northern end of the snake-like configuration. About 162,000 net usable square feet of office space will be available in the three buildings, all of which are listed in the National Register of Historic Places. William A. Hall & Associates are architects for the $15.5 million renovation.

The original D&H Building was built by Albany architect Marcus Reynolds between 1914 and 1918 and is modeled on one of Europe's most renowned monuments, the 13th-century Cloth Guild Hall in Ypres, Belgium. The 4-story Flemish Gothic concrete and steel structure, topped by a 13-story tower and replete with gargoyles, has undergone extensive interior renovation, with much of it having been entirely gutted. The building's unusual shape, more than 600 feet long by 45 to 85 feet wide, made mechanical and heating modifications expensive. New floors and ceilings modernize the space. The old windows and sashes were replaced with energy-saving, double-glazed, gray-tinted windows opening to the inside for easy cleaning.

Exterior work consisted mainly of restoring the stately facade to its original pearl-white color and reconstructing many of the ruined gargoyles. Since starlings had caused much of the damage, an automatic starling distress call was installed to keep the birds away. Finally, the 4,000-pound copper weathervane, in the shape of Henry Hudson's ship, the *Half Moon*, was cleaned.

The old newspaper building, also built by Marcus Reynolds at about the same time and in the same style, originally housed the Albany *Evening Journal*, to be succeeded by other publications. When the state decided to purchase the building for the SUNY complex, it was vacant. Interior and exterior renovation paralleled the D&H program. The Journal Building is to house the State University Construction Fund, while the D&H Building will be home to the larger central administration staff.

The Old Federal Building was designed by James T. Hill and built in 1883–84 for the U.S. Treasury Department as a combined federal customs house, courthouse, and post office. The French Renaissance structure retains a mansard roof that was once studded with chimneys. When alterations are complete, the primary occupant will be the State University Research Foundation. The building's structural strength will enable it to house the university's computers and printing machinery. Admissions and loan processing, archive storage, and public television studios will be spread, along with the Research Foundation, over the three full floors, attic, and cellar. SUNY acquired the Old Federal Building, with its 63,220 square feet of usable space, by a transfer of property rather than an actual sale.

Interior renovation will be drastic. Only the handsome old paneled courtrooms will be preserved more or less intact. First-floor partitions will be removed to make room for an auditorium seating 250 and a glass-enclosed passageway linking Old Federal's third floor with the second floor of the D&H Building. The Old Federal Building's most striking architectural feature, its interior open court, will be bridged over entirely on the second and third floors and partially on the fourth, to create 6,270 square feet of additional office space. What remains of the inner court will be incorporated into the third- and fourth-floor library, and will be naturally lit through a ceiling skylight.

Albany will benefit in many ways from SUNY's recycling of the historic lower Broadway buildings. There is no cafeteria within the complex, insuring new business for local restaurants. An old bus turnaround fronting the D&H Building has been converted into a public park and the D&H arcade has been enclosed with glass and converted into an exhibition gallery.

37

TOP: aerial view.

LEFT: before, exterior, 1974. Photo: Jim Shaughnessy.

ABOVE: during construction, interior, 1975.

The Torpedo Factory Art Center

From: torpedo factory, federal warehouse
To: art center

During both world wars, the bleak block-long factory complex on the Alexandria bank of the Potomac River manufactured torpedoes. After World War II it became a federal storage warehouse. Long considered an eyesore but too costly to demolish—its walls were designed to withstand accidental explosions—one of these three waterfront buildings is now a prominent cultural attraction. The factory was bought by the city of Alexandria in 1970 from the federal government for $1.5 million and in 1973 was selected by the Alexandria Bicentennial Commission as the site of an art center.

The Torpedo Factory Art Center now houses some 200 painters, potters, sculptors, printmakers, stained-glass workers, fiber artists, jewellers, photographers, and others. It also has 4 galleries presenting the work of 1,200 artists and craftsmen and a school operated by the Art League, Inc. Now showing a profit (most of the artists pay $3 rent per year per square foot), the 60,000-square-foot building draws some 350,000 sightseers and shoppers each year.

A rather undistinguished commercial structure with Italian Renaissance touches, the building was renovated for about $300,000, which included re-painting the battleship-gray exterior an alluring Co-lonial gold. A three-year loan of $140,000 from the city of Alexandria, which was anxious to upgrade the building as part of the historic Old Town Alexandria district, has been repaid.

Marian Van Landingham, center director, an assistant director, and two janitors are the only paid staff. Except for the installation of utilities and permanent walls by city contractors, all work on the building was done by volunteers. Ann Laddon, a kind of "design czar," oversaw interior continuity and graphics. Studios were finished by the artists themselves. One innovative aspect of the re-use is the large fixed windows that allow visitors to look into studios, thus permitting artists to work undisturbed, if not unobserved. The studios are grouped by type—that is, sculptors, who make noise and dust, are grouped in one area, while printmakers, whose chemicals create fumes that must be vented, are set apart in another.

The Torpedo Factory Art Center has been a model to other communities (and artists) of what can be done through cooperation between the civic and private sectors. It has also generated new cultural life and economic vigor in this Washington suburb.

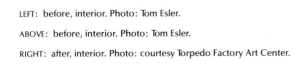

LEFT: before, interior. Photo: Tom Esler.

ABOVE: before, interior. Photo: Tom Esler.

RIGHT: after, interior. Photo: courtesy Torpedo Factory Art Center.

Barn at Lucerne

From: dairy barn
To: shopping center

The huge Barn at Lucerne once housed 250 of the finest Guernsey cows in St. Louis County, supplying 35 milk routes. In 1906, soon after the city of St. Louis had come to international attention as the host of the 1904 World's Fair, the Ganahl family employed the Swiss architect Spernelli to design the structure as part of their vast 500-acre Renaissance estate. The barn had stuccoed walls, beamed wood interiors, a tin roof, and four 60-foot-tall concrete silos that measured 16 feet in diameter and were topped by gables and spires. The barn was sold along with the rest of the estate in 1939 to the first of a succession of owners. For a time Lowell Frei preserved the structure on a 25-acre site, using it to display his collection of electric and steam-powered automobiles. The property gradually fell into decay, suffering damage from fire and vandals, until it was bought in 1962 by engineer-developer Paul Londe and a group of investors.

Londe and his associates were preservation-minded developers. They envisioned within the restored Swiss-style barn a specialty shopping and business center that would create the illusion of a Swiss mountain village. The success of the effort was all but assured by its location at the edge of St. Louis and by the county's development into a thriving residential area with scattered office and commercial complexes.

The first phase of the renovation was recently completed under the direction of St. Louis architects Jay Reiter and Helen Kessler DiFate. To make the most of what was there, they partitioned the rough interior with cedar walls, connected shops on the loft and ground-floor levels with rambling cobblestone paths, and painted the roof barn-red. One of the four silos was converted into a private dining area. The plans include an additional west wing, compatible with the original style. Purely public spaces, such as the link between the old barn and its new wing, are glass-enclosed and filled with plants to blend the indoors with the building grounds.

There are now 25 shops displaying art, local and imported crafts and fashions, workshops and offices for artists, writers, and professionals, gourmet restaurants, a discothèque, a patisserie, and a theater to attract crowds day and night. The project, which opened for a public preview in April, 1977, is graced by Thomas Lawless's outdoor limestone sculpture and a mural painted by John Odell in the spirit of the Midwest's chronicler, Thomas Hart Benton; it depicts the barn in its first years with a suggestion of the changes to come in an encounter between a horse and a 1904 truck. Eventually, the entire 25 acres will be developed for further shopping and recreation.

OPPOSITE: after, exterior. Photo: Daryl Schueller.

TOP: before, exterior.

MIDDLE: before, interior.

LEFT: after, interior.

Mount Royal Station

From: railroad station
To: classrooms, lecture hall, studios, library for art college, public gallery

Through the Italianate hall of Baltimore's Mount Royal Station once passed such famous figures as Presidents Franklin Delano Roosevelt and Dwight Eisenhower, Buffalo Bill Cody, and Romania's Queen Marie. Now the recycled station draws to its lecture hall cultural luminaries like Margaret Mead, who told an audience of art students that Mount Royal's renovation as a multi-use facility for the Maryland Institute College of Art is "perhaps the most magnificent example in the Western world of something being made into something else."

In 1827, a year after the establishment of the Maryland Institute, Mount Royal's original owner, the Baltimore and Ohio Railroad, became the first U.S. railroad to be chartered. In 1896, the B&O built a belt line that skirted Baltimore's metropolitan area and placed an uptown station along this route at the site of a terminal formerly operated by the Baltimore and Susquehanna Railroad. On a generous lot surrounded by parkland, Baltimore architects Baldwin and Pennington built a grand Renaissance Revival structure, featuring a tall central tower with a clock at its summit and a porte-cochère at its base, and a long row of double-cusped windows. The materials were granite with limestone trim and red glazed roof tiles; iron shed supports, railings, and gates were wrought in a sympathetic vein. Inside was a long, 37-foot-high galleried concourse, with marble mosaic floors, figured oak wainscoting, and a stamped metal ceiling. The furniture was of oak, supplemented in the 1920s by the rocking chairs that became the symbol of Mount Royal to many aficionados.

With rail traffic tapering off, the B&O closed the station in 1961. While it hoped to sell Mount Royal for several million dollars, in the meantime it permitted the Maryland Institute a year's rent-free use of the building. In 1964, after the station had stood vacant for two years, the B&O sold the building, its site of nearly four acres, and air rights over the tracks to the school for the nominal sum of $250,000 (the building alone had originally cost $300,000).

A fund drive to raise $1 million enabled the school to hire architect Richard Donkervoet of Cochran, Stephenson and Donkervoet, who shared the institute's desire to preserve the exterior and respect the character of the interior while subdividing it for a variety of uses. The square framed by the four central columns and entered through the porte-cochère retains its high ceiling and recalls the original lobby. To the left and right, an intermediate floor level was installed at the height of the original galleries, more than doubling the building's floor area from 22,500 to 47,000 square feet. The upper level is the Decker Library that overlooks the lobby through glazed walls. The lower-level areas, a lecture hall, and the Decker Gallery are segregated by movable wall panels that may be opened for large-scale events. Open areas, such as the baggage and waiting platforms, were enclosed and now house the graduate Rinehart School of Sculpture and a number of studios and offices, a cafeteria, a gallery, and student space. Second-floor offices and previously unused third-floor lofts became studios. At $18 per square foot, the renovation was a financial success and was received with acclaim when the station reopened in November, 1967.

In 1973 the station was added to the National Register of Historic Places. But perhaps the renovation's most dramatic effect has been to inspire a proposed congressional amendment to the National Foundation on the Arts and Humanities Act of 1965, enabling the National Endowment for the Arts to acquire unused railroad stations for renovation and free use or low rental by municipalities for cultural or civic functions. The Mount Royal Station once more proved its civic usefulness by accommodating hearings on the bill.

TOP: before, interior. Photo: courtesy B&O Railroad Archives.

BOTTOM LEFT: after, exterior. Photo: Herman Emmet.

BOTTOM RIGHT: after, interior. Photo: Ken Huston.

City Hall and Libraries

From: federal offices, private residence, library
To: municipal offices, library, museum, children's theater

Hurricane Camille was a very ill wind that—despite the massive destruction it wrought in 1969—managed to blow some good to Biloxi. The disaster prompted reconstruction of the city's main street, a sensitive, coordinated project involving several buildings and uses.

The centerpiece of the project is the Neoclassical Old Federal Building, renovated as the city hall even before Camille struck and an office annex diplomatically faced in the same gray marble as the larger structure. Across the street are a new library and cultural center, covered with white stucco to harmonize with their residential neighbors in this Gulf resort. In the library's garden stands the venerable Creole Cottage, where Mississippi's first free library was originally housed; it has been given new life as a museum dedicated to Biloxi's cultural past. Just down the street is a Spanish Colonial Revival building that sheltered the library from the time it outgrew Creole Cottage in 1925 until 1977, when the new center was completed. The most striking features of this second library building, surely Biloxi's finest example of this architectural movement, are a highly decorated main doorway with twisted columns, embellished spandrels, full entablature, and curvilinear gables. The original tile roof was damaged by Camille in 1969 and has been replaced. The building has now been freed for possible new use as a children's theater.

Construction of the Old Federal Building began in 1905, but supply failures, incompetent subcontractors, a hurricane, and a yellow fever epidemic delayed completion until 1908. The steel structure, faced in Italian marble, initially had a post office on the first floor, federal courts and offices on the second, and customs house offices on the third. In the 1950s, the building was taken over by the city in a property exchange between local and federal au-

thorities. Renovation to convert it into a city hall began in 1960 and was finished four years later. The original stairs leading to the second floor remain, their marble treads and oak railing a fitting introduction to the old second-floor courtroom, now the city council chamber. In this stately room a Doric order stands out from the wainscot to support a full Doric entablature. However, an acoustical tile ceiling has been installed below the original coved ceiling. Full-length windows look out through the main facade's projecting portico with seven Corinthian columns on a full-story base pierced by an arcade. The rounded arches of the arcade are echoed on the other exterior walls through the use of arched windows, as opposed to the rectangular windows used on the other floors.

Across the street from the city hall, the San Francisco architectural firm of MLTW/Turnbull Associates completed in 1977 the new Library and Cultural Center. The 33,000-square-foot complex is embraced by a large, curved wall. Also linking the two new buildings is a large skylit rotunda containing the library's circulation desk and the cultural center's information desk. The walled garden, opening to the street and city hall, was planned to accommodate the historic Creole Cottage, built sometime during the period from 1830 to 1870. The cottage is considered a fine example of an 18th-century style Louisiana folk plan. Long privately held, the structure reverted to public use in 1973 when its owner donated it, but not its plot, to the city, which moved it to its current site opposite city hall.

Thus, Biloxi's relief effort has proved more of a revival than a repair, in which two outstanding examples of particular architectural styles, tasteful new construction, and one of the city's most historic structures have been most harmoniously combined.

RIGHT: before, Creole Cottage. Photo: courtesy the City of Biloxi.

OPPOSITE TOP: after, exterior, Federal Building. Photo: Carlos Faul, courtesy the City of Biloxi.

OPPOSITE BOTTOM: after, aerial view. Photo: Bill Elmore, courtesy the City of Biloxi.

The Ames-Webster House

From: private residence
To: professional offices

The formidable brick and brownstone structure at the corner of Commonwealth and Dartmouth in Boston's Victorian residential Back Bay district is not just a big house. It is an urban palace, a fitting American rival to the elaborate *palazzi* of Renaissance Italy, those fortress-like residences built by the rising merchant class created by the growth in international commerce.

Designed in 1872 by Peabody and Stearns, the building was enlarged ten years later by the noted English-trained architect John Sturgis for its wealthy owner, Frederick L. Ames. The Ames and then the Webster families occupied it for another 90 years, until it was purchased in 1972 by Neil St. John Raymond. Working with vision and sensitivity in partnership with the architectural and planning firm of Childs Bertman Tseckares Associates, Inc., Raymond recycled this bastion of residential grace and respectability into a commercial space that today contains 8 professional offices with nearly 100 employees.

The interior spaces were designed for a sumptuous life style—witness the spectacular 63-by-18-foot reception room with its 18-foot ceiling. Rather than adjust those spaces to fit clients, the architects looked instead for tenants who could fit into such dignified surroundings: Raymond himself, the CBT architectural firm, lawyers, publishers, other plan-

ners. The fact that no interior partitions were added indicates the respect that characterized this conversion. It also fostered economy: Recycling costs were approximately $6 per square foot.

Almost all the original interior detailing has been retained. That is a considerable accomplishment when one is transforming a 55-room residence, with 40 fireplaces, 3,000 square feet of parquet, and priceless wood carving, plaster ornamentation, Benjamin Constant murals, and crystal chandeliers, into a place where people work. The basement offices, for example, retain the original servants' call directory, the old oak kitchen cutting slab (now a conference table), and flour and grain bins that now enclose a secretary's desk.

Raymond and CBT have not confined their recycling efforts in Boston to the Ames-Webster House. They have successfully converted 1 Winthrop Square, which was built in 1873 and, from 1924 until 1972, housed two Hearst newspapers, into a complex of shops, offices, and restaurants fronted by a CBT-designed park. Another of their projects, the Exeter Theater, constructed in 1891 as a temple for a short-lived religious sect and converted to a movie house in 1914, now contains two theaters, top-floor office space, and a glass-enclosed restaurant that brightens the area's night life.

OPPOSITE LEFT: after, exterior.

OPPOSITE RIGHT: after, interior.

LEFT: after, interior.

BELOW: after, interior.

Photos: © Robert Perron.

Faneuil Hall Marketplace

From: public market
To: food shops, specialty shops, offices

In a sense, Boston's Faneuil Hall Marketplace is an oddity in a collection of recycled buildings. It started out as a marketplace, and it remains one. But saving it required faith, love—and an extraordinary renovation effort. The central issue in the fate of the massive Greek Revival buildings was their location. Since 1742, the year that Faneuil Hall was built as a meeting place and a market, they have been part of the city center. Though the center did not move, Boston grew at a rate that the old market could not match, even with an 1806 addition by Charles Bulfinch. In 1824, Mayor Josiah Quincy ordered the building of a new complex just opposite Faneuil Hall. Alexander Parris designed a long, three-aisled granite Greek temple that was opened in 1826 and named Quincy Market in the mayor's honor. It was soon flanked by South and North Markets, privately built but to Parris's specifications for architectural harmony. All three buildings are 535 feet long and from 50 to 65 feet wide.

By the 1950s, supermarkets and trucks had rendered the market obsolete. Its decaying buildings, besides, were wedged between Boston's glittering waterfront renewal project and its new government center; nevertheless, Walter Muir Whitehill and other historians persuaded the head of Boston's Redevelopment Authority, Edward Logue, to preserve the market. But to what end?

The answer was not forthcoming until 1973, when the BRA's new director, Robert T. Kenney, designated architect Benjamin Thompson, founder of Design Research, to create a food market and general retail complex in collaboration with the James Rouse Company, a firm known for building the "new town" of Columbia, Maryland, and for designing and managing innovative shopping centers.

Even before Thompson and Rouse got the nod, facade renovation of the three buildings had been completed. Architect Theodore Stahl of Stahl, Bennett stripped the Quincy facade to its handsome granite slabs. He also restored the North and South markets to their 1820s appearance, prompting criticism that he had thereby removed a 150-year link between past and present.

In the Quincy Market building, Thompson tried to meet such criticism at least halfway, providing honest food in a cleaned-up market. He replaced the old canvas awnings with rigid glass canopies whose sides roll up like garage doors to admit customers and summer breezes. The rough old floor planks were paved with brick, and signs hung like standards above the center aisle were given a bold, unifying graphic style. Some patrons regret the affluent, organized character, while others like the style and claim that the goods are competitive with those found in grocery stores. The stalls are occupied by bakeries, produce and dairy outlets, butchers and fishmongers, and sellers of cooking utensils, and other food-related goods. Restaurants and cafés spill out onto North and South Market Streets, now closed to autos, during the summer, and are sealed off and heated during the winter. The food market occupies the building's full 85,000 square feet distributed on three levels that are joined at the center of the building by a cupola open from the ground level to the copper dome and ringed by balconies. The Bull Market, named for the weathervane atop the building's dome, is located in this space; leases of custom-designed pushcarts are available to craftsmen for as short a time as a week.

Quincy Market opened on April 26, 1976, the building's 150th birthday. South Market opened in 1977, and North Market is to open in 1978. The six-level North and South Markets, with 281,600 square feet of retail and office space, were designed for entertainment and small shops—apparel, home furnishings, jewelry, books, gifts—in the basement and first two levels, with offices in the top two levels and attic lofts. Ultimately, the entire complex is expected to house about 250 merchants.

The project also contains a flower market housed in a greenhouse, open 24 hours a day year round. The $30-million project already generates average sales from Quincy Market of $300 per square foot per year, an extraordinarily high volume that offsets the high rents.

ABOVE: before, exterior. Photo: courtesy F.H., Inc.

LEFT: before, exterior. Photo: courtesy F.H., inc.

BELOW: after, exterior, opening day. Photo: Dave Cabbage, courtesy F.H., Inc.

Institute of Contemporary Art

From: police station
To: galleries, offices, shop, restaurant

Boston's Institute of Contemporary Art was always something of a vagabond. Created in 1936 as a kind of provincial chapter of the Museum of Modern Art in New York, ICA had nearly a dozen temporary residences before finally finding a real home and settling down. Quite a home, too—a splendid example of Romanesque Revival architecture designed by Arthur Vinal in 1886 as Police Station No. 16. A 4½-story, gable-front building, it features the bold masonry detailing, round-arched openings, and short clustered columns characteristic of the influential style developed by the Boston architect Henry Hobson Richardson. An adjoining building, erected at the same time and in the same rich Romanesque style to serve as a firehouse, looks a bit like a smaller brother. That now-modernized structure remains the headquarters of Boston's Fire Department Ladder Co. 15, but the police abandoned their building in 1965.

ICA took a typically bold step and acquired the landmark from the city on an 80-year lease, undertaking a $750,000 program of renovation and adaptive re-use. The two-story stable at the rear of the station was converted into temporary office and gallery space in 1973 while work on the main building began. The original interior—prison cells, guard rooms, coal bins, and drill halls—was gutted. Cambridge architect Graham Gund designed a contemporary multilevel facility of galleries, offices, and a museum shop. The exterior was restored to near-original condition. New single-paned windows replaced the original multipaned ones, creating a more dramatic opening into the transformed interior.

An open, split-level stairwell set on a diagonal in the center of the entrance space gives the small interior unexpected spaciousness and creates unconventional viewing spaces into the galleries. In addition, the design called for a restaurant that could remain open when the galleries were closed; this was placed on the lower level of the entry space but within view of the galleries.

Although the building was structurally sound, there was a complication: a 12-inch rake on the main floor front to back, and a 4-inch rake to the side. The slant and an odd column here and there are reminders that this is an old building, whose landmark facade now leads into an elegant, exciting space.

OPPOSITE: after, exterior. Photo: Steve Rosenthal.

LEFT: before, interior. Photo: Greg Heins.

BELOW: before, interior. Photo: courtesy ICA, Boston, Mass.

BOTTOM: after, interior. Photo: Steve Rosenthal.

Women's Educational and Industrial Union

From: restaurant
To: shops, offices, studios, conference room, lounge

Founded in 1877 and one of the country's oldest social service agencies, the Women's Educational and Industrial Union campaigned in early years for shorter working hours for children, school hot lunch programs, and aid for the adult blind and continues as a comprehensive social service agency. In the early 1970s, a renewal project threatened the union's quarters in two adjoining Victorian townhouses at 264 Boylston Street; besides, the quarters had grown cramped. The union eventually purchased the old Schrafft's Restaurant Building at 356 Boylston, just down the street but beyond the renewal project, and chose the Boston firm of Shepley Bulfinch Richardson and Abbott as architects to adapt the three-story building.

The original gilded cast-iron facade with its ground-level gold leaf decoration remains essentially as it was, although new windows and a heraldic, gilded swan, which hovers over the original entrance, have been installed. The swan was chosen as the union's symbol because Boston's swanboats were launched on the Public Garden pond in the same year that the union was founded. Inside, the original vaulted ceiling has been retained, as have the old marble columns with their classical capitals, traditional structural elements that blend well with the otherwise clean and simple lines of the new interior design. The basement has been fitted with a badly needed teaching kitchen and a classroom for the union's training programs. Six retail shops that raise funds for the union's operation have been given central space on the ground floor. A staff lounge and offices are located around the periphery of the floor. Upstairs on the newly built mezzanine are the union's design studio and coffee shop.

The second floor is devoted to support services: career counseling and administrative offices as well as a 150-seat auditorium, a conference room, and a members' lounge, which looks out on the Boston Public Garden. Social services for the handicapped, disadvantaged children, and the elderly are housed in the basement.

Construction costs for the project, completed in 1976, were $927,500, or $34 per square foot. Furnishings and equipment for the new union headquarters came to $110,000. To finance the move, the union raised money largely through a public appeal, supplemented by grants.

LEFT: after, street facade. Photo: Ron Levenson of Walpole, Mass.

TOP RIGHT: during construction, interior. Photo: courtesy Shepley Bulfinch Richardson & Abbott.

BOTTOM RIGHT: after, ground-floor shop. Photo: Ron Levenson of Walpole, Mass.

Lutheran Medical Center

From: foundry plant
To: 532-bed teaching hospital

Even in as poor and rundown an area as southwest Brooklyn, the old American Machine and Foundry Company plant was considered an ugly nuisance. Abandoned in 1969, it was part of the blighted waterfront section near Bush Terminal. Yet it is now an attractive, well-equipped modern hospital, the first to be recycled from an industrial plant, and instead of being a reproach to the whole neighborhood, it is now a source of pride.

The old Lutheran Medical Center, roughly half a mile away from its new site, had outworn its facilities and outgrown its space. Realizing that community health—mental and physical—is strongly influenced by environmental factors like housing, schools, play areas, and jobs, hospital officials organized a Department of Comprehensive Health Planning that documented the area's traffic, housing, and unemployment problems. In considering new qualities, they sought a location that not only would place the hospital in the neediest area, but would also encourage community renovation efforts. The 5-story reinforced concrete building met these requirements, affording as well 514,000 square feet, floor-to-floor heights of 16 feet 7 inches, and sturdy floors capable of bearing extremely heavy loads.

The center is a general medical and surgical facility with 532 beds and a large ambulatory care unit. J. Armand Burgun of the architectural firm of Rogers,

Butler and Burgun was the partner in charge of the redesign, with the Turner Construction Company handling the unique problems of converting the old foundry building. Bulldozers were brought inside to gut each floor, leaving the shell pretty much intact. Windows were refitted with mirror glass and blocked on the inside to reduce heat loss, though individual segments were left open in patient rooms. A new front entrance and large second-floor lobby funnel visitors and new patients to the proper wings in the 700-foot-long building. The top three floors are devoted to operating, delivery, radiographic, and fluoroscopic rooms. Thanks to the building's industrial load-bearing capacity, the arrangement of equipment was dictated by need rather than structure. False ceilings installed at ten feet yielded over six feet for air conditioning, plumbing, and fire prevention systems.

Contributions from an appreciative community and from employees formed part of the $1.9 million raised from private sources to supplement federal grants of $2.8 million and a New York State loan of $63 million. The renovation, completed in 1977, came to $42.7 million, with the remaining funds going to equipment purchases. All told, renovating the foundry cost $10 million less than the price of a new hospital building.

LEFT: before, exterior. Photo: courtesy Rogers, Butler & Burgun.

ABOVE: after, exterior. Photo: Bill Maris.

RIGHT: after, exterior. Photo: Bill Maris.

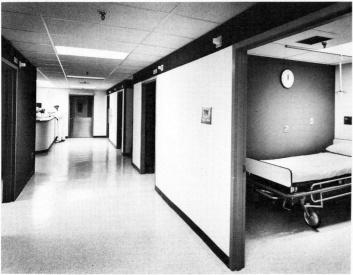

OPPOSITE TOP: before, interior. Photo: courtesy Rogers, Butler & Burgun.

OPPOSITE BOTTOM: after, interior. Photo: Bill Maris.

ABOVE: before, interior. Photo: courtesy Rogers, Butler & Burgun.

LEFT: after, interior. Photo: Bill Maris.

CHARLESTON, S.C.

Historic Charleston

Charleston is surely the prototype of urban architectural preservation efforts. The first local preservation society in the United States was founded there in the 1920s, nearly half a century ahead of much of the rest of the country. In 1931, on the advice of Frederick Law Olmstead, Jr., citizens established the first historic district zoning ordinance, a move designed to prevent post–World War I tourists from carrying off everything from Charleston's fine cast- and wrought-iron work to entire houses.

The city has a pedigree to be proud of. In 1682, the original settlement of Albemarle Point moved to the current city site on the peninsula between the Ashley and Cooper Rivers. Charles Towne, named for Charles II by the English, Bermudan, West Indian, and Irish settlers, became the seat of the South's great rice plantation and trading oligarchy. Dwellings took a characteristic form: the "single" house, one or two rooms wide, with its long flank set at an acute angle to the street to pick up ocean breezes, shaded by a veranda reminiscent of West Indies architecture and known in the South as a "piazza."

Because of the Civil War, much of Charleston remained unchanged well into the 20th century. There simply was no money for remodeling or building anew in Victorian or Classical Revival styles, so much of the city's historic district was preserved as a rare example of Colonial and early American architecture. In 1940–41, the Carolina Art Association conducted the first architectural survey in the United States, cataloguing 1,168 buildings and ornamental iron gates and fences. *This Is Charleston*, published in 1944, featured 572 of these. The effort was an alarm to sleeping neighbors like New Orleans, which established the Vieux Carré Historic District in 1937. It also alerted Charleston to the fact that the buildings needed preservation advocates, since many lay outside the original 20-block historic district. Thus, in 1947, a Historic Charleston Foundation was chartered to educate the public on the subject and to buy and restore buildings.

By the 1950s, the HCF had gathered the funds to buy and restore the 1809 Nathaniel Russell House as its headquarters. Since then, it has pioneered the idea of a revolving fund for preservation, with which it buys old properties and either resells or rehabilitates and rents them; it also grants mortgages and home improvement loans. In addition, it accepts gifts of houses with a provision that donors will have lifelong tenancy.

Historic Charleston's focus has not been so much on individual landmarks as on renovation of dilapidated neighborhoods, where private investment may later take over. The first choice was Ansonborough, a 6-block inner city slum with 135 ante-bellum houses. In 4 years, the foundation bought 26 of the houses, sold 11 to be refurbished as residences, made apartment buildings of 3, and plans to sell or renovate the rest.

An HCF subgroup, the Broad Street Beautification Committee, undertook the refurbishing of one of the city's first thoroughfares, laid out in 1673 and dotted with buildings dating as far back as the early 1700s. At its eastern end stands the 1771 Exchange Building, where the Provincial Congress met and a protest was staged against the British Tea Tax two weeks before the Boston Tea Party. City hall is also on Broad Street. So are No. 92, now a realtor's office but once the home of Dr. David Ramsey, patriot and historian, and No. 106, the Lining House of 1715, the oldest dwelling surviving from the original fort settlement. The committee prepared a master plan for repainting and refurbishing facades and replacing discordant signs, as was also to be done in Corning, New York's Market Street project.

Among property-owners persuaded to recycle by the HCF is the city itself. Its Housing Authority is now in the former Marine Hospital on Franklin Street. Cramped Charleston College expanded its offices, classrooms, and dormitories into 75 houses from the 17th and 18th centuries. The Southern Railway Company installed its Southern District offices in the former William Aiken House of 1811 on King Street. The most dramatic renovation, however, was of Rainbow Row, whose rear slum alleys inspired a stage set for *Porgy and Bess* in the 1930s. Its 18th-century houses, built for merchants who installed counting offices on the first floors, were renovated as residences by private individuals.

Some treasures were lost; the Orphan's Chapel, for example, built in 1802 by Charleston's best architect, Gabriel Manigault, gave way to a parking lot. Much work remains to be done, especially in the Wraggsborough, Harleston Village, and Radcliffeborough areas. What is more, the refurbishing of Ansonborough created new problems: The tripling of land values drove out low-income residents, a process that has come to be known as "gentrification" and is the reverse of "blockbusting" as far as the poor are concerned.

LEFT: before, Rainbow Row, 18th century. Photo: courtesy Historic Charleston Foundation.

MIDDLE LEFT: 141 East Bay, c. 1853. Formerly Farmer's and Merchant's Exchange Bank; now law offices.

MIDDLE RIGHT: after, Rainbow Row. Photo: courtesy Historic Charleston Foundation.

BOTTOM: William Aiken House, c. 1811. Formerly residence; now offices. Photo: courtesy Historic Charleston Foundation.

Chicago Public Library Cultural Center

From: public library
To: branch library, cultural center

For a stretch of a few miles, Michigan Avenue and the shoreline in Chicago are "Culture Row." Here are the Art Institute, Orchestra Hall, the Auditorium Building, the Field Museum of Natural History, the Adler Planetarium, and the Chicago Public Library, a building designed, in the words of the library board, to "convey to the beholder the idea that it is an enduring monument worthy of a great and public-spirited city."

Though Chicago's public library system was founded in 1872, it had moved a number of times before the city council in 1883 chose as its permanent site Dearborn Park, west of Michigan Avenue between Randolph and Washington Streets. The first of the city's parks, it had deteriorated to an embarrassment. Construction did not get started until 1892 under Shepley, Rutan and Coolidge, the Boston heirs of the office of H. H. Richardson, who died in 1886. Charles Coolidge was the partner in charge of the library. The library board wanted a Classical Revival building, similar to the structures being built for the World's Columbian Exposition, which was to open in Chicago in 1893. Moreover, the building was to be of masonry bearing-wall construction rather than the steel frame that had revolutionized commercial architecture in Chicago and New York and led to the skyscraper. The conservative civic image drew instead on old European prototypes and the axial and symmetrical Beaux-Arts planning reflected by the trend-setting buildings at the Exposition. Richardson had been at once a prophet of progressive austerity and a devotee of Medieval masonry; his successors must have seemed the right architects for a modern/old-fashioned design.

A five-story building in the form of a blunt-ended U was completed in 1897. Its three-foot-thick exterior walls of bluestone rest on a granite base. The first-floor facade is smooth, punctured by pairs of deep-set rectangular windows; the second and third floors share double-height arched windows; the fourth and tallest, most ornate floor is lit by narrow, rectangular windows separated by piers with superimposed Ionic columns. A frieze of garlands and lions' heads is surmounted by a denticulated cornice on brackets and a balustrade. Entrances at the north and south ends are set back 15 feet and approached by broad staircases. The Randolph Street entrance is a massive Doric portico, and the main Washington Street doorway a deep arch with a coffered ceiling and three pairs of doors in elaborate bronze frames.

The grand staircase in the Washington Street section is of white Carrara marble, its balustrades inlaid with Tiffany-style mosaics in marble and glass around medallions of dark green Irish marble. The materials were practical as well as plush: The frequent scouring necessitated by Chicago's smoky atmosphere only heightened their glory, whereas painted decoration would have been dulled through cleaning. The third-floor main reading room is roofed by an illuminated Tiffany stained-glass skylight supported on arches covered with the richest mosaics in the building. In the Randolph Street section, the stained-glass dome and marble walls of the lobby and the Civil War memorial hall upstairs have been restored.

By the late 1960s the library's central collections and functions had outgrown the building, and the central collection was moved to a temporary structure. The old Dearborn Park building, meanwhile, was renovated as a library branch cum cultural center. Designated a landmark in 1976, the building mostly required restoration, although an addition was built that filled in the U and connected the north and south wings of each floor. The work was begun by Holabird and Root in 1974 and completed in 1977. Currently, the first floor houses the fine arts division and popular library, the second and third floors, the remainder of the library collection, reading rooms, reference rooms, administrative offices, and a civic reception hall, the fourth, the audiovisual division and a children's library, and the fifth, the music section.

Museum of Contemporary Art

From: bakery, townhouse
To: art museum

The program of Chicago's Museum of Contemporary Art calls for the breaking down of the barriers between art and life. Perhaps it is just as well, then, that two years of negotiation to acquire the U.S. Court of Appeals Building for the museum failed, for in such a formal setting, the barriers most likely would have remained intact. The Museum of Contemporary Art opened instead in a bakery that was built in 1915 and later served as offices for *Playboy* magazine. Bought for $500,000, the two-level, 94-by-104-foot rectangle was renovated and furnished for another $200,000. And now the museum has just completed another transformation.

The need for a modern art museum to complement the Chicago Art Institute had long been acknowledged by Chicagoans. Plainly, the native city of Vachel Lindsay, Carl Sandburg, Louis Sullivan, and Frank Lloyd Wright required room for the future of art as well as the history of art. The effort that paid off was organized by art critics Doris Lane Butler and Alberta Friedlander, who invited a group of 30 artists and aficionados to join them in the mid-1960s in a search for appropriate quarters. In 1966, under the presidency of lawyer and collector Joseph Shapiro, the group leased the old bakery from HMH Enterprises, *Playboy* publisher Hugh Hefner's company. Hefner was one of the donors who put up $1.3 million to buy, renovate, and staff the building.

Under the guidance of architects Brenner, Danforth, Rockwell, the building donned a new white concrete face, new lighting, and an all-white interior, from the burlap-covered walls to the 9,500 square feet of tiled floor. Movable partitions and furniture by Le Corbusier, Mies van der Rohe, Marcel Breuer, and Florence Knoll define temporary galleries and reception areas and embellish permanent staff offices and workspace. Mechanical systems are a noticeable aspect of the environment. As architect Dan Brenner, a

museum trustee, sees it: "A modern museum functions like a stage in the theater, equipped with elaborate control panels for sound and light and with a structural grid which allows anything to be hung from any height at any place." The facade itself became a gallery wall with the installation of a 50-by-8-foot red copper bas relief by the Swiss sculptor Zoltan Kemeny. An eight-foot-wide, coal-filled moat kept observers at a respectful distance from Kemeny's work—despite the museum's stated intentions.

The last vestiges of that particular barrier between art and life were abolished, however, in the museum's current expansion program. This time, renovation architect Laurence Booth, of Booth, Nagle and Hartray, has done away with the moat and incorporated an adjacent three-story brownstone into the museum. The brownstone and museum fronts were unified in a single still-white facade of treated aluminum, composed of several transparent and permeable layers. Where the moat once lay is now a raised entrance promenade.

The brownstone, built in 1900 and formerly a beauty parlor, a gallery, and a magazine's test kitchen, was acquired for $250,000 and renovated for $900,000, including the overall changes to the museum. It gives the MCA an additional 14,000 square feet, including 5,600 square feet of galleries, the space needed to house the permanent collection, which is growing steadily after a decade of provocative and successful exhibitions. Those shows, originally under the directorship of Jan van der Marck, and now under the new director John Neff, will continue to encourage those living artists who were shown only sporadically in Chicago before the museum's establishment.

A later phase of renovation of the protean MCA will involve tearing down most of what used to be the bakery and constructing a new, open loft building in its place.

TOP: before, exterior.

BOTTOM: after, exterior. Photo: courtesy Museum of Contemporary Art.

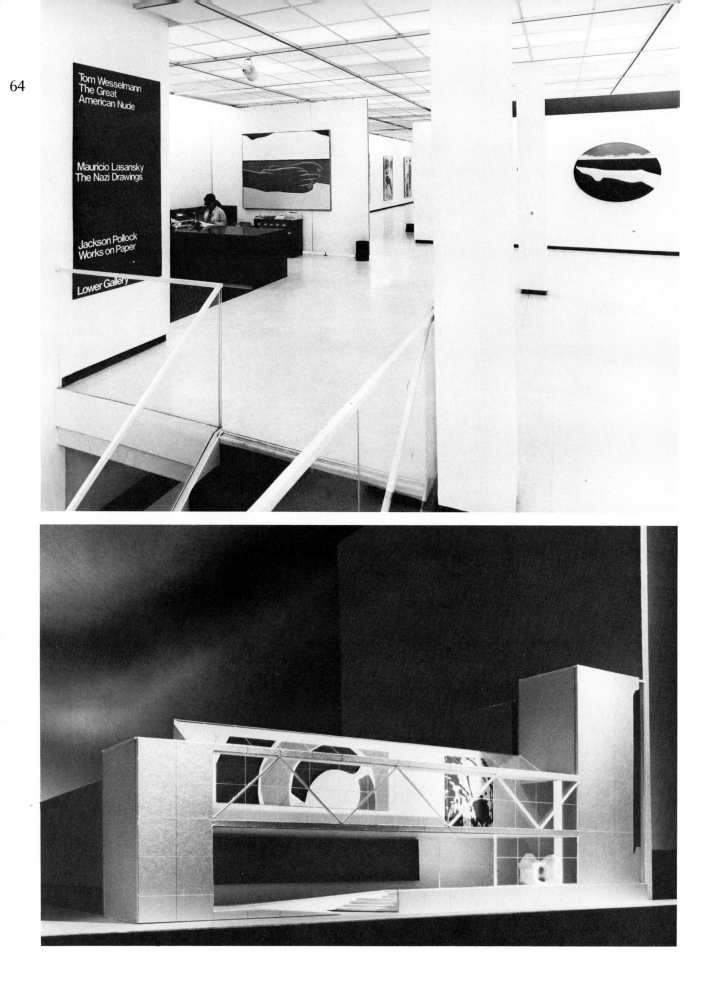

Tom Wesselmann
The Great
American Nude

Mauricio Lasansky
The Nazi Drawings

Jackson Pollock
Works on Paper

Lower Gallery

ABOVE: after, interior. Photo: Shimer, Hedrich-Blessing.

TOP LEFT: after, interior. Photo: John Vinci, courtesy Brenner Danforth Rockwell, Architects.

BOTTOM LEFT: after, exterior, model. Photo: courtesy Museum of Contemporary Art.

Navy Pier

From: recreation complex, transportation terminal
To: recreation complex

In its 62 years, Chicago's Navy Pier has gone from pleasure dome to training base to classroom and now back to pleasure dome. The 34-acre complex thrusting into Lake Michigan was designed by architect Charles S. Frost and built in 1916. The construction job was a marvel. Some 21,000 Oregon timber pilings were driven into the floor of the lake and a 292-foot-wide concrete slab was laid down, stretching 3,040 feet from the shore. Double-decked sheds lined the pier's north and south edges.

When the pier opened, swarms of excursion boats, steamers, and cargo ships moored by its sides daily, disgorging mobs of passengers. Most headed for the end of the pier, where stood a pleasure palace with high arcades, broad esplanades, an adaptable ballroom/concert hall with a high ceiling vaulted by metal ribs and two 165-foot-high concert towers that were lit at night for dancing to roof-garden bands.

With the Depression, lake traffic dwindled and business with it. In 1941, the pier was made a naval training base, and its sheds and concert halls were partitioned for classrooms and offices. In 1946 the University of Illinois, swollen with veterans, leased the pier for classroom space; until 1965, it was known as "Harvard on the Rocks." Other tenants, including the police department, the courts, and a radio station, made further changes until a maze of alterations had obscured the buildings' original appearance. The copper roofs and concrete footing, neglected and battered, began to give way to wind and water.

In 1974, the abandoned mess caught the fancy of Mayor Richard Daley, who had changed Chicago's skyline with countless new high-rises and now sought to change its shoreline. City Architect Jerome Butler and his 100-member Bureau of Architecture quickly saw the value of restoring the pier and thereby filling an ugly gap in the lakefront park that skirts the Loop. With the Bicentennial less than two years off, they began to prepare the buildings for an international trade fair and festival.

Phase one of a two-phase program was begun in 1975 on a budget of $7.2 million (later increased to more than $8.8 million), financed by the sale of municipal bonds. Twelve months of rapid work repaired the most badly damaged buildings at the end of the pier. Structural repairs on the buildings' steel frames swallowed up 20 percent of the budget. Deteriorated brick and ornamental terra cotta and window frames were matched in modern materials. The new brick was chosen for color from 15 sample panels; the cast-iron window frames were duplicated in steel; existing terra-cotta molding was supplemented with limestone at half the cost of new terra cotta; a copper-coated stainless-steel roof sealed the domed ballroom. Interiors were gutted and original skylights, long sealed over, re-opened. Artificial lighting was re-installed in the concert hall with 3,000 bare light bulbs that drew attention to the metal ceiling ribs. Work on the hall included acoustical and mechanical improvements as well as retrieval of the second-level balcony overlooking both the lake and the interior. What is now called the Shelter Building was once an open bridge connecting the concert hall to the Terminal Building; now its upper level has been glazed for viewing and for year-round comfort, while its lower deck lies open to the weather. A checkerboard pattern graces the concrete aggregate paving of the esplanades and roof gardens. Rooflines are enlivened by an animated frieze of Chicagoans. Trees, benches, and banners lend a festive air. There is a carousel for children and, for weary parents, vintage streetcars that travel the length of the pier. Parking will be accommodated in a nearby sunken plaza and along an inner strip of the pier between the rows of sheds.

Phase one was completed in time for a Bicentennial opening. An all-night restoration ball, the first in 35 years, was organized by the Chicago School of Architecture Foundation. As yet, however, the new facilities are only summer-proof. Phase two will winter-proof them and convert the great expanse of sheds between the concert hall and the shoreline into stores, restaurants, tennis and handball courts, and exhibition halls—a balance of public service and private commercial and cultural development.

More changes are in train. A marina has been proposed for the watery lot to the north of the pier. To the south, the existing Dime Pier, so named for the original entry fee, will be restored for fishermen. And on Navy Pier itself, construction plans are underway for an Energy Research and Development Administration demonstration project in solar energy: 8,000 square feet of collectors on the south shed roof will meet 35 percent of the heating needs of the Terminal Building. No longer will the windows and skylights of Navy Pier defy the sun.

LEFT: before, exterior.

BELOW: after, exterior.

TOP LEFT: before, interior.

BOTTOM LEFT: after, interior.

ABOVE: after, exterior.

Photos: Hedrich-Blessing, Ltd.

Cincinnati Union Terminal

From: railroad terminal
To: performing arts school, bus maintenance facility

When Fellheimer and Wagner designed Cincinnati's huge, $8.6 million Union Terminal, they wanted to make a statement—an optimistic one—about the future of passenger travel by rail. Completed in 1933, the terminal was one of the best Art Deco buildings in the United States. It boasted a rotunda and great semicircular facade, geometric floor paving, chrome hardware, and heroic WPA murals. Passengers had access to a nursery, newsreel theater, and barbershop, among other services. The terminal consolidated five separate stations, although the only spot where the tracks could be merged was an inconvenient edge-of-town location. The terminal's distance from the business district hastened its obsolescence; it was used to capacity as a passenger terminal only during the troop-train days of World War II.

In the early 1970s Norman Pfeiffer of the New York architectural firm Hardy Holzman Pfeiffer rediscovered the vacant building and launched a three-year study of its re-use potential; the study became a book on railroad station conversions throughout the country. Under pressure from local preservationists as well as from Pfeiffer, the city bought the building with a $1-million grant from the Federal Urban Mass Transit Administration. Pfeiffer was the obvious choice for renovation architect, and proposed a performing arts school for the upper levels, including the rotunda. The Southwest Ohio Regional Transit Authority wanted the lower levels for a bus storage and maintenance facility, and had a $13.5-million UMTA grant for the conversion.

In spite of all that support, the project failed. The case, said Pfeiffer, "illustrates almost every aspect of the conflicts inherent in the re-use of buildings."

Basically, the issue was restoration versus renovation. Ardent preservationists who had saved the building and enlisted it on the National Register of Historic Places were loath to see any changes, even those necessary for successful re-use. Some even objected to a change of function, hoping that a future revival of railroads would revitalize the building.

The architects argued that some changes were unavoidable. George F. Roth and Partners, architects for SORTA, wanted to build extensions to both sides of the building, and Hardy Holzman Pfeiffer proposed building a theater and gym above these additions. The annexes would have used the original brick, window type, and trim, and would not have been visible from the front of the building. Inside, the public would have been able to admire the murals across a low railing beyond the entrance separating public areas from the school's open classrooms and dining spaces. Although traffic would have been diverted around the rotunda rather than through it en route to the tracks, the symmetry of the terminal would have been preserved. Modern partitions in the less spectacular spaces would have contrasted with the old structure, but the original surfaces themselves would have been preserved.

Nevertheless, many preservationists were adamant that re-use was enough of a concession; alteration was out of the question. Their view prevailed, and both the Board of Education and the Transit Authority withdrew their plans. Ironically, the terminal is now endangered for the sake of its aesthetic, and it may fall victim to the bizarre logic that it is better to die young and beautiful than to compromise with real life.

LEFT: before, exterior.

TOP RIGHT: before, interior.

BOTTOM RIGHT: after, interior, model.

Photos: courtesy Hardy Holzman Pfeiffer Associates.

CLEVELAND

Cleveland Warehouse District

From: warehouses, shops, light industry
To: shops, restaurants, offices, entertainment

To the north lies Lake Erie, to the west the Cuyahoga River. And, like its bounding waters, Cleveland's historic Warehouse District was, until quite recently, in extremely bad shape. Once seriously polluted, Erie and the Cuyahoga have been cleaned up considerably and have begun to recover. So has the old Warehouse District.

The district was one of the first pieces of land settled by Moses Cleaveland and his band of surveyors at the end of the 18th century. Food, retail and wholesale clothing, and light mechanical industries grew up there through the 19th century, occupying brick buildings that made good use of the clay indigenous to northern Ohio. The structures were sober, understated, and often tastefully ornamented places of business. Berea sandstone was sometimes used to face the more elaborate buildings.

By the 1920s, the 40-acre district began to suffer as the urban center moved eastward toward Public Square, and the suburbs grew. Workers, shoppers, and merchants began moving outside the city and commuting by car, and parking space became a city-wide problem. Some historically valuable buildings, along with some thoroughly dispensable ones, were razed to make way for nearly 5,000 surface parking spaces.

In 1977 a feasibility plan for the district by William A. Gould and Associates, architects and city planners, called for revised zoning and tax laws to encourage developers to recycle worthy structures for mixed uses. The plan also called for the replacement of surface parking lots by underground and upper-level facilities. A building might, for instance, have retail and wholesale space on lower floors, parking on the middle floors, and apartments or restaurants or both above. A number of urban spaces such as miniparks would link businesses, apartments, entertainment areas, and government offices, typified by the newly constructed Justice Center east of the Warehouse District.

Signs of regeneration in and around the district were already appearing even before the Gould plan was unveiled. Of the 150,000 people employed in Cleveland's central business district, 20,000 are in the Warehouse District and 25,000 more in the immediately adjacent blocks. Nearby is an area of specialty shops and restaurants called "The Flats" that was recently developed on several slices of land between the river and the Warehouse District. In 1974 Higbee Corporation's board chairman Herbert Strawbridge announced a project called "Settlers' Landing" to be constructed on 6.5 acres near the southwest corner of the Warehouse District. The Cleveland Landmarks Commission has either designated or nominated no fewer than 34 buildings within the district.

The Gould study concluded with two specific economic feasibility studies to guide investors. The first proposed adaptive uses for the Hoyt block, a group of serene four-story Italianate buildings from 1875, ranging from a wine cellar–restaurant in the basement to three full floors of office space. With 63,261 square feet of available space, buying and recycling the Hoyt block would cost an estimated $1.6 million with a 9.5 percent return on investment using the Ohio tax abatement law. The second example is the less impressive Gilkey Building. The 53,000-square-foot structure would require $988,700 for purchase and conversion into three floors of commercial space, including a ground-floor restaurant and eight two-bedroom apartments on the fourth floor. Return on the investment was calculated at 9.7 percent.

OPPOSITE LEFT: warehouse buildings overlooking Cuyahoga River.

OPPOSITE RIGHT: before, St. Claire Avenue.

ABOVE: after, exterior detail, Western Reserve Building.

Photos: courtesy William A. Gould & Associates.

Senior Center Club

From: waterworks and powerhouse
To: center for the elderly

Mrs. Burhl Ellis recalled vividly how the men who used to work at the old waterworks building in Columbus took pride in the place, lovingly planting and tending flowers every year outside the 18-inch-thick walls of the sturdy, hip-roofed structure. Completed in 1903, the waterworks housed pumps that drew water from the East Fork of the White River. But a new pumping and filtration plant was built in the 1950s and the building was sold to the Southern Machine Company, a tool and parts maker, which remained until 1971. Columbus's redevelopment commission purchased the structure for $65,000 as part of a downtown renewal project, but left it vacant for several years. Many of the large arched windows were broken, letting in winter's ravages, and the roof began to show signs of neglect.

In 1975, the city received some $660,000 in federal Community Development funds, and announced hearings on how to spend the money. Mrs. Ellis had an idea. She was director of the Senior Center Club, which had outgrown its storefront facility on Franklin Street as its membership grew from 54 in 1965 to 1,400 a decade later. Why not give the center a new home and save a city landmark at the same time? Mrs. Ellis organized a letter-writing campaign and got more than 200 club members to attend the city community development commission hearing. The commission

decided that the senior center was a good idea.

Early in 1976, a $441,000 project was begun under Columbus architect James Paris to turn the former workplace into a building to work and play in. The old roof was replaced without altering the original style. The red brick, some of it covered with decades of coal dust, was cleaned and repaired inside and out. Broken windows were replaced and new heating and air-conditioning systems installed. The interior was gutted except for large brick support arches that now form a frame for stairways to the second level and for balconies looking down onto the ground level. Local business donated furniture, and volunteers did much of the cleanup work.

The main level includes two large recreation areas, offices, and a full kitchen. The lower level now has a television lounge at one end and a crafts area with the balance of the floor given over to Senior Products, Inc., an agency providing part-time employment for about 25 older people in local industries. Club members pay only $2 in dues a year, which entitles them to gather for cards, television, talk, and inexpensive hot meals, calling upon the club's carpool. Noting the structure's sturdiness, club member William Shafer comments: "When all the new buildings have done fallen to the ground, this old building will still be standing."

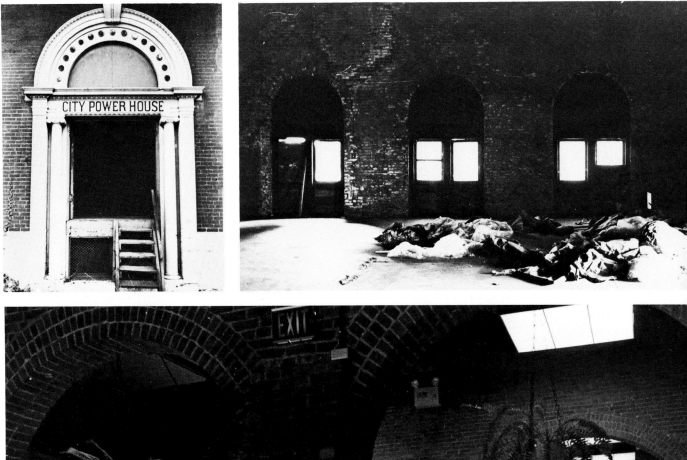

LEFT: after, exterior.

TOP LEFT: before, exterior.

TOP RIGHT: before, interior.

BOTTOM: after, interior.

Photos: Nolan Bingham and Jeff A. Marshall, courtesy James K. Paris, AIA.

Market Street

From: commercial buildings
To: shops, offices, apartments, recreation

Founded in 1835, the city of Corning did not really begin to flourish until the Brooklyn Flint Glass Works relocated there in 1868, eventually becoming the Corning Glass Works. After a number of disastrous fires in the 1850s, solid two- and three-story brick buildings went up along Market Street, but less prosperous times during the first half of the 20th century permitted only modest storefront remodeling and little new building. As a result, a typical late 19th-century street was preserved, though marred by neglect and unattractive 20th-century overlays.

For some time, the Corning Glass Center–Corning Museum of Glass, Hall of Science and Industry, and Steuben Glass Factory had been a major tourist attraction for Corning, luring 750,000 visitors a year, but relatively few of these detoured to Market Street. The Corning–Painted Post Historical Society and the Corning Glassworks Foundation began a campaign to spruce up the street as a good example of living history and as a magnet for visitors. Several things happened in 1972 to aid their efforts. In March, the foundation, at the suggestion of its new president, Thomas S. Buechner, granted $72,000 to seed the Market Street Restoration Agency. Simultaneously, Mayor Joseph Nasser established a 22-member committee to revitalize commerce on the street, still the city's prime shopping artery. Then, in June, Hurricane Agnes hurried up efforts by flooding much of Corning and leaving Market Street under 2 to 4 feet of water. Federal flood relief funds of $500,000 were used to buy new brick sidewalk paving and honey locust trees, and that helped to increase storeowners' receptivity to the agency's continuing efforts. A further boost to preservation came in 1974 when a four-block area was named a historic district and listed in the National Register of Historic Places.

The Market Street Restoration Agency emphasizes cosmetic improvements—new coats of paint, restrained but legible signs, lighting, and removal of modern metal that conceals old brickwork. Street life is also a major concern, in the form of smooth traffic flow, adequate parking, street festivals, and seasonal decorations. The agency approaches shopkeepers individually (a tactic complicated by the fact that 30 percent of the landlords are absentee) and offers free design services, including measured drawings of proposed changes to enhance the features that both distinguish a storefront and identify it as one of a coherent neighborhood of buildings, such as arched windows, decorative cornices, terra cotta, and ornamental brickwork. Much attention has gone to replacing the large, obtrusive signs with well-mounted ones or small 19th-century-style perpendicular signs announcing a store's goods.

A newsletter and walking tours encourage interest and sophistication in design. So do neighboring examples, such as the extensive facade renovation of the First Bank and Trust Company and the two Corning Glass Works adaptive re-use projects on the street. One of them, the Clubhouse Building, was built as a mill in 1878 and sold to Corning Glass in 1929, when it was adapted as a recreation center. The roof was raised 15 feet to accommodate a basketball court, a swimming pool was built, and a bowling alley was added in a rear extension. Now the building has been adapted to offices, with the pool turned into conference space.

Norman Mintz, who directs the agency's small salaried staff, says: "I tell people what a difference a simple coat of paint will make if they can afford nothing else." If one excludes three major renovations, the average expenditure by shopkeepers has been modest—$1,343—with a total of $112,000 spent to improve over 70 percent of the street's buildings in just over 3 years. Total expenditure for the agency's project comes to less than $750,000. An economic survey made possible by the National Trust for Historic Preservation in 1977 indicates that the project's intention has been realized: In 1974, about 15 percent of the stores were vacant; now vacancies are down to one and business, including tourist trade, is up considerably. Though the second floors are only 65 percent occupied, plans are in the offing for their renovation as retail space and apartments. Downtown living may become attractive again with the completion of the adjacent Urban Renewal Project Number One, including new housing, commercial, recreational, and civic facilities.

LEFT: after, exterior. Photo: Kellogg Studio, Painted Post, N.Y.

BELOW: before, exterior. Photo: courtesy Market Street Restoration Agency.

BOTTOM: after, exterior. Photo: courtesy Market Street Restoration Agency.

SEDCO Office Building

From: elementary school
To: company headquarters

Cumberland Hill was built as an elementary school for the children of the fine neighborhood houses overlooking the Trinity River. By the mid-1920s, it had been nicknamed "the melting-pot school" as its classrooms filled with the children of recent immigrants. In 1963, the imposing old Victorian Gothic building was converted into a vocational school for welders, carpenters, bricklayers, and electricians, reflecting the change from an affluent residential neighborhood to a downtown mixed-use area.

When the building was put up for auction in 1969, it was bought for $1.3 million by SEDCO, Inc., a Dallas-based international drilling, pipeline, and engineering firm. SEDCO chairman W. P. Gill Clements, Jr., who had long admired the building, planned to recycle it as a 90-employee corporate headquarters. When renovation began, a number of construction workers pledged that they would take particular care on this job: they were graduates of the old trade school.

Since 1919, the building had been haphazardly altered. Its windows no longer matched, and its high-pitched roof with crowning cupola had been replaced with a flat roof with crenellated parapets. The renovation architects, Rodger Burson and James Hendricks, with consulting architect A. H. Pierce, rebuilt the roof and windows. They also added new bay windows, entrance details, and a skylit floor-to-roof foyer beneath the cupola, giving the interior the focus it had lacked. Paint and varnish were stripped away to expose children's initials carved into the 11-foot-high cypress doors; offices were furnished with Victorian antiques or reproductions; light fixtures were salvaged from the remodeling of classrooms at Southern Methodist University's Dallas Hall. Plain, white roller shades were installed in all the windows; at the end of the day, they are lowered to half-height, as in the Dallas schools, for a tidy look.

Renovation of the 34,000-square-foot building was completed in 1971 at a cost of $1 million. The building has won numerous awards, and many Dallas citizens have written to thank SEDCO for undertaking their city's first major restoration project. One of the writers, a Cumberland Hill teacher for 27 years, sent a magnolia plant by way of thanks. It now flourishes in the newly landscaped schoolyard.

Further renovation work, perhaps encouraged by SEDCO's successful renovation, has taken root in East Dallas: A number of the Prairie School frame houses in the 13 blocks of Munger Place have been bought and renovated by individual families thanks to the revolving fund of the Dallas Historic Preservation League.

RIGHT: before, exterior, 1890s. Photo: courtesy Dallas Historical Society.

TOP LEFT: before, interior, 1890s. Photo: courtesy Dallas Historical Society.

TOP RIGHT: after, interior. Photo: William McDonald.

BOTTOM: after, exterior. Photo: William McDonald.

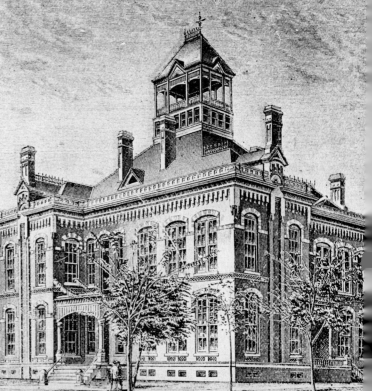

Detroit Cornice and Slate Building

From: workshop and foundry
To: restaurant, artist's studio, architectural offices

As Maggie Citrin drove past a downtown area of Detroit several years ago, a unique building caught her attention. This was an area where one structure after another had been demolished for parking lots, and the Detroit Cornice and Slate Building, with its ornamental Victorian facade, stood there all by itself. Discovering that it was up for sale, her husband Toby and his two brothers bought the building for their investment company J. A. Citrin Sons. Then they sought and gained federal, state, and city designation as an historic landmark, which legally bound the owners to respect the building's exterior.

That was fine with the architect hired for the renovation, William Kessler, who took such a fancy to the building that he later moved his firm there, taking 1½ of the 3 floors. Maggie Citrin, an artist, took half a floor for a studio, and the fashionable Grosse Point restaurant, Piper's Alley, opened a branch on the ground floor. The restaurant has brought business to the area after business hours, along with the hope that the whole downtown district will benefit from this sign of new life.

Until its purchase by the Citrins, the building had belonged to the Hesse family, for whom it was built in 1897 by Henry J. Rill. It was known for its galvanized-steel facade, said to have been designed by the founder of the business, Frank Hesse, who also handmade a huge, 150-pound zinc eagle with a 6-foot wingspread for the cornice. The facade signified the business inside, which was responsible for a number of Detroit's roofs and facade ornamentations, and which still operates, although from other, larger headquarters. After the metal had been stamped with ornamental designs, and its friezes and tympanums had been hand-hammered within the building, the facade was mounted and painted to look like stone. The trompe l'oeil process, developed in the 1840s to satisfy the desire for economy and speed in construction combined with decorative grandeur, was so convincing that the city had assessed the building as stone. In fact, the construction is part brick bearing-wall and part wood frame, an interesting but not uncommon reversal of the early steel or cast-iron construction encased in masonry walls.

Hesse's small, pre-assembly line workshop and foundry was essentially unchanged when purchased by the Citrins, except that the eagle had been stolen some 20 years earlier and there was considerable rusting in the facade, despite the zinc. A full 110 workdays were needed to restore the facade to its original luster. Inside, the architect stripped the open interior down to beams and bricks, then modernized the lofts at a cost of about $20 per square foot. The crowning touch came in 1974 when a duplicate of the stolen eagle was raised to a perch at the center of the building's cornice.

TOP: after, exterior.

BOTTOM: after, interior.

Photos: Balthazar Korab.

Fine Arts Foundation

From: private house
To: offices

When John Brown, a stonemason from Scotland, settled in Fort Wayne in 1852, he built a house and shop in what then was a flourishing part of the city: the banks of the Wabash and Erie Canal, a 458-mile waterway that served as the major commercial route into the Midwest. The building materials and stove coal that Brown sold from the first-floor shop of the two-story stone structure were probably loaded directly aboard canal boats, practically at his doorstep, and transported to markets as far south as Evansville.

Ironically, the same year that John Brown built the Canal House, as it came to be called, the Pennsylvania Railroad was born, the first of the great westward-bound railroads that eventually doomed the canal and the way of life that it had helped to spawn. Long before this deterioration began, however, Canal House had begun to change hands. Brown left it after ten years, and among its later residents were the families of three canal boat captains. In 1885 the New York, Chicago, and St. Louis Railroad bought it for use as a warehouse. For a time, local fur traders leased the structure to store raccoon pelts, but its final use seems to have been as locker space for rail workers.

In adapting the old building, the railroads removed its three chimneys and the inside stairs and changed the entrance location. The canal, in the meantime, had become little more than a muddy ditch. In 1973, as Fort Wayne civic and arts groups began making plans for the Bicentennial, a campaign was launched to restore Canal House, inspired at least in part by the historical research undertaken by

John Loveland. In 1974, the Norfolk and Western Railroad donated the house to the city. It was leased by Canal House, Inc., chaired by Karen Anderson, and in turn subleased to the Fine Arts Foundation, directed by John McKenna.

When actual restorative work commenced in 1975, volunteers did the bulk of the work. Individuals, companies, and foundations raised $25,000, and many building materials were contributed. The Construction Battalion of the local U.S. Naval Reserve unit took on the conversion as a field training project, repairing and repointing the yellow stonework, replacing the patched and disintegrating plaster walls inside, building new stairs, and replacing the old roof with cedar shingles. For the reconstruction of the three chimneys, a demolition company donated used bricks and Boy Scouts cleaned them.

By the time of Fort Wayne's Bicentennial celebrations, the former Canal House was sufficiently restored to become one of the principal attractions. Work is still going on, though the Fine Arts Foundation moved into the building in early 1977. One problem remains: New surfaces are needed in some areas to improve the acoustics, which are troublesome in a stone structure with open interior spaces.

When conversion was begun, Canal House was the only remaining structure on the dilapidated South 100 block of Superior Street. Now miniparks and new offices are being planned, compatible with the Canal House style, in an area that once was considered fit only for parking lots.

OPPOSITE: before, interior. Photo: Gabriel R. DeLobbe.

LEFT: before, exterior. Photo: Gabriel R. DeLobbe.

BELOW: after, interior. Photo: Michael Brower.

William Reuben Thomas Center

From: residence and luxury hotel
To: municipal offices, museum, cultural center, offices

In 1906, Charles W. Chase, one of Florida's first phosphate kings, began building a massive 20-bedroom house in Gainesville. When he died three years later, Major William Reuben Thomas, son of a Gainesville pioneer and himself a successful businessman and politician, took over the unfinished mansion. Thomas completed the woodwork, including a solid mahogany staircase, and roofed the central, terrazzo-paved courtyard, later covered with a louvered glass and steel ceiling.

During the Florida land boom of the 1920s, Thomas seized the opportunity to convert his house into the town's first resort hotel. He commissioned W. A. Edwards of Edwards & Sayward, a major Atlanta firm, to design an additional, larger wing. Its Mediterranean style with Renaissance motifs said to have been researched at Michelangelo's Laurentian Library in Rome was a sensation for its time, as was the interior decoration by A. Rime of Chicago's Marshall Field & Company, featuring Oriental rugs, silks, velour curtains, and art collected on Thomas's travels. The 100 bedrooms in the 3-story, U-shaped annex had private baths and central steam heat, novelties for northern Florida of that day. Oversized corridors and an entrance portico closing the courtyard gave grand scale to the hotel, which opened to public acclaim in 1928. Connected to the wing by passageways was Thomas's converted residence, containing the hotel offices and public rooms, with the main dining room in the central courtyard and additional guest rooms on the second floor.

The hotel was in operation until 1968, accommodating guests like Robert Frost, Helen Keller, and World War II officers in a club housed in its basement bar. After Thomas's heirs sold it in 1968, the new owners began looking for an office building developer to take it over. But Historic Gainesville, Inc.,

led by Samuel Gowan, stepped in to sign a purchase option. A feasibility study funded by the Bicentennial Administration and city and county commissions convinced the city to buy the hotel for $316,202.

The plan was to renovate the 1928 hotel wing for municipal offices, and the original residence as a cultural community center. Office renovation began in 1974, under project architect Murray Tuckerman of Architectural Design Associates, with advice from the National Heritage Corporation of West Chester, Pennsylvania. The most expensive element was a new roof, for which tiles were cast from the original molds by the same manufacturer, the Ludowici-Celadon Company of Chicago. Rotting cornices and decayed windows were replaced with duplicates; the plaster frieze of the courtyard was copied from a cast and reinstalled. Walls were painted pale yellow, with darker yellow trim. Most of the interior was retained, and now contains offices for the fire department, the cultural commission, municipal personnel department, and the police investigative department. The spacious and soundproof quarters cost a modest $30 per square foot.

The old Thomas residence is currently being restored with a $16,000 grant from the National Parks Service and a $1,234,000 public works development grant from the Department of Commerce, for a 1978 opening. In the ground-floor rooms, woodwork must be stripped, sanded, and revarnished by hand to prepare the 1920s period rooms for a local history museum. The isolated pagoda-roofed kitchen will become an art gallery. Offices and community rooms will occupy the upper floor. The U-shaped central court, whose acoustics make it ideal for ceremonial functions or chamber music, will accommodate cultural performances.

TOP: during construction, west side, Building B.

BOTTOM: after, west side, Building B.

Photos: McKellips & Tuckerman, AIA, Architectural Design Assoc., Inc.

The Strand

From: commercial offices, warehouses
To: shops, offices, apartments, restaurants, galleries

Once the Strand was called "the Wall Street of the Southwest"—an uninterrupted five-block avenue of fine 19th-century commercial buildings constructed between the 1850s and the 1890s in Galveston Island, Texas. When business deserted this Victorian quarter for Houston some 60 years ago, the port town of Galveston converted some of the Strand's fine old buildings into warehouses, while others became vacant.

In the 1960s, the county arts agency council, seeking to revitalize the city's sagging visual and performing arts, joined with business, minority, and preservation groups to apply for an $8,000 grant from the National Endowment for the Arts to fund a feasibility study on the Strand's renovation and re-use. The project proposed mixed cultural, residential, retail, and wholesale use in the old buildings, which were ultimately bought for those purposes with a revolving fund of more than $200,000 from foundations. Local banks established a $1-million credit line to seed the renovations. Additional grants from the National Endowment for the Arts will permit continued development. So far, recycling has cost $3.5 million.

The effort has yielded a performing arts center (in the 1894 Grand Opera House), museums, and artists' and craftsmens' studios (in the 1878 Mallory Produce Building and the 1859 Hendley Row), as well as restaurants, specialty shops, offices, and apartments.

The first major renovation in the newly designated National Historic Landmark District was of the Trueheart-Adriance Building, designed in 1882 by Galveston's foremost architect, Nicholas Clayton.

The project was undertaken in 1969 by the Galveston County Junior League, which now operates a soup and sandwich shop on its ground floor. The 1870 League-Blum Building, currently being restored by George and Cynthia Mitchell with architects Ford, Powell and Carson for a restaurant, shops, and offices, boasts the most extensive cast iron in the district. A nearby building stripped of its cast iron by a 1930s owner has undergone restoration by artist Richard Haas, who painted a trompe l'oeil mural of the missing ornamentation. Robert Lynch and Taft Architects dug out the ground-floor arcade of the 1870 Rosenberg Building from cement block, winning a Texas Institute of Architects award for transforming it into apartments and shops. The 1870 Rice and Baulard Building, built as a paint store and subsequently demoted to an electrical supply warehouse, now houses specialty stores on the ground floor and large upstairs apartments lit by skylights and an atrium cut through its wooden framing.

Such features are common in many of the neighboring renovations. Once deserted and dingy, the warehouses have been reopened to sunlight and night lights, demonstrating the feasibility of neighborhood preservation. Galveston itself, with its wide range of fine buildings, from a prefab Greek Revival house of the 1830s to the Victoriana of Clayton, has gained prominence as a city. Its 1856–61 U.S. Custom House was chosen, after its 1964 restoration, as the first subject of a series of historic preservation postcards published by the U.S. Postal Service.

TOP: before, exterior, Rice and Banlard Building.

BOTTOM: after, exterior.

RIGHT: after, interior.

Photos: courtesy Galveston Historical Foundation.

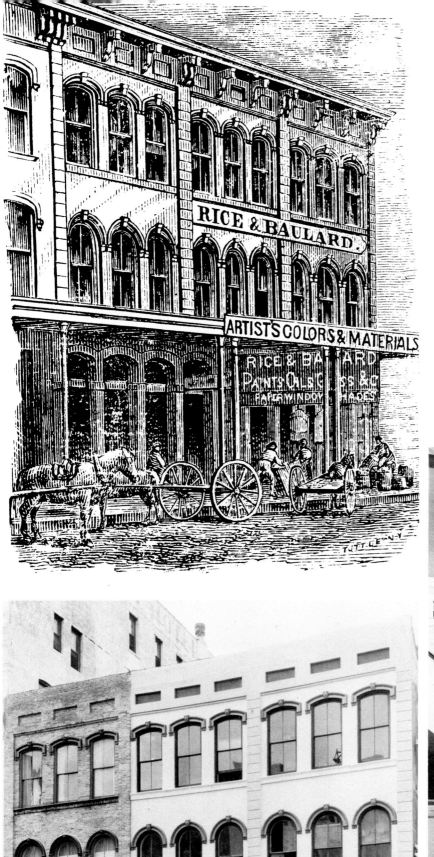

Central Grammar Apartments

From: school
To: apartments for elderly

If some of the residents of the Central Grammar Apartments in the Massachusetts port of Gloucester occasionally have a sense of déjà vu as they gaze out a window or wander down a corridor, no wonder: They went to school there, or taught there.

The 80-unit apartment building started out in 1889 as the High School. Later, it was designated the Junior High School, then the Central Grammar School, and finally it was judged obsolete and abandoned in 1971. Redundant school buildings present a problem all over the country. In New York State more than 200 elementary and secondary schools have been declared surplus in the last 3 years. But Central Grammar's 82-year life was not at an end, thanks in large part to the efforts of R. Kirk Noyes. Trained as an architect, he came to Gloucester's Action, Inc., the local antipoverty agency, to satisfy two years of alternative military service during the Viet Nam war. That was about the time of the school's abandonment, and Noyes, noting its proximity to city hall, proposed converting it into an administrative annex. The city council rejected the idea by one vote. A year later, Noyes's proposal to transform the building into housing for the elderly was approved. Even the project's detractors underwent conversion as the recycling neared completion and its economic promise became obvious.

The total cost of Central Grammar's recycling came to $1,482,350, or $20.45 per square foot. The key financing role was played by the progressive Massachusetts Housing Finance Agency, which has been unusually active in recycling. Tenants began moving in during the fall of 1975, and taxes generated during the first year amounted to $26,000. Anderson Notter Finegold, Inc., the Boston architectural and preservation planning firm responsible for the recycling, never lost sight of "people considerations"—the idea that space, light, color, and a sense of one's past are important. The 11½-foot-wide corridors and 9½-foot-high ceilings create a sense of expansiveness. Original features like the maple floors, some of the cabinetry, and even some of the classroom doors complete with the old room numbers have been retained. Such touches help prevent elderly tenants from feeling disoriented by too much that is new.

A number of projects have been conceived in Central Grammar's image. In Jackson, Mississippi, Central High had already begun conversion to a State of Mississippi office complex. Similar conversions are underway in Peabody, Needham, Marlboro, and Newton, Massachusetts. No fewer than ten Boston schools are being considered for recycling, and schools in Cincinnati, Baltimore, and Roanoke are being studied as well.

LEFT: after, exterior. Photo: © Phokion Karas.

RIGHT: after, entrance. Photo: © Phokion Karas.

ABOVE: after, interior. Photo: Jerry Klinow.

Community Arts Center

From: federal office building, courthouse, post office
To: arts center

In 1975, when Argentine-born architect Emilio Ambasz was asked to develop a design for the adaptive re-use of Grand Rapids's old Federal Building, he was intrigued by the notion of letting a single bold statement confer a new identity on the 1908 structure. He respected the old Beaux-Arts monument, by suggesting that the bulk of the building be allowed to continue to speak for itself. But he proposed a radical modification: the addition of a striking translucent inclined plane that would ascend from the street to the roof, much like the stepped side of an Aztec pyramid, inviting visitors to the new home of the Grand Rapids Community Arts Center.

The original entrance to the sturdy granite structure was on the closed side of its U-shaped plan. Ambasz would have occupants of the second- and third-floor public spaces and the fourth-floor artists' studios continue to use that entrance. But he would also flip the original plan around for his client, the Grand Rapids Art Museum, giving it a separate and grandly surrealistic entrance on the open side of the U. The architect points out that this would echo the plan of the building's prototype, the east facade of the Louvre.

The new entrance would be constructed of fiberglass resting on a metal space frame. Visitors to the museum would walk up the steps in the center of the plane and enter the Community Arts Center's second-floor grand foyer through a half-moon aperture cut into the fiberglass skin. The inclined plane is intended to serve not only as a means of access and exit but also as a protective cover for the arcade formed beneath it. Drainage is provided for by stepped, concave channels to the right and left of the entry path. On inclement days water would cascade down the sides of the plane or crystallize into icy cloudlike patches on the sky-reflecting surface.

The transfer of the now-vacant Federal Building from the General Services Administration to the city of Grand Rapids is only one instance of urban recycling in the downtown district. Nearby structures, including an old movie house, will also undergo renovation. But the inclined plane planned for the arts center would understandably dominate the surrounding scene. Ambasz would like to use it, in fact, as a symbol for all downtown recycling.

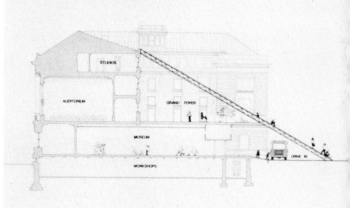

LEFT: proposed facade. Rendering: courtesy Emilio Ambasz, Architect.

ABOVE: before, exterior.

MIDDLE: section.

BOTTOM: proposed interior.

Photos: courtesy Emilio Ambasz, Architect.

The Becky Thatcher House

From: private residence
To: historic showplace, bookstore

In 1842 the Elijah Hawkins family moved from Kentucky to Hannibal with their five-year-old daughter Annie Laura. They moved into a plain, center-hall Federal-style house that had probably been built three years earlier. Across the street was the home of Samuel Clemens, later to be known to a world of grateful readers as Mark Twain. Annie Laura Hawkins thoroughly captured his fancy and became Becky Thatcher in *The Adventures of Tom Sawyer*. She remained in Hannibal when he left in 1853, and five years later married Dr. James Frazier. Frazier died in 1873, she in 1928.

Once her childhood friend had become a literary giant and his old home was opened to the public, Annie Laura's former home was turned into a rooming house for tourists. It was not until 1949, however, that the first steps were taken to preserve the dwelling, when John Winkler bought the house and set about restoring it without public funds or any other form of official public support.

Upstairs the parlor and a bedroom were restored to conform to the original pre-Civil War period; a few of Annie Laura's own things are kept in the two rooms. The first floor was turned from a living space into a book shop, responding to the community's need for a center stocking Mark Twain's works. The shop has one of the best collections of books in print by and about Mark Twain anywhere in the world.

Winkler died in 1977, but the book shop continues to thrive and has been augmented by a souvenir shop in another first-floor room. The house remains in the possession of Mrs. Winkler.

LEFT: after, exterior, 1977. Photo: courtesy Becky Thatcher Book Shop,
    Hannibal, Mo.

TOP: before, exterior, 1937. Photo: John Winkler.

BOTTOM: after, interior, book shop. Photo: courtesy Becky Thatcher Book
    Shop, Hannibal, Mo.

Helena First

From: hotels, apartments, saloons, banks, businesses
To: shops, offices, apartments, restaurants

The spillover from the California Gold Rush did not reach the mountainous territory of Montana until the 1860s. It was not until 1864 that Helena, later to become the state capital, was founded. Prospectors threw up temporary shelters on their claims and along the gulches that brought water from higher elevations. As rich lodes made the town prosperous, shacks gave way to more substantial structures, in styles ranging from granite-faced Richardsonian Romanesque mansions to the idiosyncratic Bluestone Building on a high slope overlooking Last Chance Gulch. This stream eventually dried up and became Helena's winding main street, along which the city's many newly minted millionaires built hotels, businesses, banks, and saloons. So much wealth, so quickly accumulated, helps to explain why so small a town (present population: ca. 23,821) boasts so many elegant examples of late 19th-century architecture.

In the 1950s and 1960s, suburban sprawl and urban renewal threatened Helena's unique downtown district. In 1967, however, concerned downtown merchants, bankers, and architects incorporated under the name "Helena First" to build a hotel/convention center on Last Chance Gulch. Soon the plan grew into a broadly based program for revitalizing the entire central district. Loans and relocation grants totaling $13.2 million from the Department of Housing and Urban Development plus city grants that included $1 million in model cities funds helped make it work.

Last Chance Gulch, the focal point of the plan, has been transformed into a pedestrian mall. Residential, office, and retail spaces were integrated throughout, as Helena sought to strike a balance between sensitive preservation of the best from the past and imaginative use of new technology. Nearly a score of historic buildings have been restored at a cost approaching $7 million, but 228 more were demolished.

A new 6-story Arcade Building now houses 12 businesses, 7 of which are new to Helena. A new city-county library and federal office building have altered forever the look of the downtown district. A number of public housing facilities have been added, presenting quite a contrast to the old "Upper West Side" mansions.

One triumph of the plan was the preservation of the Bluestone Building. Built in 1889 by James Stranahan, a local architect, as a wedding gift for his wife, the house stands high above Helena's old red-light district, not far from the town's old fire tower, which is also being protected. The house was eventually abandoned, perhaps due to 1935 earthquake damage. In 1976, developer Tom Lythgoe purchased the property for $9,700 and literally pulled it down stone by stone in order to rebuild it. The cost was high—nearly $100 per square foot of usable space—but today the Bluestone, with its distinctive minaret, functions as an elegant restaurant.

The first building restored under the Helena First project was the Diamond Block, designed by the Bluestone's architect and built the same year. Aside from tiny faceted mirrors in the diamond motif between the second- and third-story bay windows, the most celebrated feature of the stone and brick structure is its endearing lack of symmetry. The eight bay windows in the main facade are unevenly spaced, divided at odd junctures by smaller rectangular windows and stone pilasters, and the building itself is pie-shaped, yielding rooms of irregular shape. Originally an apartment house, Diamond Block was converted into ground-floor shops and professional offices (including that of a U.S. senator) on the upper two floors.

The Securities Building at 101 North Main, just down the street from the new Arcade Building, represents the best of Helena's classically inspired architecture: Richardsonian Romanesque with a splash of Second Empire and Beaux-Arts France. Built in 1886 of heavily rusticated local granite and sandstone shipped from Wisconsin, it has richly paneled interiors and decorative ceilings that bespoke the confident prosperity of Helena's early banking community. Nicholson, Inc., a local developer, bought the Securities Building and with architect Richard Shope of Jacobson & Shope, who also renovated Diamond Block, was able to preserve the interior, despite severe structural problems, through a system of exterior buttresses incorporated into a new complementary structure. The old banking establishment is now a mix of business offices, luxury top-floor apartments, and a lower-level bar.

TOP: after, facade, Diamond Block. Photo: Len's Visual Design.

BOTTOM LEFT: before, exterior, Bluestone House. Photo: courtesy Thomas Lythgue.

BOTTOM RIGHT: after, exterior, Bluestone House. Photo: courtesy Thomas Lythgue.

95

TOP LEFT: before, exterior, Securities Building. Photo: courtesy City of Helena Redevelopment Office.

BOTTOM LEFT: after, interior. Photo: courtesy City of Helena Redevelopment Office.

RIGHT: after, street view. Photo: courtesy City of Helena Redevelopment Office.

BELOW: after, interior. Photo: Len's Visual Design.

Old Cotton Exchange

From: cotton exchange, club, saloon, offices
To: offices

Not much of old Houston is still standing, which makes renovation of the landmark Old Cotton Exchange all the more important. Designed by the German-trained architect Eugene T. Heiner and built in 1884, the Renaissance Revival brick-and-sandstone facade on Travis and Franklin Streets has long enlivened the city's business district. Red brick pilasters with Ionic volutes contrast with brickwork of buff and white and sandstone trim. The Victorian Italianate building was finished with a bracketed white cornice of galvanized iron, which swelled into a rounded pediment above the central bay of the entrance facade. Atop the pediment sat a cotton bale surmounted by a crown; that was apt, since King Cotton long ruled Houston and its merchants, who invested their returns in the city's banks and real estate. The $32,000 building originally contained offices, quarters for the prestigious Houston Club, a posh basement saloon, and, on the second and third floors, an elegant double-height trading room decorated with sculpted wainscoting, gilding, cherubim, and ceiling murals of cotton bolls and meadowlarks.

In 1907, a fourth floor was built for added office space, to the detriment of the facade design. The trading floor was moved to ground level along with its gilding, cherubim, and murals. By 1923, the Cotton Exchange had moved to a different building altogether, and the building was taken over by the Houston Merchant Exchange. Later it provided general office space, with the trading room serving the British Merchant Navy Club in World War II.

In 1959 the building became vacant, because of location and lack of such amenities as air conditioning. In 1971 fourth-generation Houstonian Jesse Edmundson III bought it for little more than the value of the land. With John Hannah, he retained restoration architect Graham Luhn to renovate the 22,500-square-foot structure. Work, completed in 1973 at a cost of $450,000, included installation of new mechanical systems above partially dropped ceilings of acoustical tile on the top three floors and under the floor of the exchange room; building a new roof, elevator, and fire stairs; restoration of the decorative surfaces of the trading room; and cleaning and repairs of the facade. The last effort was accomplished through a matching grant of $25,000 from the Texas State Historical Survey Committee, which has reason to be grateful for the successful and handsome renovation. The office floors are now fully occupied, mostly by lawyers who appreciate the building's proximity to the courthouse. The trading floor, up for rent to a permanent tenant, currently hosts weddings, political meetings, and parties. The building was entered in the National Register of Historic Places in 1973 and declared a state landmark the following year.

99

LEFT: before, exterior. Photo: courtesy The Harris County Heritage Society.

ABOVE: after, interior, 1978. Photo: Richard W. Payne, courtesy Graham B. Luhn, Architect.

RIGHT: after, interior. Photo: Richard W. Payne, courtesy Graham B. Luhn, Architect.

Zion & Breen Office

From: grist mill
To: landscape architecture firm's offices

Built in 1695, Salter's Mill in Imlaystown was in constant operation until 1962. It took its name from Richard Salter, whose son-in-law, Mordecai Lincoln, was the great-great-grandfather of Abraham Lincoln. In 1972, a decade after it stopped functioning, the old wood frame landmark on Doctors Creek was condemned as a hazard, even though its 277-year-old stone foundation was still intact. With the building on the verge of being destroyed, Robert Zion, partner in the firm of Zion & Breen, site planners and landscape architects, stepped in to save it. Himself a resident of Imlaystown and weary of the daily 90-minute commute to his New York City office, Zion bought the mill for what he calls "a pittance." His firm then renovated it as a new main office at a cost of $100,000. Now Zion commutes on horseback, leaving his mount to graze during the day in the pasture alongside the old mill.

Working with William Short as associate architect and John Morton Levine as design consultant, Zion & Breen planned the renovation themselves. They retained most of the original mill machinery and had it cleaned and reconditioned. It now provides a dramatic counterpoint to the office spaces. Even more

dramatic is a bridge that runs from the entrance to the main-level reception area, spanning the millrace that flows under the structure.

The 6,200-square-foot building has four levels. The basement includes drafting space, an employee lounge, a galley, and a sitting room as well as the millstream and the old horizontal water wheel. On the main level, in addition to the entrance bridge, are a reception area and the main, two-story-high drafting area that looks over Doctors Creek, gardens, fields, and woods. The second and third levels contain the partners' office, conference rooms, and storage areas.

The overall effect is of airiness and dramatic space. As the partners state in a brochure on their distinguished headquarters: "Working in this historic building with the millrace coursing below us, with views over the lake and the surrounding rural countryside, we cannot help being affected favorably in our approach to design. Landscape architects too long separated from the land tend to become 'hard-lined' and overly architectonic."

OPPOSITE: after, interior. Photo: Norman McGrath, New York.

TOP: before, exterior. Photo: Robert P. Matthews, Trenton, N.J.

MIDDLE: after, exterior. Photo: Norman McGrath, New York.

BELOW: after, drafting area interior. Photo: courtesy Zion & Breen Associates.

Old Brick

From: church
To: auditorium, offices, headquarters of Iowa Division of Historic Preservation

Old Brick, the affectionate name for the former North Presbyterian Church in Iowa City, has borne its years well. It replaced an earlier church that was built on the site in 1846 and burned in 1856. Plans for new construction began the same year, in a period of optimism about the city's development. Then came the financial panic of 1857 followed by the Civil War, during which the congregation met in the roofed-over basement of the sanctuary. One newspaper correspondent described the unfinished building as "an unsightly object, its windows boarded up, its ragged eaves grinning at every passerby, and its spireless tower speaking eloquently of blasted hopes and disappointed ambition." The hopes were realized after the war, however, when the church was finished, complete with a $4,000 spire rising 153 feet above the street. When the spire was struck down by a tornado several years later, the determined congregation rebuilt the belfry as a battlemented tower, but omitted the spire.

As years passed, the building won affection for its looks and its service. Romanesque Revival in design—before that style became ubiquitous—it combined brick corbeling and window tracery with the traditional and classical New England church plan and eaves and classical pilasters. In recognition of its successful eclecticism, the building was added to the National Register of Historic Places in 1973.

Old Brick is the city's oldest church building and second oldest public building, and has served the neighboring campus of the University of Iowa since its completion. In 1914, in fact, a rear addition was built to house a campus ministry. Thus, when the congregation decided it needed new facilities and put Old Brick up for sale in 1970, it was not surprising that the university agreed to buy the building. What

shocked the community was that the university proposed demolishing it and sodding the site as a green space for students. Four citizens' committees protested.

The first group stalled the building's demolition while the local Lutheran Campus Ministry considered buying the church; the Lutherans' state executive board vetoed the idea. Even as the stained-glass windows were being removed by wreckers, the second group stayed demolition with a court injunction and a lawsuit against the state, the university's Board of Regents (the official buyers), and the congregation. The legal argument was that the demolition violated the public interest and national policy for the preservation of historic sites and buildings. A new alternative arose when Adrian Anderson, head of the Iowa Division of Historic Preservation and liaison officer for the U.S. Historic Preservation Program, proposed using Old Brick as his headquarters, ensuring federal support for the building's purchase and renovation. The third citizens' group organized to match a federal grant to meet the purchase price of $152,210.

In 1977, agreement was finally reached. The building's life was ensured, and so was its care, as a result of fundraising efforts by the fourth group, Friends of Old Brick, Inc., which leases the sanctuary for $1 per year and rents it out as an auditorium, contributing the fees toward the $150,000 renovation. The sanctuary reopened in February, 1978, with an art exhibition, and has since housed several musical and theatrical performances as well as regular Sunday Lutheran services. The structure's office space has simply been modernized, and now houses Anderson's headquarters, as well as other state and local agencies.

TOP: after, exterior. Photo: courtesy Division of Historic Preservation, Iowa State Historical Department.

BOTTOM LEFT: during construction. Photo: courtesy Division of Historic Preservation, Iowa State Historical Department.

BOTTOM RIGHT: after, interior. Photo: Sandra Eskin Collection.

Clinton House

From: hotel, shops
To: museum, professional offices, offices for nonprofit groups

Completion of the Erie Canal link in 1825 and of the Ithaca-Owega Railroad in 1828 gave the growing village of Ithaca a central location in east-west commerce. So it was that Clinton House, a three-story Greek Revival hotel with a colossal Ionic portico and an elegant pediment, was built in 1830 to serve the burgeoning traffic between New York and Buffalo. The hotel, situated in what is now Ithaca's downtown business core, was originally built with a high cupola that was removed and replaced by a smaller one and a mansard roof to suit the more coloristic French tastes of 1872. A major fire in 1901 resulted in the mansard's replacement with a reproduction of the original balustrade.

For all its new roofs, however, the hotel seemed to have outlived its usefulness by 1970, and its owner considered demolishing it to build a motel. But Ithaca preservationists had recently organized themselves into Historic Ithaca, Inc., an informational group that publishes brochures and sponsors local architectural tours. To save Clinton House, Ithaca's major architectural landmark, the group negotiated its purchase in 1973 for $86,000, the original cost to the owner. Historic Ithaca thereupon set about renovating the building for lease.

Contributions from private foundations and individuals generated the major income; loans from local banks and the National Trust for Historic Preservation and matching grants from state and federal agencies met modest architectural fees and some construction costs. A fundraising auction of hotel furnishings, tours, and bazaars, all of them volunteer-organized, contributed initial operating expenses. With professionals donating some services, laborers reducing their wages and volunteers refinishing woodwork, interior renovation of the 33,000-square-foot building was completed in 12 months at slightly more than $10 per square foot. Total renovation cost: about $390,000.

The renovation has provided the DeWitt Historical Society of Tompkins County with museum quarters on the first floor and in the basement. Two additional floors of office space are being used by doctors, lawyers, accountants, and other tenants, two of them nonprofit. The nonprofit status has meant partial exemption from expensive property taxes. Historic Ithaca reports that the building is self-supporting, and hopes for an eventual surplus to create a revolving fund for future projects.

RIGHT: before, exterior.

TOP: after, exterior.

BOTTOM: during construction.

Photos: courtesy Historic Ithaca, Inc.

Bank Building

From: commercial bank
To: apartment house

For about 50 years, Jersey City suffered a lull in real estate development. Today new projects are going up in several areas and, with support from former mayor Paul Jordon, a number of renovations were undertaken, particularly of residential rowhouses. One of the pacesetting events in this heartening trend was the conversion of Jersey City's Bank Building, a five-story structure with Romanesque brownstone facade, into 13 condominiums.

The Bank Building was commissioned in the early 1890s by the New Jersey Title Guarantee and Trust Company, which also installed the current bronze entrance in 1931. The company eventually succumbed to the Depression, and in the 1950s its vacant quarters were re-occupied by the Elk Supply Company for a paper flower factory and storehouse. When the building was abandoned and put up for sale in 1973, Arthur Abba and Jane Goldberg happened to be looking for an apartment that would be at once more distinctive than the one they had and also an easier commute to the husband's investment banking firm on Wall Street. Goldberg enlisted three friends in a partnership to buy and renovate the Title Guaranty Building: William R. Bernstein, an urban planner with experience in building renovation; Alan J. Preis, a tax accountant; and Philip J. Keifer, town administrator for Secaucus, New Jersey. All signed up for condominiums.

The partners won backing from the First Jersey National Bank, which is committed to brownstone renovation. The city also helped by providing a 25-year tax abatement after designating the building an historic landmark. Richard Dattner, a New York architect known for his adventure playground designs, drew up the plans, and Dews Construction Company handled the $650,000 project. Completed in early 1976, the apartments range from 1 to 5 bedrooms, with 14-foot ceilings that lend themselves to loft and duplex design. The apartments are served by a restored French "birdcage" elevator, embellished with wrought-iron scrollwork, and a staircase with a wrought-iron and brass banister. Other features of the original interior, such as the oak wainscoting and floor-to-ceiling windows, were incorporated into the intricate, modern units. What was once the bank vault will be a sauna, the old sidewalk coal vault a wine cellar, and the roof a sundeck. All told, there are 19,000 square feet for apartments and 7,500 square feet of common area.

The renovated building, in the Paulus Hook Park neighborhood, affords a view of the nearby lower Manhattan skyline. The area is zoned for mixed residential and commercial use and the example of the Bank Building has served as incentive for more and more renovations.

OPPOSITE: before, interior, first floor, 1913.

LEFT: exterior, 1977.

BELOW: after, interior.

Photos: courtesy Bill Bernstein.

Citizens Bank

From: fort, hotel
To: bank

In the early 19th century, long before the California Gold Rush, the great Southwest was still a pretty wild and woolly place. Comfort was difficult to come by for the stagecoach travelers, pony express riders, and merchants who worked their way back and forth across the desert. In 1822, Don Martin, who owned a freighting service on the Camino Real between Santa Fe and Chihuahua City, Mexico, established an outpost in Las Cruces, 40 miles north of El Paso. In the early days the adobe building, with its three-foot-thick walls, was used as a fortress for protection against Apache war parties. Not until 1850 was it used on a regular basis as a rest stop.

Two families, the Amadors and the Campbells, operated the hotel for long periods, but it is the Amadors who left their stamp most clearly on the fine old two-story structure. As the century advanced, Victorian tastes became evident in the furnishings, draperies, and brocade bedspreads that adorned the rooms, a contrast to the blend of Mexican and Spanish Colonial paintings and Indian artifacts that decorated the walls. The main lobby sometimes served as a stage for theatrical groups and was often the scene of Las Cruces social gatherings. The building was also used as a post office, courtroom, and jail

from time to time, but well into the 20th century it remained a hotel, with 20 rooms, a saloon, restaurant, and patio. P. G. McHenry of Corrales, New Mexico, who first alerted us to the old hotel's recycling, was struck by its charm when he stayed there in the early 1950s while doing construction work at the nearby White Sands Missile Range.

When the old building finally proved obsolete as a hotel, the Citizens Bank of Las Cruces took it over for its headquarters. Care was taken by renovation architect Gerald Lundeen to retain as much of the old décor as possible. The hotel lobby became the central banking room whose original marquetry floor is preserved beneath a carpet. In niches off the lobby are a Roman missal dated 1776 and a primitive crucifix, both of which were in the old Amador Hotel. To the rear of the main floor, where the dining room was located, are murals painted by Corina Amador, and niches containing Amador family silver, china, and cut glass. A ground-floor bedroom and a parlor have been set aside for display of original furnishings, art objects, and household goods. Upstairs, one room has become a small museum for press clippings and photographs depicting the hotel's history.

OPPOSITE: after, interior.

LEFT: before, interior.

MIDDLE: after, exterior.

BOTTOM: before, exterior.

Photos: courtesy Citizens Bank of Las Cruces.

Civic Center

From: city hall, federal offices
To: offices, performing arts theater

The proposed Lincoln, Nebraska, Civic Center involves two limestone-sheathed public buildings. One is the old city hall, a Gothic pile built in 1874 as a federal office building and used as a city hall from 1903 until 1968. It now stands vacant. The other is the Old Federal Building, a French Renaissance structure that went up in stages between 1903 and 1937 and was abandoned by the federal government in 1975. It is now half-vacant; decay and fire code regulations prohibit full use. The two buildings share a block in Lincoln Center.

In 1975, the Civic Center Corporation was formed to buy the Old Federal Building for $695,000 and to promote the idea of architect Lawrence Enersen of the Clark Enersen Partners for a renovation complex incorporating both buildings. Enersen proposed a 2,500-seat performing arts center to fill the U-shaped courtyard of the Old Federal Building; the back wall of the city hall would become the backstage wall of the center. The old buildings would be renovated for municipal office space, with 85,000 square feet in the Old Federal Building alone. The city hall, which is listed in the National Register of Historic Places, would be refitted for a museum, exhibition center, senior citizens center, and offices. The cost of the entire project was estimated at $7 million, or $25.37 per square foot, to be financed by a 20-year municipal bond issue. The city hailed the project as a bargain, noting that the actual renovation cost of $3 million should be compared with an estimated cost for new construction of $10 to $12 million.

Aside from renovating the buildings, the proposal would create a theater specifically suited to symphony, ballet, and opera, as well as a wide variety of other events. Although Lincoln has several auditoriums and theaters, none fits this formal need. The new facilities might have spurred a rise in convention and tourist traffic, as well as expansion of Lincoln's own cultural resources and the regeneration of a now-dormant city block.

When the bond issue was put to a vote in May, 1977, however, it lost by a bare 600 votes, despite an intensive publicity campaign emphasizing that the entire project would cost only 40 percent of the cost of a new theater. In a special election in November, 1977, Lincoln's voters turned down the proposal even more emphatically, 14,888 to 6,965. Whether this reflected a general resistance to new spending or a specific reluctance to spend so much money for the arts is unclear. The city still has an option to buy the Old Federal Building from the corporation at cost and already owns the city hall. Renovation of the buildings for office space alone is still a possibility.

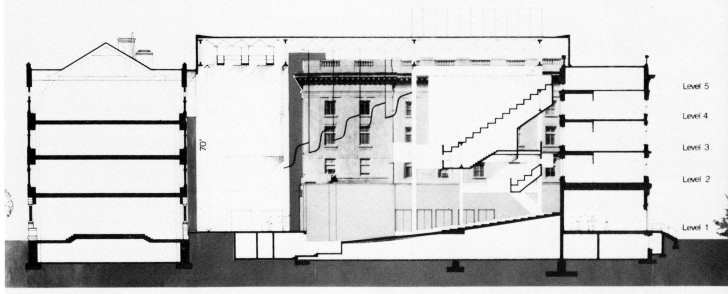

Old City Hall   Performing Arts Facility   Old Federal Building

Level 5
Level 4
Level 3
Level 2
Level 1

70'

OPPOSITE: before, exterior.

TOP: after, interior plan.

MIDDLE: before, interior.

LEFT: after, interior, model.

Photos: courtesy The Clark Enersen Partners, Lincoln, Neb.

Union Station

From: railroad depot
To: mixed-use complex

Little Rock's Union Station was so named because transportation executives hoped that it would accommodate the three railroads serving the city in the 1920s. The union never took place, but the station thrived for some 40 years as a Missouri Pacific Railroad depot. As rail use declined in the 1960s, the station grew idle and was finally bought by the Train Station, Inc., a private partnership. The new owners revived the building's use as a transportation center, adding offices and entertainment and commercial space. More significantly, they have made it the center of a mixed-use development plan for 56 acres of downtown Little Rock's historic Quapaw Quarter.

The St. Louis and Iron Mountain Railroad system built Little Rock's first station on the site of the current building in 1873, a wood frame structure that was demolished in 1906. In 1911 its replacement was completed, with Italianate touches like the tall, square clock tower flanked by entrance loggia, though these features were incongruously combined with steep-pitched roofs. The building burned in 1920 and Missouri Pacific, which had acquired the system three years earlier, undertook a speedy restoration. The company used its own architectural department in St. Louis, producing a design by architect E. M. Tucker and a building that, more than two decades later, was used by Harry S Truman for a whistle stop during his 1948 presidential campaign.

The 1921 facade was an update of the earlier design, with the pitched roofs flattened to give a clean, orderly look. The clock tower, one of the few things to survive the fire, was reinstated at the center of the building. Gray pressed bricks matching the originals were combined with marble tiles and limestone trim.

The 1971 renovation by H. Allen Gibson of Little Rock restored 1921 features like fountains and canopies, and basically preserved the interior of the four-story structure. The original waiting room, with terrazzo floor, extensive plaster molding, and columns faced to half-height in marble tiles, remains the showpiece of the project and will house some 40 retail specialty shops, on the model of San Francisco's Ghirardelli Square.

Amtrak has built a passenger station in the lower level, and the State Transit Authority has rerouted a bus line past the station. The Arkansas Department of Planning and the state attorney general were among the first tenants for the top two floors of office space. The Tracks Restaurant, on the lower level, is the major attraction, achieving the highest restaurant sales volume in the state in its first year of operation.

Renovation of the 108,000-square-foot station, at a total cost of $3 million (including purchase price and landscaping), is only the first phase of a neighborhood redevelopment project. When completed, it will result in a meeting place of renewed commercial, political, and social significance.

LEFT: after, exterior, rendering. Photo: courtesy Arkansas Historic
    Preservation Program.

TOP: before, interior. Photo: Robert Dunn, courtesy Arkansas Historic
    Preservation Program.

BOTTOM: after, interior. Photo: Robert Dunn, courtesy Arkansas Historic
    Preservation Program.

Queen Mary

From: luxury ocean liner
To: hotel, shops, marine museum, restaurants

When the Royal Mail Ship *Queen Mary* was christened on September 26, 1934, one of the guests at the ceremonies, Lady Mabel Fortescue-Harrison, said with surprising prescience: "The *Queen Mary*, launched today, will know her greatest fame and popularity when she never sails another mile and never carries another paying passenger." Since she was permanently berthed at Pier J in Long Beach and given a costly $60-million conversion, the well-traveled ocean liner has attracted several times the total number of customers on her 1,001 North Atlantic crossings. Some of these pilgrims came as wide-eyed tourists, some as patrons of the new hotel, some as diners in the restaurants, or shoppers, or marine enthusiasts anxious to study the aquaria and the multimedia exhibitions designed by Jacques Cousteau.

Long Beach won its trophy in 1967 with the highest of 18 bids—$3.45 million—to the Cunard Steamship Company, then hard-pressed by losses to air travel. The bidder guaranteed that the ship would remain publicly accessible, would retain its familiar form, and would be used in part as a maritime museum. In 1968, the ship was installed in a new berth constructed with landfill. This qualified her as a California building, technically a "nonconforming floating structure."

The *Queen Mary* was built at a time when England was part of a heated international struggle for commercial domination of the North Atlantic. At 1,019 feet and 80,000 gross tons, she was designed as a larger, swifter version of Germany's *Bremen* and *Europa*. Four 40,000 horsepower steam-operated engines drove her four 32-ton propellers. Despite the Depression, artists were sought throughout Britain to design wall tapestries, cast bronze doors, and metal bas reliefs, and to create painted, carved, and decorative murals, such as McDonald Gill's map in the first-class dining room. The cabinets were made from 56 varieties of wood.

On her maiden voyage from Southampton on May 27, 1936, about 3,000 passengers and crew members were aboard; later, she set a speed record for the North Atlantic that was to last for 14 years (3 days and about 21 hours). In World War II she donned camouflage paint and became the "Grey Ghost," safely ferrying 810,000 Allied troops all over the world. A cramped war-time bunkroom has been preserved as a reminder of that period and a contrast to the lavish three-deck-high Queen's Salon.

Seven years of renovation work transformed her. A mix of full-time services is now available on the ship's eight levels, from the bridge down to the R deck. The 400-room Queen Mary Hyatt Hotel adapted many of the staterooms and suites, adding color television, telephones, and air conditioning to the original furnishings. The prize Winston Churchill suite recalls the statesman's five crossings aboard the ship; so does the Sir Winston Churchill, one of four gourmet restaurants now serving on board. Others commemorate Lord Nelson, hero of the Battle of Trafalgar in the early days of British seafaring supremacy, and his love, Lady Emma Hamilton.

The hotel and restaurants, combined with banquet seating for more than 850 in the old public rooms, have attempted to lure numerous conventions to the ship. The former dining room and lounge also have hosted civic, professional, and social gatherings. Visitors most often come, however, to tour the museum in the old engine and boiler rooms, to view the sample cabins, officers' quarters, lifeboats, and other relics, and to browse in three malls of shipboard shops as well as a shipside shopping center designed to recall a 19th-century English village.

OPPOSITE: after, aerial view. Photo: Tom Witherspoon for Long Beach News Bureau.

LEFT: before, interior. Photo: Tom Witherspoon and Andy Witherspoon for Long Beach News Bureau.

BELOW: after, interior. Photo: Tom Witherspoon.

Actors Theatre

From: bank, warehouse
To: theater

The Actors Theatre of Louisville has a fondness for re-used spaces. The organization's last headquarters was a renovated railroad station. When the managers of the group learned that the building lay in the path of a planned expressway, they began to look for new quarters with more space at a reasonable cost. What they found were two 19th-century buildings, a superbly executed bank and an adjacent warehouse, in fine condition. The 142-year-old Bank of Louisville is used as the main lobby for the newly built, 649-seat theater behind it.

A mix of re-use and new construction designed by Harry Weese and Associates of Chicago readied the buildings for the theater company.

The bank was long thought to be Gideon Shyrock's work, but recent research seems to prove that James Dakin was the architect. Dakin fused Greek Revival elements with Egyptian influences. The facade is a temple front with two colossal Ionic columns set *in antis* between battered walls. A crowning anthemion substitutes for the usual Greek Revival pediment. This portico gives access to a large, rectangular banking room roofed by an oval dome with graduated coffers around a central oval skylight.

The theater's renovation architects designated the banking room a lobby to the modern theater behind it. The rear of the building was gutted to accommodate a simple, semicircular stage and 649 seats. Two 72-foot-long steel trusses span the room, eliminating the need for supports inside the theater. A pierced brick rear wall helps absorb sound. The basement has been excavated for use as a subscribers' lounge.

The adjacent and refurbished Italianate brick and cast-iron warehouse shelters office space in the front of its four stories and a small adventure theater at the rear. The warehouse's association with the bank building dates from its construction in the 1860s for Joshua Bowles, who helped establish the bank and served as its president for 29 years. The building was successively used in the dry goods, leather goods, carpeting, and finally furniture business before the theater acquired both buildings in early spring of 1972. The $1.7-million renovation was completed in October, 1972, and represents a saving of about $1.8 million and a year's time over new construction.

LEFT: after, auditorium. Photo: courtesy Harry Weese & Associates.

TOP: after, exterior. Photo: Steve Grubman.

ABOVE LEFT: before, exterior. Photo: courtesy Harry Weese & Associates.

ABOVE RIGHT: before, interior. Photo: courtesy Harry Weese & Associates.

Museum of Natural History and Science

From: dry goods store
To: museum

For about 10 years the city of Louisville had been looking for a home for its new Museum of Natural History and Science. Established in 1965 with a $600,000 bond issue, the museum was intended to study regional geography, flora, and fauna. Then in 1975 a site was found: 727 West Main Street, one of several buildings funded by tobacco magnate Joseph Peterson, a 19th-century Louisville businessman. A plaque affixed to the cast-iron, limestone, and sandstone facade proclaims that it was built in 1878 by architect C. J. Clarke and the Snead and Bibb Ironworks. (Louisville was the cast-iron center of the South during the post–Civil War reconstruction period.) Originally, the facade consisted of three bays of segmental arches, articulated by red sandstone Corinthian columns and embellished with incised vine-patterned panels and the sentiment, "Two Sisters," in honor of Peterson's granddaughters. The building was enlarged to its current seven bays sometime between 1895 and 1908, when its pressed iron pediment was emblazoned with the name "Carter Dry Goods Co."

The facade was restored and slightly altered for $40,000 by a commercial redevelopment company, which bought the building from the Carter Dry Goods Company in 1972 and sold it to the city for the museum three years later. The museum seemed ideally suited to its Main Street site, overlooking the Falls of the Ohio with its limestone Devonian ledge.

When the city bought the 76,000-square-foot building, it also purchased three neighboring warehouses with another 54,000 square feet renovated for additional museum space and some shops and restaurants. The peripheral warehouses serve several interests: They help the cause of Main Street redevelopment, generate operating funds for the museum, and provide reserve space for expansion. Starting with a 190,000-item collection donated by a previous city museum, the organization already has plans for exhibitions of medical research and the coal, tobacco, and distilling industries, emphasizing the cultural and natural history of the Ohio River Valley.

Funding for the purchase and renovation of the museum building came from a $2.7-million grant from the federal Commerce Department, and a $1.5-million grant from the J. Graham Brown Foundation, conditional on matching donations of $350,000 from private sources. Former Louisville mayor Harvey Sloane appointed a committee of bankers and businessmen from the area to raise the money, while project architect Jeff Points of the firm Louis and Henry handled the renovation. Extensive interior work included creation of a five-story atrium. The museum opened in July, 1977, with a gala benefit that drew many representatives of the museum world.

RIGHT: after, facade.

OPPOSITE TOP: before, interior.

OPPOSITE BOTTOM: after, plaza entry.

Photos: courtesy Louisville Museum of Natural History and Science.

Lowell National Historic Park

From: textile mills, tenements, assorted commercial enterprises
To: housing, offices, shops, recreational facilities

Before 1822, Lowell was a small collection of Indian settlements, farms, and scattered small factories. By 1850 it was the second largest city in Massachusetts, the hub of the thriving textile industry in the Northeast and known far and wide for its advanced industrial techniques and humane working conditions. Young single women from surrounding farms made up much of the labor force, and the mill-owners fostered a paternalistic arrangement that provided board, lodging, education, and cultural exposure.

From 1850 until 1920, however, waves of immigrants arrived from Europe, displacing the mill girls at work and crowding into tenements that replaced their old boarding houses. More and more mills were built, creating a dense collection of industrial buildings known as the "mile of mills" and effectively blotting out the urban amenities that had once existed. By 1900 a full 80 percent of the population of 100,000 was foreign-born.

Lowell's decline began around 1920 when the textile industry began moving South, where labor was cheaper. The period of rapid growth screeched to a halt, leaving behind a depressed populus, economic havoc, and environmental chaos. Factory buildings, agents' houses, rowhouses, and subsidiary structures were demolished or abandoned. Urban renewal efforts during the 1950s and early 1960s did more harm than good, tearing down old buildings and disrupting entire neighborhoods, leaving cheap, poorly designed replacements or vacant lots. Today, only the Wannalancit Textile Mill, also housing the Lowell Museum, is still producing cloth.

With the advent of the federal model cities program in 1966, an investigation of the city's possibilities began. Patrick Mogan emerged as the key figure in a massive program to transform the entire decaying mill area into the Lowell National Historic Park, a tribute to the city's role as the first planned industrial center in the nation. A former school administrator, Mogan became long-range planner for Lowell's City Development Authority. Along with such supporters as Frank Keefe, present director of state planning, Mogan argued that Lowell could not step into the future without doing something to preserve its past.

After two years of study and planning, the 250-page report of the Lowell Historic Canal District Commission calling for $40 million in federal aid for two five-year periods of restoration and construction was approved by Congress and signed by the President in June 1978. The funds supplement nearly $20 million pledged by the state: $9.1 million to create

Lowell Heritage State Park, a revitalization of the 5.6-mile canal system in and around the city; and $10 million from the state Department of Public Works for city transportation improvements.

The plan focuses on two concepts: an intensive-use zone and a wider preservation district. The intensive-use zone would incorporate downtown and outlying canal loops and a section of downtown Lowell that would be restored and recycled as a representative cross-section of 19th-century Lowell. The old mills, houses, shops, and commercial buildings, once preserved, will provide new space for local businesses, housing, cultural centers, and recreational facilities. Some buildings have already been individually recycled—the Pilling Shoe Factory into housing for the elderly and a warehouse into the A. G. Pollard Restaurant—and plans exist to convert the Palmer Street Firehouse into an office building. The development and design of the plan is the work of the Lowell Team, consisting of David A. Crane and Partners, Geladin/Bruner/Cott, Inc., and Michael Sand and Associates, Inc.

A good example of the plan at its best involves the Boott Mill complex, consisting primarily of the old mill and its row boarding house, once home to hundreds of mill girls. Built in 1835, the structures still stand and in 1974 were the subject of a prize-winning design by Boston architects Michael and Susan Southworth for combined housing, shopping, and cultural facilities, a center containing workshops, exhibition space, a theater, restaurants, a public library branch, and an enclosed inner courtyard plus an outdoor courtyard for staging plays and concerts.

Within the state park, the canal system, with its many locks and gatehouses, would be revitalized to accommodate pleasure boats and tourist barges. Indeed, the canal system as a source of energy is a major attraction for businesses thinking of relocating in the 1.5 million square feet of now-vacant industrial space throughout the city. Connecting the canals to the recycled old mills would be a system of promenades, parks, and gardens.

While Lowell awaited word from Congress on funding, local support mounted. The city had invested $1.6 million in downtown pedestrian improvements to reinforce the area's 19th-century flavor and offered free design services to building owners interested in restoration. By the time the report from the Canal District Commission was published, $26 million had been either spent or committed to the project by local, state, and federal sources.

LEFT: before, exterior.

MIDDLE: after, exterior, rendering.

BOTTOM: after, exterior.

Photos: Kevin Taff.

Madison-Morgan Cultural Center

From: schoolhouse
To: performing, visual, and decorative arts center

For so small a town (population: 3,500), Madison has quite an array of lovely ante-bellum homes. It also boasts one of the first graded brick schoolhouses in the Southeast, an old Romanesque Revival structure, with bell-tower, that dates from 1895 and now serves as a cultural center for the performing, visual, and decorative arts.

When the schoolhouse became vacant in 1957, the Morgan County Foundation, Inc., took it over and in turn leased it to the Uncle Remus Regional Library. When the library decided to move in 1974, the Morgan Foundation knew exactly what to do with the schoolhouse: turn it into a center serving the town and half a dozen surrounding counties.

Private foundations contributed nearly $400,000 to help renovate the building, and a membership drive in the new cultural center netted $60,000 more. Other contributions followed. The Georgia Commission for the Celebration of the Bicentennial provided a $5,000 matching grant to be used for the restoration of one of the original classrooms, down to the wood paneling, wainscoting, heating stove, and student desks. The Rich Foundation of Atlanta offered yet another $5,000 to help purchase a Steinway grand piano for use in the main-floor auditorium. The semicircular auditorium itself, with seats for more than 400, contains the original heart-pine paneled ceiling, wainscot, and interior shutters, as well as the original chairs, sconces, and chandelier. Although the audience that attended the center's opening program in 1976 may have been much more serious than the ones that fidgeted through countless school assemblies up to 1957, the room they shared has changed little.

The building houses a central art gallery, a museum of history, and smaller display rooms on the main floor, as well as a reception room decorated with a turn-of-the-century brass chandelier, velvet draperies, and English wallpaper with a William Morris design. Other parts of the building have been more freely adapted as office for the director of the Cultural Center and Chamber of Commerce, a film room, and a kitchen and dining facility used not only for special receptions but also for community cooking classes.

Four Georgia architects helped with much of the recycling: Thomas Collum and Kempton Mooney of Atlanta, Edward Neel of Columbus, and Albert James of Madison. Total cost of the job: $400,000.

RIGHT: after, exterior. Photo: Bob Moore.

TOP LEFT: before, interior, auditorium. Photo: Bill Ponder.

TOP RIGHT: after, interior, auditorium. Photo: Bob Moore.

OPPOSITE BOTTOM: after, interior, Museum of History. Photo: Bob Moore.

Butler Square

From: department store, warehouse, offices
To: commercial, retail, and office space

Butler Square, a partially renovated warehouse on the edge of downtown Minneapolis, seems to be an idea whose time has almost—but not entirely—come. Difficulties have arisen in a more or less constant stream since 1974, when developer Charles Coyer found the 534,000-square-foot project, half-developed and perhaps one-third occupied, uncomfortably sitting in his lap. The economic recession was at least partially to blame. Butler Square was then taken over by the First National Bank of St. Paul, and finally purchased, more than three years later, by James Binger of Minneapolis. Although Binger, the former board chairman and chief executive of Honeywell, has no fixed plans for the undeveloped portion of the building, its future success now seems assured.

Coyer, developer of Washington's Canal Square, was the first person to propose a workable renovation program for the immense, nine-story pile that had stood vacant for a decade. He knew that a major downtown freeway had been proposed to pass behind the building, providing a potential "gateway" situation with high visibility. Ironically, it was the displacement of railroads by highways that had led to the building's abandonment. Butler Brothers Department Stores used to run boxcars out of the building on a rail spur to distribute goods to their chain of small-town stores. When truckers, urban congestion, and the building's multistory design rendered it obsolete for its original purpose, it was turned into a storehouse for ten years, and then fell empty until 1972, when Coyer bought it.

The building's interior was structurally sound and functionally flexible, and its exterior was valued by preservationists. Designed in 1906 by Minneapolis architect Harry Wild Jones, the building has full facades on all four sides. Its windows are vertically arranged within elongated Gothic arches between a corbeled parapet and a high basement story. Perhaps the most unusual architectural feature is its wood post-and-beam structure of Douglas fir columns which taper from a 22-inch square on the first floor to 8 inches on the ninth.

Although Minneapolis was already well-supplied with standard offices, there seemed to be room for specialty office and retail space and a new downtown hotel. A two-phase development program was launched, the first phase stressing offices and shops and the second a future 300-room hotel.

The Minneapolis firm of Miller, Hanson, Westerbeck, Bell, Architects, with Arvid Elness as project architect, completed work on the first phase in 1974 at a budget of $20 per square foot. Brick walls and heavy timbers were sandblasted clean and left exposed; mechanical systems were run beneath new raised floors so as to preserve the raw ceilings. The brick archways through which freight cars once entered were transformed to shops and restaurant alcoves. The hallmark of the design was the creation of an irregularly shaped skylit atrium rising the full height of the building. Offices are lit either by enlarged floor-to-ceiling windows in the outside wall or by light pouring down from the atrium skylight. The cutaway idea was particularly suited to a renovation: It reduced the square footage of an oversized building, admits light to the interior, and draws businesses and customers to the glass walls.

TOP: after, exterior.

BOTTOM: after, interior.

Photos: Phillip MacMillan James.

Department of Pensions and Security

From: general hospital
To: government offices

Its face gives it away—a colonnade of giant Tuscan columns, each 32 feet 5 inches tall. The building could be nothing less than a distinguished public servant. In fact, that is how it began its life (as the old City Hospital) and that is how it is continuing (as the Mobile County Department of Pensions and Security).

The old City Hospital, completed by builder John Collins to plans by William George in 1838, is one of the finest examples of Greek Revival style in the Southeast. The yellow fever epidemic of 1819 spurred the city to build the hospital between 1833 and 1838 to replace inadequate facilities at the Spanish Royal Hospital. Between new waves of the fever in 1853 and 1894, it served Confederate soldiers during the Civil War and, after Mobile's fall in 1865, Union soldiers. A pioneer in social services, the hospital admitted female patients and the female staff to care for them as early as 1841; slaves and freemen were admitted as early as 1852. In 1859, teaching was added to the hospital's activities.

When City Hospital moved to a new building in 1966, the Mobile Historical Development Commission began looking for an adaptive use. J. Linyer Bedsole, a civic-minded businessman, endowed a $500,000 trust for the renovation in memory of his sister, Lorraine Bedsole Tunstall, who was nationally recognized as a pioneer in child welfare legislation. The Alabama Child Welfare Department, which she founded, was the model for the current Department of Pensions and Security.

Renovation, aided by a city and state gift of $1.2 million augmenting Linyer Bedsole's donation, was designed by architects Grider and Laraway of Mobile, in consultation with George M. Leake. The facade was cleaned and restored. The interior, with little ornament beyond a graceful and now restored circular stair, was remodeled. A major part of the job involved pouring concrete foundations, for the building had previously stood without structural grounding. Now, with support not only from modern finance and civic bureaucracy but also from modern technology, the foundation for a new career is well-laid.

LEFT: before, exterior. Photo: Paul Thompson, courtesy Mobile Historic Development Commission.

TOP: before, interior. Photo: Paul Thompson, courtesy *Mobile Press Register*.

BOTTOM: after, board room. Photo: Frank Chandler, courtesy *Mobile Press Register*.

Historic New Harmony

From: farm village
To: historic memorial

In 1814 a visionary German Lutheran preacher named George Rapp brought 800 followers to the banks of the Wabash River and established the religious colony of Harmonie. A year later Rapp wrote: "The woods are green, the herbs are growing. Everything is moving to a new birth. Flowers blossom. . . . It is surely a joy to live here." The Harmonists worked hard within the square mile that comprised Harmonie itself, and on the 2,000 acres of farmland that they cultivated, exporting surplus crops and manufactured goods as far afield as New Orleans and the East Coast. They made bricks in their kilns and used timber processed by their Wabash-powered sawmill to build 150 residences, stables, large dormitories, two distilleries, a brewery, a granary, a cannery, and factories for manufacturing cotton, wool, and silk. Determined to relocate closer to their burgeoning market, Rapp sold the town to a different kind of Utopian, Robert Owen, for $150,000 in 1825, and moved his followers to Pennsylvania.

A Welsh-born Scottish industrialist, Owen renamed the place New Harmony and set about building an "empire of good sense" based on scientific knowledge rather than religious authority. But the scientists and dreamers he imported lacked agricultural expertise, and by 1827 the official experiment was terminated. Owen returned to Great Britain, where he later founded what is now the Labour Party, but many followers and all four of his sons stayed on. The eldest, Robert Dale Owen, became a congressman and helped found the Smithsonian Institution. Another son, David Dale Owen, built the laboratory from which the nation's first geological surveys were launched.

The town has been credited with an astonishing number of other "firsts"—America's first public school system, kindergarten, trade school, free public library, and women's club. But that record did not prevent changing trade patterns and the advent of the automobile from turning it into a backwater. New Harmony slumbered until the 1940s, when Jane Blaffer Owen, wife of Robert Owen's great-great-grandson Kenneth Dale Owen and herself the heiress to a Texas oil fortune, began acquiring buildings with her own funds. Not until the 1970s, however, was Historic New Harmony, Inc., created to direct a comprehensive restoration plan.

Sturdy old Harmonist structures were restored, and shops were leased out to give the dying business district new life. Celebrated architects were commissioned to help create a blend of old and new: Philip Johnson's roofless church, adorned with Jacques Lipschitz's sculpted bronze virgin, is an example.

The last three years have brought the most striking progress, under the guidance of Ralph Grayson Schwarz, president of Historic New Harmony, Inc., and a team of restoration experts. Scores of buildings have been refurbished and restored by this team and the state of Indiana. Among the most notable projects: Dormitory Number Two, which originally housed single men and women, later served as a school, offices, a tavern, library, post office, and telephone exchange, and is now a museum for early artifacts; the Labyrinth, a shrubbery-bordered maze of paths leading to a small round temple, reconstructed on land adjacent to its original site; the Owen block, several buildings erected as an agricultural warehouse for an Owen descendant in 1882 and now restored on the outside and gutted inside for use as the New Harmony Gallery of Contemporary Art and a specialty food store; the Solomon Wolf House of 1823, built for a Harmonist shepherd and now restored as a typical brick dwelling of the period and used by the Historic New Harmony tour guides.

Today, properties owned by the state of Indiana are maintained as state memorials. Historic New Harmony owns 79 parcels of property in the town and has raised over $10 million in philanthropic funding. All told, more than $30 million has been spent on community renewal, restoration, and rebuilding. The anticipated result: up to 400,000 tourists a year.

TOP LEFT: before, exterior. Photo: James Boucher.

TOP RIGHT: after, exterior. Photo: courtesy Historic New Harmony, Inc.

BOTTOM: before, exterior. Photo: courtesy H.A.B.S., Library of Congress.

OPPOSITE TOP: after, interior. Photo: James Ballard.

OPPOSITE BOTTOM: before, exterior. Photo: courtesy Historic New Harmony, Inc.

LEFT: after, exterior. Photo: courtesy Historic New Harmony, Inc.

BELOW: during construction, relocating the Solomon Wolf House. Photo: courtesy Historic New Harmony, Inc.

Howard Library

From: memorial library
To: law offices

The authorship of the great stone fortress at Lee Circle has long been disputed. An anomaly among the breezier Greek Revival and Italianate concoctions in wood, plaster, and brick in New Orleans, the Howard Library illustrates the thinking of Henry Hobson Richardson, now lauded as the best architect America had produced up through his time.

A Louisiana-born émigré to Brookline, Massachusetts, Richardson was famous in his day for his robust, monumental stonework and Romanesque-inspired designs—a homegrown answer to the crowd of European styles that posed on American facades. This particular commission in his native state was built after his death in 1886 by his architectural heirs, the Boston firm of Shepley, Rutan and Coolidge. As late as 1976, the Chicago chapter of the American Institute of Architects maintained that Richardson had designed nothing south of St. Louis, but more recently research by Carolyn Ross has revealed otherwise. It seems that Richardson, in conjunction with Shepley, Rutan and Coolidge, designed an 1886 entry to the Hoyt Library competition in Saginaw, Michigan, which he lost. The firm then modified the Hoyt design to suit the needs of the Howard Library, endowed in memory of Charles T. Howard by his daughter. The architects credited Richardson with the design by carving his letter seal monogram into the capital of the column separating the front doors. The random ashlar facade of sandstone, guarded by turrets, gables, steeply pitched roofs, and a cavernous arched entryway, is unmistakably Richardsonian. Carvings designed and executed by Bostonian John Evans, including the New Orleans seal, completed the hybrid building.

From the announcement of this $115,000 gift to the city in January, 1887, to its formal opening on Mardi Gras in 1889, the library had excited much local interest and a number of stories in national magazines. One German observer sent from Berlin to study the building a few years after its opening wrote to the librarians: "Within this last year only the golden gate of [Louis Sullivan's] Transportation Building in the World's Fair, which shows original characteristics like the works of the late Richardson, has aroused greater interest in Berlin than your library building."

The library collection grew badly cramped by the 1930s and in 1940 was moved to larger quarters, while the building itself faced the threat of demolition. Public authorities rejected a number of suggestions for a new use, including one that it be made a branch of the neighboring Confederate Museum. Finally, private enterprise saved it. Between 1946 and 1959, it was used as a radio station owned by the Times-Picayune Publishing Corporation. Other users have included building corporations and oil companies. Recently covered with ficus vine, this city landmark was bought in 1970 by the large law firm of Kullman, Lang, Inman & Bee. When they took over the 13,000-square-foot building, they commissioned Stanley Muller to renovate it. The old reading room has been rehabilitated as the library, and upstairs rooms were gutted for added office space for the 22 lawyers.

TOP: before, interior. Photo: courtesy *The Times-Picayune*, New Orleans.

BOTTOM: exterior, 1977. Photo: Steven A. Robbins, courtesy New Orleans Historic District Landmarks Commission.

United States Mint

From: mint building
To: shops, restaurants, museums, tourist center

The grand Greek Revival structure that occupies a full city block at the edge of New Orleans's French Quarter is the oldest surviving mint building in the United States. The work of the nationally famous Philadelphia architect and engineer William Strickland, it was completed in 1838 at a reported cost of $185,000. A tall iron fence guards the courtyards and grassy fringes around the imposing structure. The ashlar facade, severe but gracefully proportioned, culminates in a slightly projecting central bay with an Ionic portico. The second-floor balcony is graced by a spidery iron railing, the kind characteristic of the historic district.

The Mint building has seen its share of history, and has already been recycled several times. During the Civil War, it served as the Mint of the Confederate States of America. In 1909, it was taken over by the U.S. Public Health Service, the Veterans Bureau, and a naval recruiting station. In 1931 it underwent its most dramatic transformation, becoming a federal prison with cell blocks on the upper floors and bars on its graceful windows. The Coast Guard took over the building in 1943, and when it moved 20 years later, the old Mint became vacant.

After its designation as a National Historic Landmark in 1975, the state of Louisiana invited pro-posals for its recycling. The New Orleans architectural firm of McNaughton Biery Toups Lemann, Joint Venture submitted the winning plan, calling for a mixed-use complex of commercial space, restaurants, a Mint museum library and archive, and a state tourist center. Shops, restaurants, and the Mint Museum would occupy the first floor, and the New Orleans Jazz Museum, Jazz Hall of Fame, Museum of Louisiana Folk Life, and tourist information center would fill most of the second and third levels, which would include substantial exhibition space and a 250-seat theater. The architects propose turning some of the jail cells on the upper levels into dining rooms—some small and intimate, some enlarged by breaking through the walls of the old cells. A Cell Block Bar would also be included. Other cells would be converted into library archives and stacks.

Except for reopening the attic level to make use of an existing skylight that would provide natural illumination for parts of the building, the architects propose few structural changes. Their view is that the building should not be restored to reflect any one period, but should retain the flavor and eccentricities of its varied, 143-year history.

OPPOSITE: before, exterior. Photo: Steven A. Robbins.

LEFT: before, interior. Photo: Stephen Duplantier.

BELOW: architect's drawing, view from courtyard. Courtesy McNaughton
    Biery Toups Lemann, Joint Venture Architects.

From: free public library
To: theaters

John Jacob Astor, the German immigrant who made a fortune through fur trading, dealings in Manhattan real estate, and slumlording, decided late in life to give some of it back to the city. On the advice of Washington Irving, among others, he bequeathed $400,000 for the construction of New York's first free library for the benefit of working people. The Astor Library opened in 1854, an Italian Renaissance palace in a Victorian translation by Alexander Saeltzer. A particularly splendid touch: The great second-story Library Hall, reached by a flight of 38 marble steps, is decorated with 26 cast-iron columns on three levels finished in imitation Italian marble and crowned, 50 feet above, by a huge skylight flanked by two smaller ones. Two new wings were added to the north of the original building in 1859 and 1881.

Unfortunately, the library's closed stacks of 200,000 volumes were available for reference use only in reading rooms that kept the gentlemanly hours of 10 to 4. Part of the reason was a lack of artificial lighting. In 1911 the free library was merged with the Lenox Library and the Tilden Trust to form the New York Public Library and was moved uptown to the public palace created by Carrère and Hastings in Bryant Park.

With that, Astor's building passed on to another charitable service, housing the Hebrew Immigrant Aid Society from 1920 until 1965, when the society negotiated a sale to an apartment house developer who planned the building's demolition, but the newly created New York City Landmarks Preservation Commission swung into action to save it. Thus, when Joseph Papp, director of the innovative theater company that had produced free Shakespeare in Central Park for seven years, called the commission for sug-

gestions for new headquarters, the solution was right at hand. The developer was reimbursed and Papp's group had a home.

Papp's Shakespeare Company is the country's largest performing arts institution, operating as many as seven theaters at once in the Astor Library's old reading rooms. Renovation has been a costly but careful and successful venture under the direction of Giorgio Cavaglieri, a New York architect noted for his preservation work. Though the Landmarks Preservation Commission only required the preservation of the building's facade, Papp and Cavaglieri willingly scaled down their original plans for an 800-seat theater to avoid tearing apart the Library Hall. The result is the Anspacher Theater, whose 300 seats are encircled by the original two-tiered cast-iron colonnade, restored and touched up with gold leaf. The open stage fills one wall, two of whose columns have been stripped down to accommodate the superstructure of the stage-lights. The open stage, with no proscenium, became the model for the other theaters in the complex. Acoustics are excellent and space is bountiful in the three-story structure, which has 220 feet of frontage on Lafayette Street in Manhattan's East Village.

Money has flowed in readily from federal, state, corporate, and private sources to fund over $3 million worth of renovation. Between $1.4 million and $1.9 million of work is still to be done, with total estimated costs of $4.5 million to $5 million. One of the contributions came from the developer who lost the building to the Shakespeare Festival Public Theater—one more instance in the building's history where culture conquered and converted capital.

OPPOSITE: after, exterior.

LEFT: after, interior.

BELOW: after, auditorium.

Photos: George Cserna.

Bridgemarket

From: farmers' market
To: market, restaurants, shops

After the Queensborough Bridge spanning the East River was completed in 1909, the cathedral-like space below the Manhattan approach housed a bustling farmers' market. About 40 years ago the market was closed, and today the area is an underutilized municipal sign shop and garage. Now this huge, vaulted space, 120 by 270 feet and ranging in height from 30 to 60 feet, will be restored to its original use as a glassed in market—with shops and restaurants as well.

The space was designed and built by the Raphael Guastavino Company, which specialized in a Catalonian system of vaulting using thin, quickly laid-up, self-supporting tiles. The company created spectacular spaces in hundreds of structures, including New York's Cathedral of St. John the Divine and the Oyster Bar in Grand Central Station.

The proposed re-use will reflect changes in both culinary taste and shopping styles. The complex will house a carefully selected variety of independent food dealers and ethnic restaurants. The great markets of Europe and the great success of the recently recycled Quincy Market in Boston serve as prototypes.

The modern developer, Harley Baldwin, engaged Hardy Holzman Pfeiffer Associates to design a two-level facility, with small food stores at the first level and restaurants on an open balcony that will be built above. An open-air plaza to the south will be designed by landscape architects Zion & Breen Associates; the plaza will include a greenhouse and farmers' market. Step one in the $4-million renovation will be to restore the vaulting, which has been damaged by water and salt seepage from the roadway above. The main structural addition will be the restaurant mezzanines, connected by footbridges.

The first re-use proposal was for the American Cinémathèque film theater complex and museum, but the recession put an end to those plans. A second proposal was for creation of a food market, but the developer backed out, and Harley Baldwin, who originally was interested in a more varied shopping complex, adopted the idea. To gain community approval for the venture, Baldwin conducted an extensive public relations campaign, including more than 130 community meetings and presentations over a two-year period.

The city is to receive a minimum rent of $54,000 a year for the space, increasing to $130,000 in the 20th year of the lease or a percentage of the project's income, if that is the larger figure.

OPPOSITE LEFT: before, exterior. Photo: courtesy Baldwin & Associates.

OPPOSITE RIGHT: before, interior. Photo: courtesy Baldwin & Associates.

LEFT: exterior. Photo: courtesy New York Landmarks Preservation Commission.

BELOW: after, interior, rendering.

Cooper-Hewitt Museum

From: private mansion
To: design museum

For decades, the Cooper-Hewitt design collection was considered by those in the know to be "the best-kept secret in New York." A superb collection spanning 3,000 years of man's efforts to shape his surroundings, it featured textiles, drawings, prints, wallpaper, woodwork, furniture, ceramics, glass, a 25,000-volume library, and an archive of 1.5 million photographs and reproductions. But since 1897 it had been hidden away on the fourth floor of the Cooper Union for the Advancement of Science and Art in downtown Manhattan. The school was founded by Peter Cooper, the iron and steel mogul; the museum was started by the three Hewitt sisters, his granddaughters, who had admired the South Kensington Museum in London (now the Victoria and Albert) and the Musée des Arts Décoratifs in Paris.

When financial crisis hit the school in 1963, Cooper Union decided that the collection was expendable, but a group of citizens appealed to the Smithsonian Institution for help, and in 1967 the collection was adopted and subtitled the National Museum of Design. However, it still had to find operating funds—and a building to operate from.

Coincidentally, Andrew Carnegie's 64-room mansion on Fifth Avenue and 91st Street was about to become available. Carnegie, another iron and steel magnate, conceived the four-story, Neo-Georgian pile as the "most modest, plainest, and most roomy house in New York." Designed by Babb, Cook & Willard between 1901 and 1902 for $1,500,000, it was richly endowed with wood panels decorated with

Indian work and installed by Lockwood de Forest, Lincrusta panels, a glass and iron entrance canopy from Tiffany's, and elaborate gilt, plaster, and stencil decoration everywhere. One of its most intriguing features: a two-level boiler room with pairs of dynamos, pumps, tanks, and coal-burning steam boilers (the duplicates in case of a breakdown), the whole served by a coal car that ran on tracks to a 200-ton coal bin.

Since 1946 the house had been occupied by the Columbia School of Social Work. With institutional zeal, the school had slapped green paint over every carved, paneled, and painted surface. After it moved on to other quarters, the Carnegie Corporation donated the house to the Cooper-Hewitt in 1972. With the mansion went the large garden and the 39-room Miller House, which the Carnegies bought in 1919 as a wedding present for their daughter, Margaret Carnegie Miller.

The museum was reopened in 1976 after 13 long years without a home. Eventually lectures, films, workshops, and so on will be moved to the Miller House. Plans are in the works for archives of industrial and advertising design and a laboratory for holography. Mrs. Taylor proposes that in these ventures the Cooper-Hewitt study the process as well as the products of design. That process, in fact, is vividly exemplified in the thoughtful adaptation of the old Carnegie mansion, itself a museum of 19th-century crafts and technology.

TOP LEFT: after, facade. Photo: courtesy Cooper-Hewitt Museum/Smithsonian Institution.

TOP RIGHT: before, hall. Photo: courtesy Hardy Holzman Pfeiffer Associates.

BOTTOM: after, entry. Photo: Norman McGrath.

Custom House

From: customs offices
To: federal offices, exhibition space

In the days when the Custom House at Bowling Green was built, between 1901 and 1907, duties on the cargo brought into New York Harbor yielded the government's largest source of income. The collection process accordingly was thought to merit a place of architectural importance equal to this practical role. Moreover, the site itself carried signficant associations for New Yorkers. Situated at what was once the southernmost tip of Manhattan, it was the port of Dutch entry in the 17th century and is said to have been the place where Peter Minuit made his $24 deal with the Indians for the island.

New York partisans built Government House on the site as a presidential mansion, hoping that their city would be named the national capital. That was not to be, and the building served instead as the governor's mansion until 1799, when it was adapted as a customs house. After it burned in 1814, a block of Federal-style houses was built on the site by wealthy merchants, who abandoned the area a decade later, leaving the houses to shipping firms that turned the block into "Steamship Row." Then the U.S. Treasury, needing a large and permanent customs office building, bought and razed the site and, in 1892, announced a competition.

The winning architect was Cass Gilbert, who designed an opulent $7-million structure. He endowed the entrance lobby and the elliptical skylit rotunda just beyond it with walls of cream- and rose-colored marble and green marble columns. Dolphins cavort in overhead bronze grills, ships' prows in bronze loom at the elevators, and the scallop shell and eagle are omnipresent. Outside, the four continents most relevant to commerce at that time sit before the entrance. They are the sculptural masterpieces of the building, carved by Daniel Chester French, also known for his statue in the Lincoln Memorial. Each of the 44 Corinthian column capitals outside the seven-story Beaux-Arts building supports within the entablature a sculpted head of Mercury, the Roman god of commerce. Granite keystones over the second-floor windows represent the 8 races of man, and 12 marble statues standing on the cornice line in silhouette against the slate-covered mansard roof symbolize the world's great commercial centers. The decoration was completed in 1937, when the Ash Can School painter, Reginald Marsh, executed the rotunda murals under the auspices of the WPA.

The building survived years of use, but in 1973 the Custom Office abandoned it for the World Trade Center, throwing the building's fate into question. With downtown office space going begging, the prognosis for re-use of the Custom House's 45,000 square feet was grim. Nonetheless, while awaiting a workable re-use proposal, the General Services Administration, the Custom House Institute, and the New York Landmarks Conservancy sponsored an initial $200,000 restoration of the exterior and the main floor.

In the fall of 1977 GSA Administrator Joel Solomon proposed a $20-million federal renovation. The plan, currently being readied for congressional review, proposes federal offices on the upper levels and continued cultural and educational functions on the first and second floors (a number of successful exhibits were held there in 1976 and 1977), the most appropriate design to be determined by national competition. In addition, the Museum of the American Indian, the foremost collection of native American artifacts, has expressed interest in moving downtown to the Custom House's lower floors.

In any event, Solomon assures that federal building policy has been revised to favor landmark rehabilitation, as evidenced by the rescue of the old St. Louis Post Office and the Washington, D.C., Post Office from demolition.

Before, exterior. Photo: © 1975, Nathaniel Lieberman.

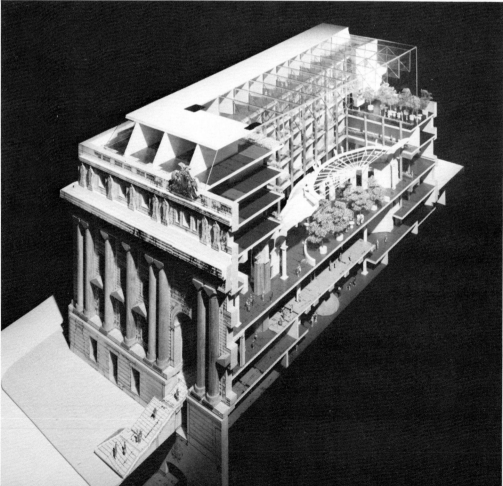

OPPOSITE TOP: before, interior. Photo: © 1975, Nathaniel Lieberman, courtesy New York Landmarks Conservancy.

OPPOSITE BOTTOM: after, interior, model. Photo: © 1975, Nathaniel Lieberman.

LEFT: before, interior. Photo: © 1975, Nathaniel Lieberman.

BELOW: before, interior. Photo: Steven Zane, courtesy New York Landmarks Conservancy.

Edward Mooney House

From: private residence
To: Off-Track Betting parlor, offices, apartments

Although Edward Mooney's vocation was wholesale meat merchandising, his avocation was breeding race horses, so it is entirely appropriate that his 18th-century residence should now house one of New York's Off-Track Betting offices. In 1785, only two years after the British evacuation of New York, Mooney purchased a plot of land at the southeast corner of Pell Street and Bowery, and began construction of a townhouse. The building was completed in 1789, the same year George Washington was inaugurated president in a ceremony held not far away, in the Wall Street area. Today, the building is considered an important example of the domestic architecture of the period. The three-story house is early Federal with a finished attic beneath a gambrel roof. Two features in particular document the building's age:

the hand-hewn timbers framing the roof, and the breadth of the front windows in proportion to their height. Most of the windows are capped by the original splayed stone lintels with double keystone blocks. From Pell Street, one can see in the gable the arched window, with the original wood tracery of its upper sash, which lights the attic. Among the remaining interior architectural details are the original window frames and trim. A Pell Street extension, equal in size to the original building and also finished in brick, was added in the first decade of the 19th century.

New York City's Landmarks Preservation Commission awarded the structure landmark status in August, 1966. Five years later, 18 Bowery was renovated as a betting parlor of OTB at a cost of $46,000. Apartments and offices are planned for the upper floors.

After, exterior. Photo: courtesy Eugene Grossman.

Federal Archive Building and U.S. Appraisers' Warehouse

From: customs appraisals
To: shops, offices, semipublic space, apartments

Designed by Willoughby J. Edbrooke in 1891 in a style greatly influenced by Henry Hobson Richardson and the Chicago School led by Louis Sullivan, the U.S. Appraisers' Warehouse is considered one of New York's finest examples of Romanesque Revival architecture. It is the largest building in Greenwich Village, a massive, square-block, ten-story brick pile with 506,000 square feet of usable space—more than an acre on each floor. The block on which it stands, bounded by Christopher, Barrow, Greenwich, and Washington Streets, is irregular in shape, and the building, in consequence, is a trapezium. The dark red structure features heavily arched bays at ground level and, at the top, three-arch groupings separated by bricked-in arches, producing, by comparison, an almost delicate effect. The third through seventh floors are unified by a series of vertical arched recesses containing pairs of double-hung windows. This progression from heavy to light treatment as the eye travels upward, one of the tenets of classical architecture, is particularly well-handled in this building. The brickwork is of fine quality, with a pink-tinted mortar. The corners of the building are rounded, emphasizing the smoothness of the exterior.

The old building was originally used to receive, examine, test, and appraise items entering the country from abroad. In 1938, the interior was remodeled as office space, and the building became the National Archives Record Center; it also housed a branch post office and a number of other federal agencies. The remodeling did not alter the building structurally. The large freight elevator shaft was maintained at the central core, capped by a large metal and glass gable-roofed skylight.

In 1974 the archives center moved and two years later the building was declared surplus. When the building was vacated, the General Services Administration asked New York's Landmarks Conservancy to study new uses, and Columbia University's Graduate School of Architecture and Planning began a feasibility study. That led to a proposal in 1975 for conversion to a mixture of revenue-producing and community uses. In 1976 New York City applied to the federal government for transfer of the building under a law enabling Washington to turn over federally owned historic properties to city, county, or state governments at no cost—assuming federal approval of the re-use plan and provided that all net income is used for "public historic preservation." In this case the income may go into a revolving fund for further preservation projects in New York City. The city will lease the building to the Landmarks Conservancy, which in 1977 chose the Rockrose Development Corporation, in collaboration with the New York State Urban Development Corporation, to handle the recycling job.

Detailed plans have not yet been completed, but Rockrose has determined certain guidelines. By community request the entire third, fourth, and fifth floors will be reserved for cultural tenants and semipublic uses such as medical facilities, a day-care center, a dance group, and a local planning board. If suitable tenants cannot be found to rent the unfinished space at $6 per square foot, or maintenance cost, it will be converted into apartments. As of now, the upper half of the building is distributed in 267 units to be condominiums, rental apartments, or Section 8 housing. John Belle of Beyer, Blinder, Belle Architects has been chosen principal architect for the planning and design of the project, whose cost could come to $20 million.

TOP: before, exterior. Photo: Steven Zane, courtesy New York Landmarks Conservancy.

BOTTOM LEFT: after, section. Photo: courtesy Beyer Blinder Belle, Architects.

BOTTOM RIGHT: after, interior, rendering. Photo: courtesy Beyer Blinder Belle, Architects.

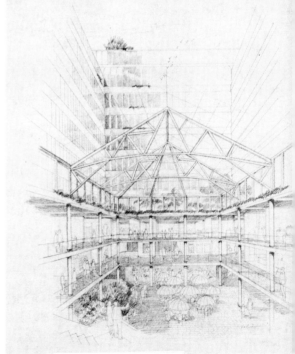

Jefferson Market Library

From: city courthouse
To: branch library

Soon after the gaudy, Victorian Gothic Jefferson Market Courthouse was completed in 1877, American architects voted it one of the ten most beautiful buildings in the country. By the 1960s, as architecture critic Ada Louise Huxtable wrote in *The New York Times*, "any popularity poll would have made it one of the ten homeliest." Yet, thanks to a revival of eclecticism, a wave of preservation, and some extensive repairs combined with skilful adaptation to use as a library, the building survives as one of the most beloved, though not one of the most distinguished, in Manhattan.

Designed by Frederick Clarke Withers and Calvert Vaux according to John Ruskin's Victorian interpretation of 14th-century Venetian Gothic architecture, the building's romantic silhouette has long dominated Greenwich Village and endeared itself to local residents. Gables and turrets pile up to a massive 10-story-high clock tower that points up the Avenue of the Americas, giving some character to an otherwise faceless thoroughfare. Atop the tower is an enclosed fire lookout with a great bell, surmounted by a four-faced clock. The building, which is set on a low granite basement, is polychrome brick, emblazoned with courses of yellow-gray sandstone; the horizontal banding is sometimes referred to as the "Lean Bacon Style."

Even by the early 1900s, this fantasy building was looked upon as ungainly; to the later modernists, it was downright disreputable. Having lost its original function as a courthouse, it served for a time to house various departments of the city bureaucracy and a police academy, but by 1946 it had been vacated and sealed. With the city seemingly ready to demolish the building, private individuals moved to save it. First they shrewdly formed the Committee of Neighbors to Get the Clock on the Jefferson Market Courthouse

Started. Money was raised, the clock was electrified, and the old building was very much in the news. A committee that included architectural historians Alan Burnham and Margot Gayle, Lewis Mumford, and e.e. cummings urged that the courthouse be recycled as an enlarged library branch to replace one nearby that was looking for larger quarters. Finally, Mayor Robert F. Wagner threw his support to the preservationists and against the New York Public Library, which wanted a new building to standard specifications.

The architect for the renovation, Giorgio Cavaglieri, happens to be of Venetian birth, but he limited his Italianate Gothic sympathies to repairs. New partitions and fixtures were done in a crisp modern idiom (travertine-lined doorways, black or deep-bronze fixtures), but without violating the high Gothic windows and elaborate woodwork. Specially trained craftsmen of the old school were needed for some repairs; two of the plasterers who worked on the molded ceilings were over 70 years old. The main, first-floor courtroom became a children's reading room with 20-foot ceilings; the original judges' chamber and the 37-foot-high second-floor courtroom became the adults' reading room; the low, vaulted basement, with salmon brick columns and arches, the reference room.

The adaptation cost more than a new building would have, largely because the heavy masonry walls and high ceilings did not lend themselves readily to refitting. The final bill in 1967 after three years of construction came to $1.3 million (including books and furniture), but the results seem well worth it: a fine library, a cut above the boxy, undistinguished buildings currently being built for branches; a landmark preserved. As much as the books it now houses, the building itself is part of history's record.

TOP LEFT: during construction. Photo: courtesy New York City Landmarks Preservation Commission.

TOP RIGHT: before, interior. Photo: H.A.B.S., Library of Congress.

BOTTOM: after, interior. Photo: Marc Neuhof.

Nesbitt Studio

From: slaughterhouse
To: artist's studio, residence

Lowell Nesbitt, a New York painter who works on a colossal scale, needed colossal quarters to replace the SoHo loft that he outgrew in the early 1970s. He found what he needed in Greenwich Village: an abandoned three-story warehouse built in the 1850s. The building's somewhat unsavory past—initially a slaughterhouse, and until recently a police stable—and its location near a current meat market, were more than offset by the appeal of 18,000 square feet of usable space enclosed by cast-iron columns, brick walls, and plank floors. What is more, recent history has so inverted values that a building with such a past rates as desirable.

Nesbitt bought the building in 1974 for $138,000, a bargain given its location and size. Renovation cost $260,000, which is far from excessive considering that it involved cutting an atrium through the center of the structure and installing a sizable swimming pool. Two friends, Edward F. Knowles, one of the architects of

the new Boston City Hall, and interior designer Mara Palmer, designed the renovation in close consultation with Nesbitt.

Since the only windows in the building were in the 63-foot-wide street facade, the architect opened a light well 25 feet square in the building's center. Beneath the glass and aluminum skylight that he installed is a 20-by-14-foot fiberglass pool. New sheetrock partitions enclose bedrooms, baths, and kitchen surrounding this core. The lacquered bedroom walls and floor carpeted in brilliant reds by Palmer shock the eye grown accustomed to the aged brick of the original walls, where Nesbitt's generously proportioned paintings hang.

Originally, Nesbitt intended to fill his new quarters with his own works. Now he intends to open his second-floor gallery and entertainment area to work by selected artists. They will be getting quite a dramatic showcase.

OPPOSITE: before, exterior. Photo: courtesy Edward Knowles.

ABOVE: after, interior. Photo: Richard Champion, as appeared in April, 1977, *Architectural Digest,* courtesy Edward Knowles and Mara Palmer.

MIDDLE: before, interior. Photo: courtesy Edward Knowles.

BOTTOM: after, interior. Photo: Richard Champion, as appeared in April, 1977, *Architectural Digest,* courtesy Edward Knowles and Mara Palmer.

The Printing House

From: printing house
To: shops, offices, apartments, restaurant

When the 1976 Owens-Corning Energy Conservation Awards were announced, Stephen B. Jacobs & Associates won a prize for their plan to adapt an old printing house at 421 Hudson Street in New York's Greenwich Village. In this eight-story mercantile building constructed before World War I, the few remaining commercial tenants had long since ceased to cover the operating costs. The building was purchased for $597,000 from the Lawrence Wien estate in August, 1975, by Mountbatten Equities, whose owners have shown keen interest in creative re-use projects. The 100-by-200-foot building will be converted into 188 family-size duplexes with commercial space on the first two floors and a health club and restaurant on the roof.

Owens-Corning singled out the project because of a special feature on the roof: about 300 solar energy panels, or 6,000 square feet of flat plate collectors, that will be installed around and above the restaurant and health club, making innovative and economically sound use of the unusually large rooftop area. The solar collector system will provide the hot water for the residential portion of the building. In addition to the solar system, recycling work includes construction of a water-to-air heat pump system in every apartment, permitting heating and cooling without an external heat source.

The ceilings in the roomy loft building are 17 feet high, allowing for duplex apartments combining double-height rooms with two living levels. The building is situated in a low-rise neighborhood; this, coupled with the large, factory-dimension windows, will bring an enormous amount of light into each apartment. The ground-floor rear of the building is being transformed into maisonettes, apartments with their own street entrances. These will face a mews that was created after the acquisition of additional property.

The estimated cost of conversion is $27,000 per apartment, including land costs. Construction was scheduled to be completed in spring, 1978. Rents are projected at $120 to $145 per room or $600 to $700 for a two-bedroom duplex, a not-uncommon rate in Manhattan. In fact, the neighborhood, on the western edge of West Greenwich Village, has attracted considerable recycling activity partly because of even higher rents in the better-known area around Washington Square and lower Fifth Avenue.

The renovation of 421 Hudson was made possible by a $110,163 grant from the Department of Housing and Urban Development, which allocated $6 million nationwide in 1977 to help finance 169 projects involving alternative energy sources. When completed, the 421 Hudson project will also qualify for New York City's J-51 tax abatement program.

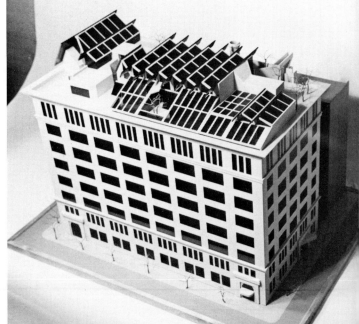

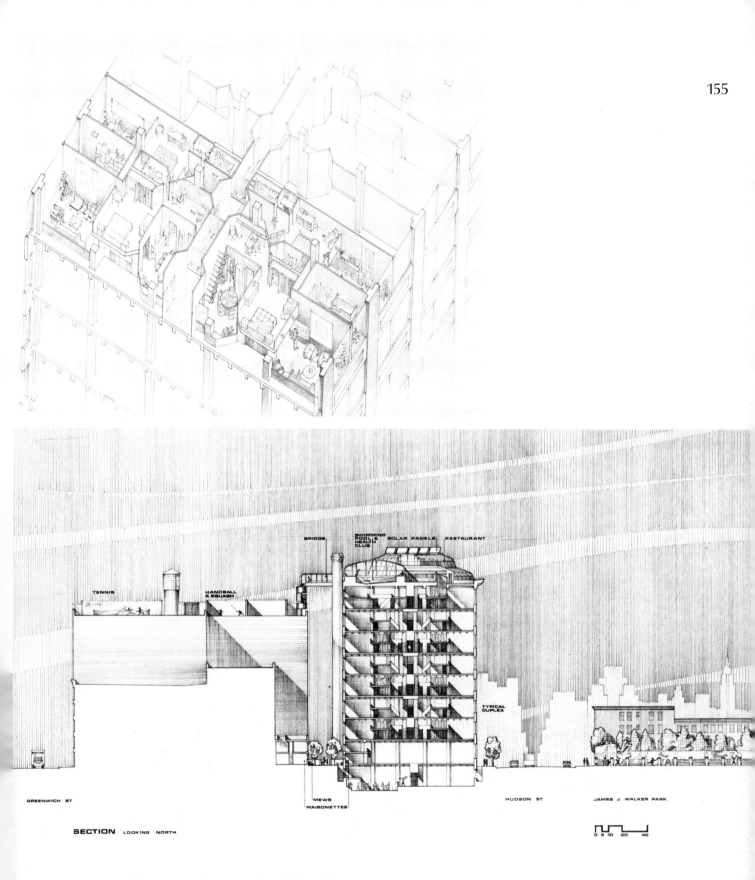

SECTION LOOKING NORTH

GREENWICH ST

MEWS
MAISONETTES

HUDSON ST   JAMES J. WALKER PARK

TENNIS   HANDBALL & SQUASH   BRIDGE   SWIMMING POOL & HEALTH CLUB   SOLAR PANELS   RESTAURANT   TYPICAL DUPLEX

0 5 10 20 40

OPPOSITE LEFT: before, exterior. Photo: James Bret, Mt. Kisco, N.Y.

OPPOSITE RIGHT: after, exterior, model. Photo: James Bret, Mt. Kisco, N.Y.

TOP: after, interior. Rendering: J. Rolland Ristine, R.A.

BOTTOM: after, section. Rendering: J. Rolland Ristine, R.A.

Puerto Rican Traveling Theatre

From: firehouse
To: theater, workshops, offices

The firehouses of any city produce street theater of the purest kind—unrehearsed, unplanned. When one of these structures is abandoned, what better way to re-use it than for a genuine street theater company that goes out in a truck giving performances in parks and on city streets?

The architectural firm of Napoleon Le Brun & Sons built quite a number of 19th-century New York firehouses, completing the one on 47th Street in 1887. The facade shares its combination of red brick and white trim—typical of the Victorian architecture of its decade—with the neighboring hotel. Yet its small, tidy scale and the gaiety of its corner pinnacles and fields of angled brickwork immediately spell firehouse to a knowing eye.

When Engine Co. 54 recently abandoned the building, the city had no further use in mind for it. But

Miriam Colon, director of the Puerto Rican Traveling Theatre, happened to be looking for winterized quarters, since her mobile drama company was restricted to a summer schedule. Not only was the firehouse vacant, roomy, and suitable in spirit, it also stood on the edge of the Broadway theater district. Two years of negotiations with the city earned her a long-term lease. A renovation plan by Peter Blake and Brian Smith will permit year-round performances and expansion of the company's free dance and theater workshop. The 1978 conversion, at an estimated cost of $310,000, involves solely construction of third- and fourth-floor offices, a lounge and training room; a basement shop; and an open stage, raked orchestra and balcony in the 28-foot-high space of the combined first and second floors. The original cast-iron circular staircase will be saved and re-erected.

OPPOSITE LEFT: before, exterior. Photo: Brian Smith.

OPPOSITE RIGHT: after, model. Photo: Ken Howard.

TOP: before, interior. Photo: Ken Howard.

BOTTOM: before, interior. Photo: Ken Howard.

SoHo Cast-Iron District

From: factories, warehouses, showrooms
To: artists' lofts, studios, apartments, factories, commercial space

Cast iron was pioneered for structural purposes and then popularized for decorative purposes in 18th-century England. But the world's greatest concentration of cast-iron architecture is found in New York's 19th-century SoHo Cast-Iron District, comprising 26 blocks between Houston and Canal Streets.

As early as 1794, when the district was still mostly farmland, Joseph Blackwell had established a cast-iron foundry there. It was not until the 1850s, however, that commercial structures with cast-iron fronts began to dominate the scene. Two of the best known now are the 1857 Haugwort Building and the Arnold Constable Store, which illustrate the two most common facade types: the full cast-iron front, a curtain wall independent of the brick-bearing walls and cast-iron interior supports behind it; and the ground floor with cast-iron columns supporting an old-fashioned masonry facade for the stories above.

Initially, design in cast iron imitated that of stone work, first in the Italianate style and later in French Second Empire and Neoclassical styles. Voluptuous detail could be supplied in cast iron at the same cost as a plain masonry wall, and much more quickly. Cast-iron members could also be thinner and could span larger openings than masonry; cast in a mold, they lent themselves to repetitive, rhythmic effects, and combinations which ultimately affected masonry design. The results of such open yet intricate design can be seen in another district landmark, Ernest Flagg's 1903–1904 Singer Building.

The two greatest American popularizers of cast-iron architecture ran their businesses in the district: James Bogardus, who advanced the iron frame buildings, and Daniel Badger, whose foundry produced iron fronts like those of the Detroit Slate and Cornice Company. The difference between Bogardus's special interest in the structural use of cast iron and Badger's decorative use is not as great as it may seem. Both involve the prefabrication of identical units. Moreover, the concept of the curtain wall underlay the skyscraper and the modernist aesthetic of repetitive decentralized design, made to appear weightless by large expanses of glass. The steel skeleton, however, soon replaced cast-iron framing for technical and stylistic reasons, and by the end of the 19th century stone and brick were again the main building material, and terra cotta had become the new, cheap means of decoration.

Badger's factory was an early member of a growing number of factory loft buildings, which overtook the district by the 1880s and 1890s. The neighborhood became the warehouse and showroom center for the nation's fabric business. While retail sales took place elsewhere, major buyers came here to inspect goods and admire the companies' buildings.

By the end of the century, however, the major businesses had moved north, following the city center, and marginal industries filled their places. By the 1960s, the trend among New York artists to paint big led them to the large, low-rent lofts. One of the pioneers in this movement was filmmaker Charles Leslie, who bought up 1,800 square feet of loft space in a brick and limestone Edwardian store and factory building with iron entablature on Prince Street. The building had fallen into disastrous shape since erection in 1903 by architect W. Pigueron, and the initial work involved removal of crumbling tin ceilings and rotten floor boards. Once renovated, the loft provided Leslie with equal amounts of living and studio space, including room for editing, rehearsals, and filming titles for documentaries.

Through zoning changes the city encouraged the co-existence of manufacturing and this special class of residents. SoHo became known for avant-garde art and chic galleries, but also for its own architectural and historic merits. It was declared a New York City Historic District in 1973, and has become a model of adaptive re-use for sturdy but under-used warehouses across the country. Hardly a building can be found there that still serves its original function.

TOP: before, exterior. Photo: courtesy Charles Leslie.

BOTTOM LEFT: exterior. Photo: Mark F. Goldfield.

BOTTOM RIGHT: after, interior. Photo: courtesy Charles Leslie.

The Villard Houses

From: private residences
To: hotel

When publisher-financier-rail magnate Henry Villard commissioned a splendid palazzo at Madison Avenue between 50th and 51st Streets in 1882, the location was socially desirable and slightly rustic. St. Patrick's Cathedral was across the avenue; the twin Vanderbilt houses were under construction a block away; Columbia College's Tudor Gothic library and Hamilton Hall were just to the south. Now, of course, the area is one of the world's choicest pieces of real estate, and that fact very nearly meant the destruction of the Villard Houses.

The U-shaped brownstone complex was one of the first essays by McKim, Mead and White in the Neo-Italian Renaissance style that they later brought to a number of New York glories—the Metropolitan Club of 1893, the University Club of 1899, the Racquet and Tennis Club of 1918. In proportion and detailing, the model for the Villard Houses was the seminal, late 15th-century Palazzo della Cancelleria in Rome. Completed in 1884, the building's three wings contained six private houses, enclosing a central courtyard with an arched wrought-iron gateway to the street. A hipped roof of brown tiles caps the four-story facade with high rusticated basement and attic. Quoins weight the corners and band courses set off the floors, with a cornice of dentils, egg-and-dart molding, and foliated modillions at the roofline. The central pavilion features a five-bay arcade; side wings are approached by pedestal stairs and a simple doorway with plain frieze and projecting cornice. Flanking Florentine lamps match the one that hangs from the courtyard gate.

Villard, owner of the New York *Post*, president of the Northern Pacific Railroad, son-in-law of abolitionist William Lloyd Garrison, and father of the editor of *The Nation* magazine, lived in the houses less than a year. Because of his railroad's decline, he was forced to sell. The new owners had similar interests in publishing and finance. Elizabeth Mills Reid, who bought the south wing in 1886, was married to Whitelaw Reid, editor of Horace Greeley's *Tribune*, ambassador to England and Spain, and Republican vice-presidential candidate in 1892. The Reids commissioned a seven-story corner tower from McKim, Mead and White in 1910 and occupied the building until its sale to the Archbishopric of New York in 1948. The central pavilion, 453 Madison Avenue, was owned by lawyer Artemas H. Holmes until his death in 1917, when it became part of the Reid holdings. Part of the north wing, 455 Madison, was bought by Edward Dean Adams, a business associate of Villard's and a patron of the arts. Harris C. Fahnestock, a banker, bought 457 Madison, then two separate houses. In 1922, these north-wing houses were combined by Charles A. Platt for William Fahnestock, who founded a Stock Exchange firm and directed the Lackawanna and Western Railroad Company. The family sold the wing in 1945 to Joseph P. Kennedy, who, in turn, sold the following year to Random House Publishers. From 1921 to 1949, Harris Fahnestock's daughter, Helen Campbell Hubbard, simultaneously owned both 455 Madison and 24–26 East 51st Street; the latter property had first been occupied by Roswell Smith, founder of *Scribner's Monthly* and *Century* magazines.

The south wing's interior is the most sumptuous, representing the combined efforts of some of the period's foremost artists and decorators. Included are stained glass by Louis Tiffany and the La Farge Decorative Glass Company, murals by George W. Breck and John La Farge, marble sculpture by Augustus Saint-Gaudens, architectural woodwork by Joseph Cabus, and superb decorative painting, gilding, mosaics, and paneling. The Belle Epoque Music Room, or Gold Room, with its Italianate ceiling, gold brocade walls, La Farge murals illustrating Art and Music, and white mahogany and English oak floors, is one of the most acclaimed interiors in New York. So is the library, walnut-paneled with a painted ceiling and adorned with the crests of publishing houses.

With costs rising steeply, both the Roman Catholic Archdiocese and Random House moved their offices elsewhere in the 1960s and tried unsuccessfully to find new tenants. Meanwhile the AIA, the State Council on the Arts, and others searched in vain for an adaptive re-user. Developer Harry Helmsley made the only feasible proposal: a 51-story hotel to be designed by architect Richard Roth, Jr., of Emery Roth and Sons on a lot equal in size to but behind the Villard lot. A portion of the Villard Houses would serve as the hotel frontispiece, and the developer's rent on the property would accrue to the church. The facades of the Villard Houses came under the protection of the New York Landmarks Preservation Commission, but the interiors did not; they were designated "significant interiors" several years before preservation law was broadened to give selected interiors, as well as facades, landmark status and protection. The Gold Room would have been demolished because of a discrepancy in floor levels between old and new buildings.

After considerable public protest and two new design efforts, a way was found to preserve both the Gold Room and the library as public hotel rooms. Roth redesigned the skin of the hotel in bronze anodized aluminum and dark glass to give the Houses a neutral background. The hotel's window and cornice lines were aligned with the Villard band courses. Formal entrance will be through the Villard courtyard, which will be given over to pedestrians and a fountain rather than the current crowd of parked autos, and through an arcade in the central wing. The Palace Hotel logo will be incised in masonry above the arcade, which will be glazed to afford a view of the split-level interior and its grand staircase linking lobby with ballroom and restaurant. Plans were finally approved in 1976, and completion is scheduled for 1980.

LEFT: after, the Palace Hotel, model. Photo: Steven Zane, courtesy New York Landmarks Conservancy.

TOP: before, exterior. Photo: courtesy H.A.B.S., Library of Congress.

BOTTOM: after, rendering. Artist: Vijay Kale.

Westbeth Artists Housing

From: telephone laboratories
To: apartment complex

Westbeth Artists Housing, the world's largest living and working facility for artists, furnishes 384 apartment-studios to writers, painters, sculptors, dancers, composers, filmmakers, and musicians for subsidized rents ranging from about $100 for an efficiency to $170 for a 1,300-square-foot, three-bedroom unit. A great deal of money—some $10 million—and even more imagination were required to recycle the 625,000-square-foot, block-square Bell Telephone Laboratory. The 11-to-13-story behemoth, actually an amalgam of 13 separate steel-and-concrete frame commercial buildings built between 1898 and 1920, is named for its Greenwich Village location. Situated on Bethune and West Streets, it overlooks the Hudson River and affords southern-exposure apartments stunning views of lower Manhattan.

The project was born of an alliance between the National Council on the Arts and the J. M. Kaplan Fund, which provided seed money to buy and begin renovating the building when it came on the market in 1967. The Federal Housing Authority provided the bulk of the financing. Richard Meier and Associates, a prominent New York architectural firm known for its housing work and avant-garde aesthetic, undertook the plans.

With large windows, thick masonry walls, fire-resistant construction, and ceilings at least ten feet high, the building was ideal for conversion. Apartments surround a central courtyard that was once a roofed loading area for trucks. The renovators removed the roof and two stories above the court, opening it to the sky, and converted the space into the main apartment entrance and the locus of projected shops, galleries, and community facilities, including an 800-seat theater, playground, darkrooms, and soundproof film and rehearsal studios. A circulation ramp was built to give access to mezzanine shops. Two pedestrian arcades, one leading to the street and the other to the 13,000-square-foot Westbeth Park with its sparkling fountain, were also built. The original cast-iron gates at the main entrance were preserved.

The basic structure of the building is unchanged, influencing the varied layouts of the apartments, with their undulating, vaulted ceilings. The interiors have almost entirely open plans, the only fixed and enclosed areas being kitchens and bathrooms. Residents are free to partition their lofts by building their own walls or by shifting around the modular closets supplied by the building to double as partitions.

Such open plans had never before been sanctioned by the FHA, but, in a revolutionary turnabout, the authority permitted the architects to substitute dotted lines for actual walls in their plans, signifying potential space distribution. Government flexibility was a vital ingredient in the project, which has already inspired a modified counterpart in the Piano Craft Guild in Boston, built in the big old Chickering Piano Factory.

RIGHT: after, interior. Photo: Ezra Stoller, © ESTO.

OPPOSITE TOP: after, exterior. Photo: Ezra Stoller, © ESTO.

OPPOSITE BOTTOM LEFT: after, courtyard. Photo: courtesy Richard Meier.

OPPOSITE BOTTOM RIGHT: after, exterior. Photo: Ezra Stoller, © ESTO.

Chamber of Commerce Building

164

From: private academy
To: offices

The Greek Revival building that Thomas Ustick Walter designed in 1840 for the Norfolk Academy is solid evidence that adaptive re-use is neither novel nor ephemeral. Over nearly 140 years, the academy's classrooms, library, and large lecture hall have housed not merely a school but also a hospital during a 19th-century yellow fever epidemic, a post office during the Civil War, a Red Cross station during World War I, the local Juvenile and Domestic Relations Court, and, since 1975, the Norfolk Chamber of Commerce.

When the building was abandoned in 1971, the Norfolk Chamber of Commerce acquired it for $3,500 from the Norfolk Redevelopment and Housing Authority. The decision to restore the landmark was not easily reached, since the cost of renovation was estimated to equal the cost of a new building. What is more, the academy's status as a registered historic landmark meant that it could not be enlarged in the future. Still, there were powerful arguments in favor of renovation: the promise of a $90,000 federal grant toward the cost of restoration, the building's location on St. Paul's Boulevard and, most important, the architectural significance of both the building and its

architect, for Thomas Walter also designed the wings and the spectacular dome of the nation's Capitol in Washington, D.C.

A 46½-foot-long structure, the academy was modeled on the Temple of Thesis at Athens, which Walter had seen on a tour of European buildings sponsored by a wealthy patron, Nicholas Biddle. It is encompassed by an unbroken entablature on pilasters along the side walls and Doric porticos at each end. When the interior was cleared, the restoration architect, Sheldon J. Leavitt, found that some of the original features, such as Walter's two entrances, ideally suited the new occupants' needs. As for the exterior, a technician from the Colonial Williamsburg restoration peeled the paint down to the 1841 coating and a gorgeous array of colors emerged: white on the cornice and columns, stone gray on the walls, reddish brown on the column capitals, glazed chestnut brown doors and frames, Chianti red windows and trim. Unfortunately, plans called for a uniform white finish, the kind we mistakenly associate with ancient Greek buildings. Upon Leavitt's recommendation, it was repainted in 1978 in the original colors.

OPPOSITE: before, exterior, 1900.

TOP: before, exterior, 1969.

LEFT: before, interior, 1971.

Photos: courtesy Sheldon J. Leavitt.

Old Market District

From: produce market
To: restaurants, shops, offices, apartments, entertainment

Unlike San Francisco's Ghirardelli Square, Denver's Larimer Square, and most of the other carefully planned and financed redevelopments in American cities, Omaha's Old Market just grew. There was no master plan, no thick sheaf of blueprints, no fretful financial committee. In fact, the shopkeepers and restaurateurs who began transforming the district in helter-skelter fashion in the late 1960s were skeptical of an offer by a local businessman to take over the project with an $11-million investment.

Omaha's food district grew up between 1887 and 1900. The Italianate brick buildings with cast-iron storefronts erected during those years were owned by wholesale and retail produce companies. In the broad city streets of the district under sidewalk canopies, early-rising truck farmers held an open-air market. Some of the neighboring multistory industrial buildings—factories and wholesale outlets—are among Omaha's oldest. But the rise of the suburb, the shopping center, and the supermarket began to kill Omaha's entire central business district in the 1950s, and the farmers' market along with it. The market's few remaining customers were individuals and restaurateurs who placed their orders by phone.

As the old business center continued to decay, private citizens began looking for ways to preserve the social and financial benefits of city marketing and entertainment. In 1968, one of the Old Market's biggest landlords, Sam Mercer, an Omaha native practicing law in Paris, proposed redeveloping his property for shops and restaurants. Mercer was neither a wealthy·developer nor an on-site entrepreneur, and he left much of the realization of that idea to his new tenants. Within a few weeks, the first business had leased a store—a British imports shop—and 11 more followed within a year. Mercer's own contribution proved highly significant: a gourmet French restaurant installed in a renovated cast-iron and glass storefront, and operated by a Parisian chef and a former night-club manager. It soon began drawing the day and evening crowds long absent from the district, and as they browsed through the new shops of the neighboring streets and alleys, these Omahans realized that the Old Market was in the midst of a renaissance.

The shops increased in number and income— cafés, bookstores, gift shops, boutiques, cinemas, galleries, and artists' studios—until the district began attracting tangible support from the city government. New gas lamps were installed in 1969; the brick-paved streets were restored in 1973 with the elimination of ugly cement patches; street trees were planted in 1975. As public interest grew in overall redevelopment, the Old Market was often cited as proof that it could succeed.

Today, the Old Market is attracting offices and apartments for the upper stories of its shops and cafés. Eventually, it will be connected by a greenway to a new Central Park Mall: a major open space spine. And it will benefit further from the conversion of a nearby warehouse district into living lofts.

RIGHT: before, 1106 Howard, 1894.

OPPOSITE TOP: after, street view. Photo: Vera Mercer.

OPPOSITE BOTTOM: after, interior. Photo: Vera Mercer.

Omaha Building

From: life insurance company offices
To: law firm offices, bank offices, retail space, parking

When the New York Life Insurance Company Building went up in Omaha in 1888, the Italian Renaissance style was in vogue. The famous New York architectural firm of McKim, Mead and White created an elegant exemplar of this fashion: an H-shaped masonry structure with flat twin towers, a profusion of arches, and horizontal bands of multicolored stone. The building was sold in 1910 to the Omaha National Bank and took the new owner's name. In 1970, Omaha National moved its headquarters across the street to the new, modern Woodmen Tower, and the old Italianate fortress stood vacant for several years, known simply as the Omaha building. At one point, it was on the verge of being torn down to make way for a 28-story office building.

In 1977 the bank signed a long-term lease with the Omaha law firm of Kutak Rock Cohen Campbell Garfinkle & Woodward, which is renovating the Omaha Building for re-occupancy in 1978. While the firm will be the prime occupant, the Omaha National bank will use one floor.

The architects of the $4-million project, Kaplan/McLaughlin of San Francisco, plan to enliven the dreary rear courtyard with a glass-enclosed greenhouse atrium—a series of open, heavily landscaped, two- and three-story courtyards filling most of four floors. The facade will be cleaned. Interior marble columns and woodwork will be restored and the entire interior fitted with brass fixtures.

The Omaha Building is now listed in the National Register of Historic Places. The city of Omaha as well as the bank that once abandoned it are delighted that the imposing old structure was not only saved but also recycled for a variety of new uses.

BELOW: before, interior.

RIGHT: before, exterior.

Photos: courtesy Kaplan/McLaughlin, Architects/Planners.

Great Falls Historic District

From: textile mills, factories, power plants
To: museum, arts complex, school, apartments, industry craft workshops, artists' lofts, offices, shops, restaurants

From the earliest Colonial days, the 77-foot cascade at Great Falls, New Jersey, was a powerful tourist attraction. But it took Alexander Hamilton to recognize the waterfall's industrial potential. Having made this discovery, perhaps while camping on the Paterson site with George Washington and his Revolutionary troops, Hamilton decided to try to harness the resource to power an independent native industry. In 1791 he helped to found the Society for Establishing Usefull Manufactures (SUM). Pierre Charles L'Enfant, planner of Washington, D.C., designed the Great Falls Raceway and Power System, a grand, multitiered scheme for channeling water to the mills that SUM planned to build. A simpler, less expensive plan by Peter Colt was eventually adopted.

By 1792, Paterson had become the country's first planned industrial city, initially attracting cotton textile mills and factories producing mill machinery. When the Civil War cut off cotton supplies from the South, manufacturers turned to producing industrial machinery and silk, and by 1870 most of the silk made in the United States came from Paterson. The Colt revolver, the Wright airplane engine, and the Holland submarine were also developed there, but locomotive manufacture did even more to replace the textile mills. Thomas Rogers, a former manufacturer of textile machinery, was particularly noted for producing steam locomotives that helped to win the West, supply Union troops during the Civil War, and even traverse Siberia.

The Rogers shops are the focus of a renovation plan administered by the city of Paterson, which bought SUM in 1945. In the mid-1960s highway building plans threatened the Great Falls raceway system and many of its old mill buildings with destruction. Paterson citizens formed the Great Falls Development Corporation, which saved the district and even acquired $340,000 in Highway Department funds for an archaeological dig into the ruins of the Rogers works. (Industrial archaeology, originating in Britain in the 1950s, has proved necessary to trace the unrecorded development of 19th- and even 20th-century industrial techniques.) The diggers' biggest find in Paterson was one of the first three raceways of the power system, a brick-faced tunnel that had been thought destroyed.

Research and archaeological finds helped get the district listed in the State and National Registers of Historic Places, but the biggest boost came in 1976 when President Ford declared the 119-acre site the country's first industrial National Historic District. The designation made available a $330,400 grant from the Economic Development Administration to restore Rogers's Locomotive and Erecting Shop. In 1977, EDA awarded an $11.1-million Title IX grant to restore and develop the district as a Federal Demonstration Project. Together with a city investment of $6 million, the grant will fund multi-use retail, residential, and industrial development.

Already one building, the Union Works, has been privately purchased and houses a primary school and electronics assembly firm. When completed, the Rogers Erecting Shop will serve as a museum and cultural arts complex. The development plan also calls for historic mills to be converted into craft studios, specialty shops, and art galleries. Developers have submitted plans for the conversion of the Essex Mill into living/working lofts for artists. Construction is underway on a $1.4-million tree-shaded park along the upper raceway, and a 6½-mile bicycle path linking the historic section with Paterson's parks and central business district.

TOP: before, exterior, Rosen Mill. Photo: courtesy Archives, Paterson Free Public Library.

BOTTOM LEFT: before, interior, Rogers Locomotive. Photo: courtesy Archives, Paterson Free Public Library.

BOTTOM RIGHT: after, interior, Rosen Mill. Photo: M. Sporzarsky, courtesy Archives, Paterson Free Public Library.

171

Alley Friends Architects

From: food storage warehouses
To: architectural offices

Designers Richard Stange, Alan Johnson, and Bruce Millard needed space for their business, which encompasses everything from architecture and interior design to set design and inventions. In 1973 they found what they were looking for—or almost: seven interconnected buildings that provided ample room (20,000 square feet), the right price ($17,500), and basically sound construction. It was up to them to get the buildings into shape.

Their new quarters are on the northeast corner of Vine and Front Streets in the heart of what used to be Philadelphia's food distribution center. Architecturally, the structures are far from first-rate, but the views of the Delaware River and the Ben Franklin Bridge were appealing, and the roof lent itself to "planting and relaxing and viewing Camden through the telescope," as one of the partners puts it. So they set out to convert the dilapidated old interior into functional work space that would be presentable to the public; the upper floor was converted later into living and dining space.

Built in the 1850s, the old food processing, storage, and refrigeration structures had spartan but sound interiors, including concrete floors that had been scrubbed daily during the buildings' previous life and heavy-duty glass-block windows. The earlier wooden double-hung windows were still stored on the top floor and were used to contribute to the transformation of the living-dining area. Previous repairs over the years had been crudely executed, with no attempt to match mortar or brick to the original. The buildings' exterior had remained half-hidden by the nearby elevated subway, an eyesore that the city removed in June, 1977.

The recycling of this group of contiguous buildings is still in progress, but, as Richard Stange has remarked, referring to the disappearance of the old overhead transit line, "Now we're exposed, and the job gets more interesting." One of the most interesting aspects is the rooftop installation of a gravity-feed solar hot-water collector, which supplies 130-degree water to a 40-gallon tank. On the top floor, now used as dining space for partners and employees, walls have been sandblasted and left unplastered to show off the curves of the copper solar pipe and electrical conduit. A Fisher woodburning stove provides 75 percent of the heat during the winter. A skylight brings in natural light and intentionally blurs the distinction between the inside, where plants hang from the water collector, and the rooftop outside, which serves as a deck and is hedged by Ailanthus trees growing up the side of the building.

The entrance lobby has been painted black and furnished with objects that have recycling histories all their own: a light sculpture from the 1964 New York World's Fair, a light globe that used to hang from the elevated subway, and one of the old butcher-block tables from the warehouse. The glass block (with clear panes inserted to take advantage of certain views) has been retained throughout, as have the concrete floors. Stainless steel was used to complement the glass and concrete with a touch of refinement. In the gallery, where photographs and three-dimensional models of past and current projects are displayed, an undulating ceiling was fashioned as an alternative to the sheet rock surface that might otherwise have been used to replace the old water-damaged ceiling. The undulations refer to the flowing Delaware outside the window.

In the conference/projection room, one of the original freezer doors now serves as a table, while the benches were retrieved from old locker rooms. The principal drafting area is divided into loosely defined offices with the use of graphic cutouts, thus avoiding the construction of new interior partitions.

TOP: before, exterior.

BOTTOM: after, interior.

Photos: Joseph Mikoliak.

Design Research

From: private mansion
To: retail furnishings and accessories store

One of the most splendid buildings on Philadelphia's elegant Rittenhouse Square is the Van Rensselaer Mansion, an imposing Renaissance Revival structure with a granite facade, designed by the Boston architects Peabody and Stearns and built in 1897 for Sara Drexel Van Rensselaer. The family lived in it until 1942; then it was occupied by a number of clubs, including the Penn Athletic Club. But by 1972, in the face of rising costs and less than adequate maintenance, the house was abandoned and demolition became a real possibility.

At that point, Benjamin Thompson's Design Research of Cambridge, Massachusetts, entered the picture. A retail operation specializing in contemporary furnishings, fabrics, and accessories, Design Research was looking for a Philadelphia location in which to open its 11th store. For the company, the concept of selling its modern wares in a historic building was not new; the DR store in San Francisco is situated in Ghirardelli Square, and the store on New York's 57th Street is in a renovated townhouse. In 1974, the firm signed a 20-year lease for the Van Rensselaer Mansion at $100,000 a year, and in 1975, the store opened.

The designers, Architectural Resources Cambridge, Inc., originally proposed gutting the interior.

But strong opposition from the Philadelphia Historical Society, the Historic Preservation Commission of the local AIA chapter, and other preservationists resulted in a compromise: the two-story dining room was to be preserved, as was the central stained-glass skylit dome, now set over a new open-tread spiral stairway. The rest of the interior was redesigned in a contemporary idiom with multilevel shopping areas opening off white-painted steel balconies. The elaborately detailed rooms have been replaced by simpler but more dynamic open spaces interconnected by vertical wells and horizontal passageways. Sales areas take up 11,000 of the mansion's 17,000 square feet of space, with offices in the attic.

The old dining room, now furnished as a contemporary living room, was preserved in close-to-original condition. Figures, festoons, anthemia, cartouches, and other elaborate detailing adorn the ceiling, the modillioned cornice, and the mosaic fireplace. On the ceiling are portraits of the doges of Venice and four popes that Mrs. Van Rensselaer, a converted Catholic, bought in Italy; hence the name, "the Popes' Room." Yet somehow, the contemporary furniture seems quite at home in the ornate surroundings. Cost of the renovation: $1.2 million.

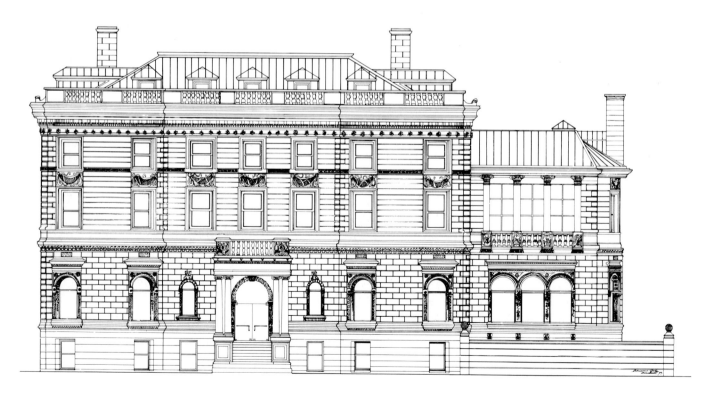

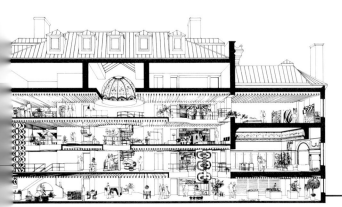

OPPOSITE: after, exterior, rendering. Photo: courtesy Architectural
Resources, Cambridge.

ABOVE: after, interior. Photo: Tom Crane, Philadelphia.

LEFT: after, interior, rendering. Photo: courtesy Architectural Resources,
Cambridge.

Station Square

From: railroad station
To: residential, recreational, and commercial complex

Turn-of-the-century Pittsburgh was a rapidly growing industrial center, thanks largely to the rich mineral deposits nearby and to the swift expansion of the American rail system. Three large railroad terminals were built at that time: the Pennsylvania; the Wabash; and the Pittsburgh and Lake Erie. Two were demolished in the 1950s, but the P&LE Terminal, smallest of the three, has taken an interesting turn.

Having survived the decline of rail service and the ravages of urban renewal, it is now the focal point of a $30 million shopping, working, and entertainment center along Pittsburgh's riverfront, just across the Monongahela from the Golden Triangle, sponsored by Pittsburgh History and Landmarks Foundation. The Allegheny Foundation, chaired by Richard M. Scaife, provided $5 million to the Landmarks Foundation in initial funding with two goals in mind: to make the buildings a major adaptive use project for downtown Pittsburgh and to revitalize the riverfront.

The first five-year phase of the project aims to restore the terminal building itself; convert Shovel Warehouse into the Great Landmarks Office Building; convert the Freight House, a one-story warehouse next to the terminal for 100 shops; and construct a new hotel-convention center. In addition to the existing 50,000 square feet of office space, another 260,000 square feet will be renovated. The overall 12-year plan calls for a $250 million residential, commercial, and recreational development of 40 acres along the Monongahela River from Panhandle Railroad Bridge to Ft. Pitt Bridge. That makes it the largest private commercial recycling project currently underway in the United States and the largest renewal project in Pittsburgh's history.

Pittsburgh's History and Landmarks Foundation, formed in 1964, has directed planning of the Station Square project; all income from the project, after taxes, will go to its historic preservation programs in Pittsburgh. Chairman Charles Arensberg and President Arthur Ziegler sought advice from representatives of similar projects like Salt Lake City's Trolley Square and Denver's Larimer Square. The people who planned Disneyworld conducted the marketing study.

Restoration and partial conversion of the elegant Beaux-Arts terminal building became the project's natural cornerstone. Designed by architect William George Burns between 1898 and 1901, the structure has never stood empty. The P&LE line's offices will stay on the terminal's upper floors even after conversion of the ground-floor Grand Concourse, an impressive, baroque interior that evokes the romance of our great age of railroading. The symmetrical facade with its generous windows and frieze depicting a chugging locomotive required little repair. The lavish interior, bedecked with massive marble columns, carved banisters, paneling, and waiting-room pews, and a mosaic floor, is crowned by a coffered vault with a stained-glass skylight. The conversion of the area into the Grand Concourse Restaurant, seating 500, has been accomplished by the C. A. Muer Corporation at a cost of over $2 million.

The main shopping area, however, will be in the Freight House next door. From 75 to 100 specialty shops, outfitted with artifacts rescued from demolished Pittsburgh buildings, will fill some 85,000 square feet of retail space. Box and flat cars, transformed into shops and placed on the interior train tracks that still run through the warehouse, will anchor the center of the building. The last wooden caboose to make regular runs in and out of Pittsburgh will be among them. Exterior renovation has involved replacing the rusted corrugated siding with wood siding. For display, bay windows have been created in the old truck bays where goods were once handled. Inside, the ceiling's steel trusses are being sandblasted and painted and will be left exposed.

Next to the Freight House, the old six-story Shovel Warehouse is being converted into 360,000 square feet of office space, with 60,000 square feet of retail space on its first floor. Not far away, a 250-room luxury hotel designed to complement Station Square is rising. It will overlook the river, the projected marina for riverfront traffic, and nearby buildings. All the area's overhead electrical wiring, long an element of industrial gloom, is being buried.

Before, overview.

RIGHT: before, exterior.

BELOW: before, interior.

TOP: after, exterior, rendering.

LEFT: after, interior.

ABOVE: after, interior.

Photos: courtesy Pittsburgh History and Landmarks Foundation.

Guernsey Hall

From: private mansion
To: condominiums

When Guernsey Hall, a 42-room Italianate mansion, came on the market in 1970, it was too large to sell as a single-family residence. Yet it has been successfully preserved essentially as it looked for two-thirds of a century through its conversion into five condominiums plus a caretaker's apartment.

The house exemplifies the Italian villa style introduced to the United States by its architect, John Notman. It was built around 1850 for Richard Stockton Field, a New Jersey supreme court justice and U.S. senator, who had assembled the surrounding farmland to provide a 40-acre landscaped setting. In 1887, the estate was bought by Allan Marquand, who named it Guernsey Hall after the Channel Island where his ancestors had lived. Allan Marquand founded Princeton University's art history department and collected Renaissance art. Eleanor Cross Marquand, who was a horticulturalist, landscaped the grounds. In 1912, the family had the house modernized and enlarged by the New York firm Cross and Cross.

In 1970, architect and Guernsey Hall neighbor William Short with others set up a limited partnership corporation to preserve the building, then up for sale. By that time, all but 2½ acres of the grounds had been sold off, over half to be used as Princeton Borough parkland. Short dismissed institutional use for the building as impractical because of the excessive wear that it would undergo and the amount of parking needed. The ultimate solution, luxury condominiums, filled a need for families whose children had moved away and who wanted to shift from large houses into smaller but comparably comfortable quarters. Tax assessments from five such apartments proved equal to or greater than those projected for five new houses, an alternate development solution for the land; the occupants' use of schools, roads, and other public facilities, moreover, proved to be lower. The town, reluctant to lose one of its landmarks, was persuaded that Short's proposal would maintain the character of the neighborhood and granted a variance from the existing single-family zoning.

Guernsey Hall lent itself readily to conversion. The intent was to preserve as much as possible of the original interior and, to that end, the central hall and some of the architectural detailing and plasterwork were protected by restrictions written into the deed. The apartments surround an octagonal, 40-foot-high stairwell with a glazed dome. The house was built with high-ceilinged, elaborately plastered rooms for the owners' use and lower-ceilinged service areas and servants' quarters. The apartments were laid out so as to provide four of the five units with at least one of the original formal rooms for a living room. The bearing-wall masonry construction helped to meet fire code specifications. All apartments were completed and occupied by the summer of 1974. They sold for $95,000 to $115,000 per apartment, with annual operating costs of $7,000 each, which includes the caretaker/gardener's salary. The total cost of interior and exterior renovation was almost $500,000, with interior construction costs running $29.58 per square foot for top-quality work.

According to William Short, the project's success makes it a model for the rehabilitation of many once-elegant estates around the country which now face either demolition or restoration as museums. Guernsey Hall expands the repertoire of proven alternatives for old and usable structures. And while luxury housing is not a priority to most Americans, Guernsey Hall did perform a public service by maintaining the building's exterior and thereby preserving a community resource.

OPPOSITE: after, exterior.

TOP LEFT: after, interior.

BOTTOM LEFT: after, interior.

TOP RIGHT: before, interior.

ABOVE: before, interior.

Photos: Otto Baitz, courtesy Short & Ford, Architects.

Whig Hall, Princeton University

From: debating society headquarters
To: debating society, classrooms, offices, public spaces

After Whig Hall, a Neoclassical temple built by A. Page Brown at Princeton University, was gutted by fire several years ago, the architectural firm of Gwathmey/Siegel was asked to undertake a challenging task. The firm was engaged to rebuild the hall, providing 10,000 square feet of usable space where previously there had been 7,000. The building, constructed in 1893, was to remain the home of the university debating society, but additional classrooms and public spaces were needed.

Gwathmey/Siegel felt that to extend their design beyond the original structure would be disastrous in terms of "historical architectural precedence, the university's traditional architectural interpretation and the site references." This was particularly so since the building has a twin, Clio Hall, which stands alongside it; together the two enclose Cannon Green.

The architects sought to emphasize positive precedents, including the Classical Roman temple and Le Corbusier's Maison Dom-ino proposal, with its interior columns instead of walls supporting the roof and its "free-floating" stairways. What Gwathmey/Siegel did was construct a new building within Whig Hall's remaining marble shell. A new structure was inserted in the existing shell, with reinforced concrete columns and floors. Four floor levels replaced the original three to provide the added 3,000 square feet. The most radical change was the removal of most of a side facade to expose the open plan of the interior with its stucco walls. Not everybody approved of this departure; one local newspaper called it "Dairy Queen" architecture. Nonetheless, this radical—and, in some eyes, witty and elegant—solution won the designers a 1973 Progressive Architecture award.

LEFT: before, front facade. Photo: Gwathmey/Siegel, Architect.

TOP: after, lobby. Photo: Norman McGrath.

BOTTOM: after, side facade. Photo: Norman McGrath.

Rhode Island School of Design Architectural Studies Building

From: iron works
To: classrooms, studios, faculty offices

Since 1968, enrollment at the Rhode Island School of Design in Providence has grown by 34 percent, creating an intolerable space squeeze. The school had hoped to build a new structure for classrooms and design studios, but had to abandon the idea in 1975 because of the price tag: $4 million. Then one of RISD's own architecture students came to the rescue. In her senior thesis, Clara Marx Dale ('74) had proposed the re-use of the vacant Phillips Lead Supply Company Building, a spare, well-proportioned warehouse only two blocks from campus, as a shopping and entertainment arcade. A professor brought her work to the school's attention, and with her permission, RISD used her findings in considering its use.

The red brick building with granite lintels and Greek Revival detail had been built on the Providence waterfront in 1848 for the Fall River Iron Works. The Rumford Chemical Company, which produced baking powder, took it over in 1885. From 1927 until 1962, Phillips Lead Supply, a wholesale plumbing supplier, used it for offices and a warehouse. For nearly 15 years the city's urban renewal agency tried unsuccessfully to find a new owner. The greatest interest was shown by Mrs. Dale, who had to get permission from the agency to enter the building and, with pigeons for company, conduct her studies by searchlight.

In the end, RISD proved the only serious bidder, and got the building for $115,000 and an annual payment to the city of $2,000 in lieu of taxes. The renovation job went to an RISD graduate and teacher, Irving B. Haynes, and his five associates, all graduates of the school, who specialize in renovation. In consideration of the needs of 330 architecture students and 45 faculty members, Haynes provided simple, spacious studios, faculty offices, classrooms, corridors lined with red lockers, green and blue stairwells, and a first-floor gallery and lecture hall. The top-floor interior with dormers and angular arches formed by exposed beams was converted into a drafting studio for sophomores. An exhibition area, seen through the altered main entrance, is designed to attract passersby to browse through student and faculty work.

The new building, dedicated in April, 1978, joins such earlier RISD conversions as the 1864 Woods-Gerry House (administrative offices) and the 1763 Market House (graphic design department). The project cost $1.25 million, providing 53,000 square feet and a new home for the scattered architecture department for perhaps a third of what a new building would have cost.

LEFT: before, exterior engraving. Photo: courtesy Rhode Island School of Design.

ABOVE: before, exterior. Photo: Warren Jagger, courtesy Rhode Island School of Design.

LEFT: before, exterior. Photo: courtesy Irving Haynes Associates.

BELOW: during construction, fourth-floor design studios. Photo: courtesy Irving Haynes Associates.

OPPOSITE TOP: after, fourth-floor design studios. Photo: courtesy Irving Haynes Associates.

OPPOSITE BOTTOM: rendering, top-floor studio. Photo: courtesy Rhode Island School of Design.

The Register/Jamaica Arts Center

From: city offices, archives
To: art center, offices, galleries, workshops

When the Greater Jamaica Development Corporation was formed to find ways to reverse the steady deterioration of the Jamaica section of Queens, its members came up with a wide variety of ideas. They wanted to attract business, of course, but they also weighed the city university's plans to build a new campus (today's York College), as well as ways to increase the amount of office space in the community and to create vocational workshops. The idea of incorporating an arts program into an early phase of the plan was also advanced—an innovative step in a world where consideration of the arts is often relegated to an icing-on-the-cake position in community development priorities.

The direct result of this thinking was the creation of the Jamaica Arts Center, which began operating in 1972 with a budget of $10,000. Two years later, the operating budget was up to $225,000 and the JAC had moved into its new home, the old City Register Building on Jamaica Avenue, probably the finest example in Queens of Renaissance Revival architecture. Since its erection in 1898, the building has been an architectural anchor in the community.

For 75 years the three-story structure, still called "The Register," housed property records for the borough of Queens. It was vacated by the city in 1973 and taken over by the Greater Jamaica Development Corporation soon afterwards. In 1974 the building was awarded landmark status by the New York City Landmarks Preservation Commission.

Architecturally, the building can be traced to Renaissance prototypes that represent some of the finest examples of palatial design. Its rusticated ground floor, punctuated with deeply recessed windows on either side of its central arched doorway, gives the structure the solid base that 15th- and 16th-century Italian urban dwellers preferred. In classic style, the facade lightens as the eye travels upward to the second and third floors, both with symmetrical fenestration and courses to mark the breaks between floors. The vertical and horizontal symmetry and the ornamental devices in the old Register Building echo the principles of precision and balance that guided Bramante in his many Vicenza palace facades and Sangallo and Michelangelo in their 16th-century design of the Palazzo Farnese's east facade in Rome.

Now that the former city offices and their files have been cleared out of the stately structure, The Register has become a multi-use facility that is almost half renovated under urban designer Peter Engelbrecht. Occupants include the Jamaica Arts Center; the Queens Council on the Arts; Jamaica Art Mobilization, a group of about 80 artists living in the district and eager to promote community involvement in the arts; the Mayor's Office of Development; the Greater Jamaica Development Corporation; and a community planning board.

The recycling concept requires that income generated by office and retail space partially cover the maintenance and rental costs of the spaces occupied by the arts. The Jamaica Arts Center fills more than half of the building's 22,700 square feet. Its facilities include a ground-floor gallery and shop, designed by Bernard Wolff, photography, pottery, and silkscreen workshops, and multipurpose areas for demonstrations, classes, visual media, and performing arts programs. The gallery intends to give equal time and space to traditional or European-derived arts and to the work of Black and Caribbean cultures.

Although large parts of the upper floors remain unrenovated, offices for the tenant organizations have been completed and workshop areas have been created to accommodate such widely varied events as Saturday puppet shows, demonstrations of Chinese calligraphy, jewelry fabrication, and quilting. As renovation progresses, an experimental theater, bookshop, sculpture court, and restaurant will be added to the complex.

TOP LEFT: after, exterior. Photo: H. Beck.

TOP RIGHT: before, interior. Photo: Bill Tchakirides.

BOTTOM: after, interior. Photo: Bill Tchakirides.

Schlegel Corporation Headquarters

From: mansion
To: corporate offices

In 1976, the Tax Reform Act passed by Congress carried with it a preservation amendment giving to registered landmarks the kind of tax breaks that new buildings previously enjoyed. At the time the act became law, the Schlegel Corporation of Rochester, a producer of sealing systems, was already beginning to renovate the old Hiram Sibley family mansion in the East Avenue Preservation District. Richard Turner, Schlegel's chairman and president and a longtime member of Rochester's effective Landmarks Society, initiated his firm's application for accelerated depreciation under the new law. That made Schlegel the first corporation in the United States to do so.

Hiram Sibley, first president of Western Union, had the house built in 1868 in a grand Italianate style. In 1900, his son, Hiram Watson Sibley, had the exterior completely altered, removing the porch, cupola, and heavy cornices, reducing the windows to a more classical scale, and installing Ionic pilasters and a brick facade. The Italian Renaissance country villa had become a Greek Revival temple. A second major alteration was undertaken in 1911, when a new wing was added, giving the house an L shape, and also a side doorway that became the main entrance.

In 1975, when a later Sibley wanted to sell the 15,000-square-foot building, the Schlegel Corporation happened to be looking for space. The firm, which has 15 plants in 9 countries, had long since outgrown its headquarters, situated in its main manufacturing plant. By 1976, Richard Turner was able to convince his board of directors that the firm should move to the Sibley place, which would provide "a work setting for 57 people at the same cost as new space for 40."

Architect Paul Malo, author of *Landmarks of Rochester and Monroe County*, was consulted on adaptation plans, which were carried out by the architectural firm of Northrup, Kaelber & Kopf and interior designer Beverly Hufner. Noting the mixture of architectural styles, Malo commented that "the house is no period piece warranting careful restoration." But rather than gut and rebuild the interior, the architects respected its mix of styles as natural stages in the structure's development. The large dining room, added in 1911, was subdivided into 3 offices; 24 other rooms became single offices. An attic loft was converted into open offices with skylights. A trophy room became Richard Turner's new office, the library a board room, the kitchen-pantry a mailroom, copy center, and kitchenette. The basement laundry was transformed into a self-service lunchroom. No elevators were installed in the three-story structure, but the original central staircase was restored and enclosed in fire-resistant glass to satisfy both the building code and the owners' preservationist intentions. To provide parking for 50 cars without destroying the old mansion's natural setting, Turner skillfully negotiated for a vacant lot behind the church next door.

When Turner first proposed the move, he wondered whether his employees would resist the shift to a neighborhood so close to Rochester's old center, but the employees found that as a result of the well-publicized conversion, their firm, little-known because its products are so specialized, was gaining recognition. It was a public relations triumph, as well as a laudable example of preserving a piece of the past by refitting it for the future.

TOP LEFT: after, exterior. Photo: courtesy Schlegel Corporation.

TOP RIGHT: before, interior. Photo: courtesy Schlegel Corporation.

BOTTOM: after, interior. Photo: John Griebsch, Rochester, N.Y.

Residence

From: church
To: private residence

In 1850, members of the newly formed Presbyterian parish of Roslyn on Long Island divided over the question of hiring an architect or a builder to construct their first church. Some argued that public buildings were always architect-designed, but a majority disagreed, and the result was a fine example of country Greek Revival carpentry, perhaps by Thomas Wood, one of Roslyn's more prolific builders of that period. Built for $1,900 in 1851, the simple two-aisled hall lacked an apse or transepts, but boasted Greek Revival moldings, a choir supported by two cast-iron columns, a belfry with a shingled steeple, and a hospitably enclosed porch. One of the church's loyal contributors, trustees, and worshipers was the poet and journalist William Cullen Bryant, who cherished its rural character.

By 1928, the growing congregation abandoned the church for a new building. The 1851 building was deeded to the Junior Order of United American Mechanics, who removed its steeple and replaced its cast-iron columns. After a period of vacancy the building was occupied by groups of artists, one calling itself the "Church Mice," who reopened it as a gallery and classroom. One of the Church Mice de-

cided to renovate it for his family residence.

In 1972, the current occupants bought the building with the same idea. They were attracted by the possibilities of designing an open, modern layout in a historic structure in the middle of the village, and hired architect Guy Ladd Frost and interior designer Phyllis Hoffzimer to help them realize their plans. The partitions previously erected were removed to create a great, 18-foot-high main space, 33 by 23 feet. The airy feeling was enhanced by the original tall double-hung church windows. The original choir loft, now a sitting room, was matched by the balcony of a new two-level bedroom wing created at the opposite end. The kitchen and a breakfast room were tucked into the 1860 vestibule, next to the entrance foyer that feeds one of the original doorways into the central living space. The owners finished the new woodwork in the spirit of the old detailing and restored or replaced the old chair railings, wainscoting, and yellow pine floor. The old steeple removed by the Junior Mechanics was never restored, but virtually every other part of the old structure has been recycled to roomy, lofty effect.

LEFT: after, exterior.

ABOVE: after, interior.

Photos: © 1978, Robert Perron.

The Logan Leader/The News Democrat Building

From: hardware and feed store
To: newspaper offices and printing plant

In western Kentucky's Logan County, not far from the Tennessee border to the south, the town of Russellville has new reason to be proud of its old square. A two-story, 19th-century building that faces the square and once contained a combined hardware and feed store was purchased in 1973 by Logan Ink, Inc., publisher of *The Logan Leader/The News Democrat* newspapers, and converted into publication and printing offices by David Zuern of the Louisville architectural firm of Ryan, Cooke and Zuern Associates. Logan Ink needed space in which to expand and liked the idea of siting the production end of its business in a part of a building that would be visible from the street and the square beyond.

The first task for the renovation team was to strip away the various earlier remodeling attempts that the building had undergone during its 100-year life. When the original cast-iron and brick facade was revealed, restoration work began. All new woodwork was compatible with the original doors and trim. The first floor was converted to accommodate a reception area, the newsroom, advertising offices, a conference room, the publisher's office, a lounge, and darkroom facilities as well as an employees' entrance in the rear, and bathroom and storage areas. At the back of the second floor are a darkroom and composition area, where the papers are laid out. The front half of the floor is reserved for expansion.

To the side of the six-bay building is an attached, one-story, three-bay structure once used for grain and feed sales and storage and now used for the printing shop. The masonry load-bearing structure was adequate to house the heavy printing equipment, but its oak floors had to be removed and a new concrete slab poured on engineered fill to accommodate the presses. The floor boards did not go to waste; they were recycled for partition paneling and new stair construction. The brick walls were cleaned of plaster and left exposed; original paneled ceilings were also cleaned and retained. New mechanical, electrical, and sprinkler systems were installed throughout. Total cost of converting 7,400 square feet of space: $95,500, including fees and furnishings, but excluding costs of the buildings ($50,000) and the new presses.

The view from the town square is now impressive. Glazed bays on the main floor reveal a modern reception area and small-scale graphics on the publishing side and a mural of the American flag, signifying freedom of speech, on the printing side, as a backdrop for the presses. The second floor of the main building has six simple arched windows with classical moldings and keystones, beneath the original broad cornice and a mansard roof. The crumbling sidewalk that fronted the building was replaced with new concrete and brick paving, and three trees were planted to complement the greenery in the town square.

OPPOSITE: after, exterior. Photo: Balthazar Korab.

LEFT: after, interior. Photo: Balthazar Korab.

MIDDLE: before, interior. Photo: Robert Stuart for *The Logan Leader/The News Democrat.*

BOTTOM: before, exterior. Photo: Robert Stuart for *The Logan Leader/The News Democrat.*

Heilbron House

From: private residence
To: savings and loan branch

News of the gold discovered by Johann Augustus Sutter and his fellow colonists on the banks of the Sacramento River in the 1840s inflamed the dreams of adventurers all over the world. August Frederick Heilbron was one of those who went to California to seek his fortune, but not by panning for gold. An emigrant from Germany at the age of 17, he found his way via steamer to Nicaragua and thence to California, where he headed for the booming, newly founded city of Sacramento to join his brother. Rather than board one of the 50 stage coaches that assembled every morning before Sacramento's hotels to carry prospectors to the mines, the brothers set up a grocery and meat market to feed the diggers. Soon they expanded into wholesale meatpacking, and then into breeding and raising their own herds of Herefords and Durhams on 69,000 acres of Spanish land grant territory.

The widespread, if ephemeral, prosperity of the 1870s and 1880s gave rise to a number of Victorian mansions in Sacramento. Some of the greatest, including the Gallatin House, now maintained as a museum by the state, came from the designs of Nathaniel Dudley Goodell. An early gold-seeker, Goodell left a successful architectural career in Ware, Massachusetts, for an unsuccessful stint in the California mines before returning to his proven skills in Sacramento. When Heilbron and his German wife Louisa decided to build a mansion large enough for a sizable family (it eventually grew to eight children), they commissioned Goodell. His Victorian design was relatively restrained and compact, to suit German tastes. The two-story building (plus attic and lower level) features a mansard roof, a Corinthian portico, high, ornamented ceilings, hand-rubbed paneling, and walk-through closets that served as additional exits in the event of one of Sacramento's frequent floods. Another precaution was the construction of the first floor at eight feet above ground level; servants' quarters and storerooms were below.

In the mid 1880s, when the Heilbron House was built, the San Diego Federal Savings & Loan Association, a home-financing venture, was getting started 600 miles to the south. This savings and loan association, with offices throughout California, bought the house in 1973 and renovated it as its Sacramento branch office. The association's president, Gordon C. Luce, had come to know the house after its incarnation as Antonine's Restaurant following the Heilbrons' sale of the mansion in 1953.

The association re-opened the house in January, 1974, a monument to prosperity past and present, with tours of the house, an exhibition of original Heilbron furnishings, and modern investment services. The renovation architects (William C. Krommenhoek and Associates of San Diego) left the facade of the building untouched. Inside, the chief changes were the installation of a vault and elevators. Drive-in teller service was provided at a new gazebo, built in Victorian style. Decorator Brenda Mason of San Diego furnished the offices in a fashion faithful to the original character of the interior. Perhaps the installation of a development concern in renovated historic quarters will encourage general recognition by the financial community of the economies and riches of recycling.

LEFT: after, exterior. Photo: courtesy The San Diego Federal Savings and Loan Association.

TOP RIGHT: after, interior. Photo: courtesy The San Diego Federal Savings and Loan Association.

BOTTOM RIGHT: after, exterior. Photo: Kenneth Shearer, San Diego.

Flagler College

From: luxury resort
To: four-year college

On April 5, 1967, the first annual Ponce de León Scholarship Ball was held to mark the end of one era and the beginning of another. The Ponce de León Hotel, one of America's great luxury resorts, was being converted into a four-year college that would open its doors to women in 1968 and, two years later, become a fully accredited co-educational school. Somehow it seemed fitting that the hotel named for the explorer who scoured the Southeast in quest of the fabled fountain of youth should be transformed into a liberal arts college attracting students from 30 states.

The ornate Spanish-style four-story structure was built between 1885 and 1887 by Henry Flagler, a businessman who first became acquainted with historic St. Augustine during a vacation from his job as treasurer of John D. Rockefeller's Standard Oil Company. Flagler built the Florida East Coast Railroad, bought up 3.5 million acres of Florida real estate, and launched a series of luxury hotels to accommodate the growing exodus of winter-weary tourists from the northern states. Hotel Ponce de León was the Flagler flagship, and despite temporary setbacks like the yellow fever epidemic of 1888, the great freeze of 1894–95, the Depression, and World War II, when the hotel was a Coast Guard training depot, the resort flourished. Florida's big development boom of the 1920s and the post-war tourist flood helped bring on the resort's golden days. But as increased use of the automobile changed the traditional pattern of tourism, with nomadic wandering replacing long rests confined to one locale, once-magnificent, self-contained holiday centers everywhere began to suffer. In 1967 the hotel closed.

When it re-opened 18 months later as Flagler College, students filled the old courtyard where guests had once sunned themselves in rows of green rocking chairs. The renovation architect, Craig Thorn, cast the courtyard as the setting for outdoor concerts, ceremonies, and other campus gatherings, while the former hotel rooms have become dormitories. Initial repairs and alterations cost $200,000, but the rehabilitation is ongoing and the old parlor, temporarily a library, will become a museum commemorating the hotel's past. The dining room is now a cafeteria for the school's 700 students. The boiler room coal bunkers are science labs, and what had been artists' studios provide some of the classroom space. Administrative offices are housed in the old barber shop and ladies' billiard room.

Many of the original furnishings are still in use. Louis Tiffany was commissioned to do the stained-glass windows, which remain intact. So do murals by George Maynard and Virgilio Tojetti. Little structural work was necessary, because extensive repairs had been made in the late 1940s. Situated in the sandy pine marshes of Maria Sanchez Creek, the building was constructed of coquina (shell composite, mixed with concrete) cast *in situ*. The original cost of construction: $2.5 million.

Architecturally, the eclectic Ponce de León is a complex arrangement of pavilions organized around two 165-foot-tall towers that once held the hotel's water tanks. Mosaics, the red tiled roof, and salmon-tinted terra-cotta ornamentation provide a colorful contrast to the neutral facade and the site's tropical vegetation. Flagler's architects, recommended by the New York firm of McKim, Mead and White, were young John Carrère and Thomas Hastings, whose later designs included New York's Public Library and the Frick Museum.

Although Flagler College spreads over 16 acres in downtown St. Augustine, the old Ponce de León is the center of campus activity. In the words of history professor Thomas Graham, who was instrumental in the hotel's listing in the National Register of Historic Places, the complex "gives us a great sense of cohesion, while the art and architecture cast a distinctive atmosphere over the institution."

Before, exterior.

ABOVE: before, exterior.

RIGHT: after, exterior.

OPPOSITE TOP: before, interior.

OPPOSITE BOTTOM: after, interior.

Photos: Flagler College, St. Augustine, Fla.

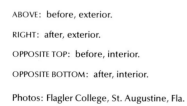

Landmark Center

From: federal office building
To: arts and community center

What is now called the "old" Federal Building in St. Paul is an exuberant embodiment of the late 19th century's preference for Beaux-Arts architecture, a bulky beauty featuring turrets and gables, arched entryways and thrusting clock towers. Designed by Willoughby Edbrooke, supervising architect of the U.S. Treasury, the five-story Romanesque Revival building is constructed mainly of granite with a frame of cast iron and steel and a profusion of carved mahogany, cherry, and marble in its high-ceilinged interior. It was begun in 1892 and took ten years to complete, at a cost of $2.5 million.

For 65 years the building was the center of federal government activities in St. Paul, housing at various times the city's main post office, armed forces recruiting stations, offices of the justice, treasury, and agriculture departments and, on the upper floors, the elaborately appointed courtrooms of the U.S. district court and the U.S. circuit court of appeals. The Barker-Karpis gang and Evelyn Frechette, girlfriend of the notorious John Dillinger, were tried there.

During the 1950s and early 1960s, however, buildings like this were having a rough time. They were not old enough to be considered historically valuable, and modernists viewed them as fussy, oversized relics. In the mid-1950s the General Services Administration, housekeeper for the federal government, began planning a new federal building for St. Paul, and maintenance of the old one slacked off.

For seven years historians, architects, and other concerned citizens worked to save the old Federal Building. In 1969 the Minnesota Historical Society placed the building on the National Register of Historic Places. In 1971 Betty Musser, president of the St. Paul Council of Arts and Science, expressed an interest in relocating there. The council handled fund-raising and administrative services for the Minnesota Museum of Art, the Schubert Club, the St. Paul Chamber Orchestra, and other groups. The purchase price set by Washington, however, had been a stumbling block for years. Then, in 1972, President Nixon signed into law a bill enabling the GSA to transfer federal surplus buildings of historical and architectural merit to local authorities for profit-

making use. The old Federal Building was saved, and was in fact one of the first buildings transferred under the new law.

In 1973 Betty Musser became chairwoman of the Old Federal Courts Building Committee and soon began the task of making essential repairs. Years of surface abuse had to be corrected. The exterior was cleaned and the roof's asbestos shingles were replaced with clay tiles made from the original molds still owned by the Ludowici-Celadon Company, founded in the 16th century in Italy. Brown linoleum was removed from counter tops and from some of the maple floors, and the original surfaces were restored. Fluorescent egg-crate fixtures, installed in the 1950s, were replaced. Much of the leaded stained glass and beautiful Vermont and Tennessee marble had been painted over with coats of government #102A paint; so had some of the paneling in the once magnificent courtrooms. This too was painstakingly removed. Three of the courtrooms were restored to public use and meeting halls. The center court skylight was stripped of the cement asbestos that had been swathed on it when leaks developed.

Richard Dober of Boston's Dober and Associates was planning consultant and the team of Stahl/Bennett, Inc., of Boston and Winsor/Faricy Architects, Inc., of St. Paul handled interior restoration and renovation. A second phase of renovation involved installation of new mechanical and electrical systems. A 280-seat auditorium below ground level was readied, and a rathskellar will eventually be opened there as well. The main floor and floors looking out on the court were given priority to allow agencies needing new space to move in.

Three of the St. Paul Council of Arts and Science's member agencies, along with the Ramsey County Historical Society and Minnesota Landmarks, Inc., moved into Landmark Center offices before renovation even began. The center will also house a community arts agency and a learning center for the Minnesota Metropolitan State University. Eventually there will be 175,000 square feet of usable space within the center, renovated at an estimated cost of $8.5 million.

TOP: exterior. Photo: courtesy Minnesota Landmarks.

BOTTOM LEFT: after, interior. Photo: courtesy Minnesota Landmarks.

BOTTOM RIGHT: after, interior, rendering. Photo: courtesy Stahl/Bennett, Architects.

Royal Palace Restaurant

From: synagogue
To: restaurant

The menu at the Royal Palace Restaurant features the cuisine of six countries. The building is no less cosmopolitan, having begun life as a synagogue, inspired by a great temple in Berlin and designed by a German architect. Eighty years later, it was recycled into a restaurant by two brothers from Iran, Maleck and Ali Manteghi, who moved from Tehran to Salt Lake City in 1970.

In 1890, Berlin architect Philip Meyer was brought to the United States to design the B'nai Israel Temple; its construction was supervised by the local architect Henry Monheim. Though its prototype (destroyed during World War II) was German, the style is basically Richardsonian Romanesque, with some Moorish touches. The gray facade is of cut Kyune stone, with pressed brick forming the sides and rear.

Though known as the Mormon capital, Salt Lake City then, as now, had a large Jewish community. When two temple congregations recently consolidated and moved to a new and larger synagogue in the suburbs, the old building became available to the Manteghi brothers, who also own restaurants in Aspen, Colorado, and Park City, Utah. For $260,000 they bought the temple, a Utah landmark recently nominated for listing in the National Register of Historic Places. With another $1 million, they converted the interior into the largest independent restaurant between the coasts, capable of seating 500 diners and boasting a 4,000-square-foot kitchen.

With Aspen architect, Nasser Sadeghi, the Manteghis altered the nave, with its 40-foot-high ceiling, to accommodate six different décors for six cuisines: French, Persian, Greek, Italian, Spanish, and American. The dining areas are set apart by partial new walls and velvet draperies tied to new wooden columns replicate of the existing ones. The brothers reopened the balcony arches, once enclosed as classrooms. They also restored the stained glass of the choir loft, now a bar. On the site of the altar, a 3-foot stage was built for nightly chamber music performances. The altar backdrop remains in place.

By stripping away some of the less felicitous changes wrought by several generations of worshipers and by usefully restoring a national landmark, the Manteghis reversed a wave in the tide of international architectural exchange that has washed a great deal of American design up on Iran's shores. Since New Year's Eve of 1976, when their new palace opened, it has reminded the customers of the pleasure and profit still to be found in their own architectural heritage.

OPPOSITE: before, exterior.

ABOVE: after, interior.

LEFT: after, exterior.

Photos: courtesy Royal Palace Restaurant.

San Antonio Museum of Art

From: brewery
To: art museum, shop, offices, restaurant

It started life as the Lone Star Brewery, one the biggest in Texas, with 1,500 feet of frontage on the San Antonio River. During Prohibition, it briefly became a cotton mill, and later headquarters for a chain of ice and food stores. Now, after a long period of abandonment, the old brewery's complex of massive brick buildings built at the turn of the century is being recycled as the home for the new San Antonio Museum of Art.

The San Antonio Museum Association acquired the complex, which is listed on the National Register of Historic Places, in 1972 for $375,000. Cambridge Seven Associates of Cambridge, Massachusetts, plan to complete the project at a cost of $4.1 million. That figure includes not only the actual recycling of a half dozen existing structures, but also the addition of auxiliary buildings and landscaping. Part of the financing comes from a $2.5 million grant from the Economic Development Administration, awarded in recognition of the project's effect on the tourist industry. San Antonio's city council has voted an additional $425,000 in Community Development Act funds to the new museum. The balance has been privately funded by individuals and regional foundations.

The brick brewery was executed in a modified Italian Romanesque style with arched windows, decorative parapets and corbeling, stone trim, and cast-iron columns. Certain structural features proved particularly adaptable to the museum's needs. The interior spaces were enormous, defined by high, vaulted ceilings and massive walls—a setting of maximum flexibility for exhibiting the museum's collections of contemporary and 19th-century paintings, Southwest Indian art, Texas decorative arts, pre-Columbian and Spanish Colonial art. Natural light, a consideration of vital importance to any display area not relying entirely on artificial light, was missing in the original building. Skylights were liberally installed, alleviating the brewery's industrial gloom by bringing the entire group of buildings into closer harmony with the sunny outdoors.

A key addition was a fourth-floor bridge connecting the two towers of the main structure, formerly the old brewhouse. The passageway has exposed trusses and a transparent glass vault. Viewed from above, through the bridge, or from below, through the skylights, the museum itself becomes a kind of permanent collection of design forms.

In addition to the exhibition areas, the recycled center, opening in early 1980, will house an auditorium, administrative and curatorial offices for the San Antonio Museum Association, a museum shop, and a restaurant in its 78,554 square feet of interior space.

207

LEFT: before, exterior. Photo: San Antonio Museum Association.

TOP LEFT: before, interior. Photo: San Antonio Museum Association.

TOP RIGHT: after, interior, model. Photo: San Antonio Museum Association.

BOTTOM: after, exterior, model. Photo: courtesy Cambridge Seven
     Associates.

Ghirardelli Square

From: chocolate factory
To: shops, restaurants, galleries, cinemas, offices

This is the granddaddy development, the revitalization project that inspired similar efforts in Atlanta, New York, Denver, Cleveland, and almost everywhere else. Completed in stages between 1964 and 1968, Ghirardelli Square cost $12 million, including purchase. But the impact it has had is beyond calculation.

The square took its name from Domenico Ghirardelli, who learned the confectioner's craft in Genoa before setting off at age 20 to open a chocolate shop in Lima. When news of California gold reached Peru, Ghirardelli headed for the Sierra and pitched a tent shop there in 1849. Eventually he moved to San Francisco, and in 1867 hit on a formula for stone-ground chocolate called "broma," which made his firm famous.

Domenico's sons bought up the current Ghirardelli block on the city's north waterfront in 1893. One of the buildings on the site was the Woolen Mill of 1860, the oldest extant factory in the West. The sons added a number of structures, including the Cocoa Building in 1900 and the Chocolate Building 11 years later; both were crenellated brick structures with quoins, cornices, crests, and voussoirs of poured and molded concrete, designed by architects William Mooser, Sr. and Jr. Most intriguing architecturally, and still the symbol of the square, is the 1915 Clocktower Building, modeled on the tower of the 17th-century Chateau at Blois in the Loire Valley, designed for Louis XIII.

The chocolate business prospered, outgrew its site, and moved in 1960. Demolition of the buildings seemed imminent. But in 1962, Lurline Roth and her son William, members of the Matson shipping family, bought the property for $2.5 million in hopes of preserving it. Their farsighted action led to the first major redevelopment of the city's north waterfront and catalyzed the recent movement throughout the United States to preserve whole districts and complexes of buildings, rather than isolated landmarks. The Roths called on the architectural firm of Wurster, Bernardi and Emmons, design consultant John

Matthias, and landscape architects Lawrence Halprin and Associates to prepare the block for a mixture of restaurants, galleries, and small specialty shops. Service facilities and large-scale ventures like department stores were vetoed for lack of space, setting the example of the recreational specialty shopping center followed in the nearby Cannery, and as far away as Faneuil Hall Market in Boston.

Renovation began at the eastern end of the square, while the Ghirardelli Chocolate Company continued to produce sweets at the western end. Costs were high, especially because of the need for a subterranean garage and for structural reinforcement of the buildings to meet the earthquake-conscious city's codes. The facades of all the buildings were retained, except for a 19th-century wooden box factory that was torn down. A new Wurster Building, named for the architect in charge of the project, closed the gap. The original huge sign that had advertised the firm until the World War II blackouts was relit in 1964.

The 60,000-square-foot central courtyard, one of the complex's most alluring features, has broad terraces stepping downhill. Iron galleries and stairways give access from the uppermost buildings to the plaza's olive trees, sculptures, and sculptural fountain by Ruth Asawa. Street furniture, lamps, banners, and information kiosks orient newcomers to the complex.

With the square's breathtaking view across the bay to the Marin Hills and Mt. Tamalpias, the architects focused on the public open space, permitting tenants to make their own improvements on their leased shells. Though the complex has 176,000 square feet of rentable space, the one- to five-story buildings, ranging from 100 to 10,000 square feet, are decidedly human in scale, and most are family-run establishments. So is the new Wurster Building, whose brick walls and tile roof harmonize with the old. Among the project's fourteen design awards is the AIA Medal for Collaborative Achievement, awarded only once before.

TOP LEFT: after, exterior. Photo: courtesy Ghirardelli Square.

TOP RIGHT: before, exterior. Photo: courtesy Ghirardelli Square.

BOTTOM: after, exterior. Photo: Roger Sturtevant, courtesy Wurster, Berhardi and Emmons, Architects.

Ice Houses

From: ice manufactury and cold storage warehouse
To: showrooms, offices

Until the 1870s, the schooner *Zenobia* and her sister ships brought cargoes of Alaskan ice to San Francisco's waterfront for sale to packers and private citizens—sometimes at a price of $1 a pound. Then artificial production made such importation unnecessary. San Francisco's National Ice and Cold Storage Company, founded in 1892, was a result of this technological revolution. When the company built new warehouses in 1914 and 1915—two spacious buildings comprising the biggest ice house in existence—the site was not far from the wharf where the *Zenobia* once docked. Ironically, the new warehouse used the same storage technique as did the *Zenobia:* insulating the ice with redwood sawdust. North Beach children, after swimming off the docks, would run to the warehouse to dry off by rolling in the sawdust. In those pre-refrigeration days, ice was sold in the streets from horse-drawn carts; with the advent of refrigeration and trucking, the warehouse continued to serve the surrounding produce dealers and packers. When the produce district moved to a new location, the buildings were abandoned.

Acquired by the North Waterfront Associates in 1967, the Ice Houses were to be renovated in the first stage of a projected five-block International Market Center. Community resistance helped to forestall that plan, but the Ice Houses were converted into showrooms for the wholesale furniture and decorating trades. That recycling spurred piecemeal residential and commercial redevelopment of an even larger area.

With their 10- to 17-foot-high ceilings and blind arches in the facades, which could easily be pierced for windows, the buildings proved hospitable to their new tenants. The two structures were built of brick with timber and steel frames and heavy floor joists. The bricks were sandblasted and the beams exposed. The original bridge joining the buildings was replaced by a glass connector 20 feet wide and rising the full height of the building, providing a central focus visible from outside. The alley between the buildings is now paved and landscaped as the entranceway to the lobbies beneath the bridge. The top level of the bridge is a cafeteria, while other levels serve as display space and also as corridors to the various tenants' showrooms.

The buildings yielded 160,000 leasable square feet from a total of 225,000. The renovation, completed in 1969 by the architectural firm of Wurster, Bernardi and Emmons, the veterans of Ghirardelli Square, cost $19.50 per square foot.

RIGHT: before, exterior. Photo: courtesy Wurster, Bernardi and Emmons, Architects.

OPPOSITE TOP: after, exterior. Photo: © Morley Baer, courtesy Wurster, Bernardi and Emmons, Architects.

OPPOSITE BOTTOM: after, interior. Photo: © Morley Baer, courtesy Wurster, Bernardi and Emmons, Architects.

Jessie Street Substation

From: utility generating station
To: commercial, office, and retail space

In 1905 William Bourn, founder of the Pacific Gas & Electric Company, asked architect Willis Polk to enlarge and modify his Jessie Street substation of 1881, creating a model for the giant utility's later buildings. Polk was a master of the late 19th century's Neoclassical style and had worked for Bourn before. He had already designed Bourn's townhouse on Webster Street, now a San Francisco landmark, and his country house in San Mateo. The PG&E building—then called Substation C and now the Jessie Street Substation—was the first public building that Bourn commissioned from Polk.

The substation, one of a trio of historic structures in the Yerba Buena district off San Francisco's Market Street (the other two are St. Patrick's and the Mercantile Building) has survived some harrowing struggles. In February, 1906, it was destroyed by fire, and two months later, just as reconstruction was getting underway, it was destroyed again by the great San Francisco earthquake and fire. That October, Polk and Daniel Burnham enlarged the original plans to include additional motor generator space and a battery room, and extended the south facade to include the entrance ornamented with the often-photographed cherub cartouche. In 1909 another major addition to the east end expanded the building to its current proportions.

In 1971 PG&E sold the building to the city for demolition, to make way for an open plaza to serve as a gateway to the entire Yerba Buena Center, an urban renewal project then being planned by the San Francisco Redevelopment Agency in conjunction with the Department of Housing and Urban Development. No action was taken immediately, however, and by 1974 preservationists had challenged the planned demolition. The Jessie Street Substation was soon included in the National Register of Historic Places and designated a landmark by the San Francisco Planning Commission. The substation was saved, but the task of turning it into a useful, functioning building remained. To that end, the National Trust provided $7,500 in matched funds for a study of adaptive re-use alternatives.

In weighing possibilities, project coordinator John Weese and chief architect William Arno Werner of W. A. Werner Associates were well aware that San Francisco's voters had approved the so-called Proposition S, giving the green light to an $85 million convention center for Yerba Buena. Their final design proposal emphasizes the old substation's favorable location—at the gateway to Yerba Buena, 2½ blocks from Union Square, the city's major shopping district, and at the southwest edge of the financial district. The brick, glass, steel, and terra-cotta building thus enjoys easy access from a number of directions.

The study team settled on a mixed-use plan that would combine retail and office space, with the possibility left open for additional uses in the future. At 70¢ to 80¢ per square foot per month, office space in the Jessie Street Substation complex would fall between rentals in the older financial district and those in newly constructed buildings.

The building's interior is now a mere shell since PG&E removed most of its heavy equipment years ago. Structurally, the building is divided into an east bay, a west bay, and three middle bays. Each has a skylight and a ceiling network of steel trusses. Ceiling heights range from 29 to 33 feet. The adaptive re-use proposal would convert the central bay into a public mall, making use of the large skylight and creating a pedestrian traffic tunnel from Market Street into the Yerba Buena Center area north of the substation. To complete this plan, a new opening would have to be cut in the north facade. Retail spaces would front both sides of the mall. The ground-floor east and west bays would be converted into restaurants, with potential outside café expansion onto the landscaped pedestrian plazas.

Second- and third-floor levels are to be built in the east central bay. Office and retail space would mix on the second floor with some 3,400 square feet of retail space and 3,600 square feet on the ground floor. The third floor would consist entirely of offices. The major new construction would be an addition to the north side of the building. This narrow extension would provide entrance to second-floor shops and offices and house the building's mechanical systems.

The original substation covered 16,000 square feet of property. The Weese-Werner plan would create a total floor area of 47,060 square feet. Projected cost of the conversion: $2.5 million.

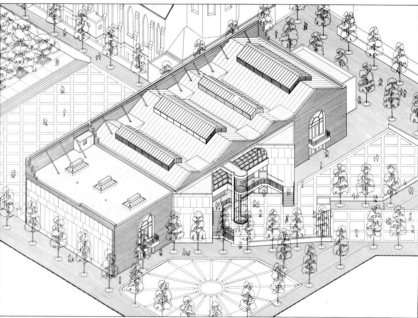

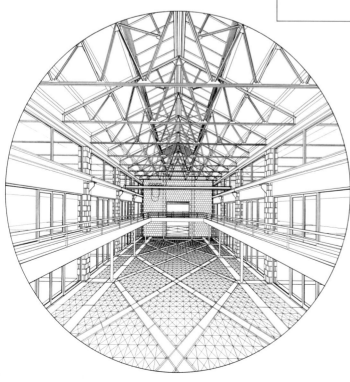

TOP: before, exterior. Photo: William Arno Werner.

MIDDLE: after, exterior, rendering. Photo: courtesy William Arno Werner Associates, Architects.

LEFT: after, interior, rendering. Photo: courtesy William Arno Werner Associates, Architects.

Lower Campus, San Francisco University High School

From: parking and service garage
To: school classrooms, offices, gymnasium

Even though the service and parking garage on Washington Street in San Francisco was noisy and unattractive, local residents were concerned when a private high school across the street acquired it for additional classrooms and a gymnasium. However, extensive public hearings held in 1976 calmed the community's fears that the school would be even noisier than the garage: there would be acoustically dampened interior walls, ceilings and floors, double-glazed windows on the gym floor, and special acoustical concrete fill in the new mansard roofs. The renovation, designed for the expanding San Francisco University High School, could proceed.

The old garage, built in 1922, had a main facade that was symmetrically divided into five balanced bays on the ground level, consisting of two entrance drives, two exit drives, and a central auto parts shop. On the second floor, rectangular windows repeated the rhythm established below. A flat wood roof capped the reinforced concrete structure which, due to neglect and insensitive cosmetic alterations, was in poor condition before its conversion in 1977.

Exteriors walls, however, needed structural repair, as did the floor beams. The interior finishes consisted of little more than the exposed structural concrete.

Roof columns and ramps leading from the main level to the basement and the upper floor had to be completely removed. Once the garage debris was cleared away, the largely open spaces were prepared for the reconstruction of existing exterior walls, addition of new interior walls, and the installation of new mechanical and lighting systems.

The former basement was recycled to accommodate four classrooms, two faculty offices, the mechanical equipment, a computer facility, and storage areas. A large hallway lined with stock lockers runs through the center of the basement. The first floor contains offices, art studios, two science labs, photographic labs, toilets, and the front lobby. The top floor is now the school gymnasium, where basketball, gymnastics, and volleyball are the main sports. Gym seating is movable, allowing for maximum floor space when needed.

Some 22,500 square feet of new high school space was created by the architectural firm of James E. Palmer & Associates at a cost of $1.1 million. Construction lasted eight months, with the first students attending classes in the recycled building in September, 1977.

215

OPPOSITE: before, exterior. Photo: courtesy James E. Palmer, AIA & Associates.

TOP: before, interior. Photo: courtesy James E. Palmer, AIA & Associates.

LEFT: after, interior. Photo: Gerald Ratto, San Anselmo, Calif.

BELOW: after, exterior. Photo: Gerald Ratto, San Anselmo, Calif.

Christiana Offices

From: paint factory
To: homebuilding company headquarters

From the outside, the offices of Santa Monica's Christiana Company, a California homebuilder, are purposefully anonymous and industrial. The company inhabits a steel frame shed, erected along with countless siblings in 1954, that served as a paint factory and later as a warehouse. But the doors, a large wooden square set into the metal panel facade, hint at a change of character within—rather like a wooden Islamic door in the tall, austere outer walls of a courtyard house. The office courtyard is a circular indoor pool, lit by a skylight. Surrounding office spaces gain additional light from two clerestories running the length of the shed. A ramp crosses the interior, circling the pool en route from front door to rear wall. It is the major axis in a seven-level maze of office areas radiating from the pool, separated by redwood partitions and railings, and connected by carpeted steps.

For the architects of the 1971 renovation, Kaplan/McLaughlin of San Francisco and Denver, variety was the design intention in every respect: lighting, texture, circulation patterns, spatial division. The preexisting steel frame was painted bright blue. A huge wine vat was installed and converted into a circular conference room. The furniture is custom-made, although from inexpensive materials like old doors; carpeting is wall-to-wall; partitions, reflecting level changes, are immovable. The cost: about $19 per square foot, including furnishings, carpeting, and air conditioning; and about $35 per square foot, when all costs including land and professional fees, are included. Comparable office space in a downtown Los Angeles tower costs $70 to $80 per square foot.

Kaplan/McLaughlin thinks that renovation calls for ingenuity, idiosyncracy, knowledge of building codes, the ability to convert apparent liabilities into practical or decorative assets, and adaptability. Christiana was their first example of the landscaping approach to raw loft interiors that they call "terrain design." It has had the desired effect: The management claims that applications for employment have increased markedly since their move to the warehouse, though it is some distance from the standard office employment areas in Los Angeles. What is more, Christiana has inspired the conversion of other neighboring industrial buildings into offices and workshops.

BELOW: after, exterior. Photo: Joshua Freiwald, San Francisco.

TOP RIGHT: before, interior. Photo: courtesy Kaplan/McLaughlin, San Francisco.

BOTTOM RIGHT: after, interior. Photo: Joshua Freiwald, San Francisco.

William Taylor Store

From: cotton warehouse
To: loft apartment, studio, boutiques

In 1818, when cotton was king and Savannah its consort, rice and cotton merchant William Taylor was so busy that he had to enlarge the facilities servicing his dock on the Savannah River. The three-building complex that went up in that year is now the oldest intact cotton warehouse in the United States. It has the added distinction of having docked the S.S. *Savannah*, the country's first steamship, and of being part of a neighborhood that is now listed in the National Register of Historic Places. Riverfront warehouses there were built from the ballast stones (coral, Roman tile, and lava among them) brought in empty ship holds, and were fitted with iron balconies. Cotton merchants traveled the warehouse circuit along second- and third-level bridges, known as "factors' walks," that were suspended above the cobblestone streets.

Such a factors' walk gives entrance to the renovated loft of Lamont and Ann Osteen in the top floor and attic of Taylor's five-story store. Ann Osteen, a painter and interior designer, and Lamont Osteen, with professional building experience, who turned to medicine, brought the first loft living to Savannah from its origins in New York and San Francisco. They settled early on the Taylor store as their site, though the Factors' Walk neighborhood was then a rundown industrial and wholesale distribution area by day and a red light district by night.

In 1971, when their two children were old enough to willingly leave their old neighborhood, the Osteens bought the Taylor house and spent some years

of their own labor on renovation. They later hired an architect from Argentina, Juan Bertotto, to finish the 2,800-square-foot duplex, incorporating contoured walls and a north light clerestory. Below the living-room ceiling hangs the great wheel that operated the pulley system for lifting cotton bales. The third floor of the warehouse is now Ann Osteen's studio, and the lower two floors rent as boutiques.

This store renovation was a variant on the house restoration movement that has drawn participants to Savannah from across the country. Under the guidance of the Historic Savannah Foundation, more than 800 houses of vastly different architectural styles have been restored in the last 20 years. The Savannah Landmark Rehabilitation Project was subsequently founded to buy 600 slum houses in the city's Victorian district and rehabilitate them for federally subsidized rental to low-income neighborhood families.

As the Osteens anticipated, tourists began to flock to picturesque neighborhoods like Factors' Walk, which has since been renovated for shops, restaurants, and museums through a $7-million federal grant. The adjacent Taylor warehouse buildings have been sold twice at a profit since they moved into their pacesetting property, but the Osteens intend to stay.

The city itself undertook to renovate the Central of Georgia rail terminal, built in 1857. Architects Gunn and Meyerhoff converted the building into the Savannah Visitors Center with help from Ann Osteen, who researched the paint colors in accordance with Savannah's architectural tradition.

RIGHT: after, exterior. Photo: Van Jones Martin.

OPPOSITE TOP: after, interior. Photo: Van Jones Martin, from *Savannah Revisited*, The Beehive Press.

OPPOSITE BOTTOM: before, river facade. Photo: Louis Schwartz, courtesy H.A.B.S., Library of Congress.

Pioneer Square

From: marginal commercial district
To: shops, offices, entertainment, possible housing

The decaying area, long a haven for derelicts, gave the term Skid Row to the language, yet today Seattle's Skid Row has been both renamed and remade—as Pioneer Square—in civic recognition of the site of the pioneer village that preceded the city.

The historic district, covering more than 20 blocks on the fringe of downtown Seattle, was first the site of an Indian village. In 1852, it was recommended as a settlement site to a pioneer doctor by the chief of the Duwamish tribe, Sealth, whose name the city carries. Other pioneers by then were settling alongside the deep natural harbor and establishing the steam-powered lumber mill on Puget Sound that gave the city its economic impetus. The logs that were skidded downhill to the waterfront mill gave the area its nickname—"Skid Road," later modified to "Skid Row"—and produced a sprawling city of wood frame buildings. When a fire razed 25 downtown blocks in 1889, the district was rebuilt with a number of masonry buildings of Romanesque design by the city architect, Elmer Fisher. The most notable was the recently renovated Pioneer Building.

After gold was discovered in the Klondike in 1897, many buildings (including Pioneer Square's Grand Central Building, also recently renovated) were converted into hotels to accommodate the miners who were flocking north. Half the miners' funds were invested in banks, such as those in the Pioneer Building, which became the most elegant business address in town. Within 20 years, the commercial boom had ended, business shifted northward, and the district ran down.

As early as 1954, a contest was held to promote suggestions for renovation. But not until the early 1960s did architect Ralph Anderson start a trend by buying and rehabilitating an old office building for his own office. Soon flophouses were being recycled as art galleries, design offices, a law firm's quarters, bars, and cafés. A Seattle historian, Bill Speidel, reopened the underground sidewalks with their original storefronts, left over from the time when Seattle's streets lay below high-tide level. To eliminate sewage problems, the city had raised the streets and shops 10 to 30 feet, abandoning the old ones and building new sidewalks atop them; now business has resumed underground where Speidel conducts tours.

When a proposal was made in the 1960s to run a freeway through the district, with accompanying garages, Speidel, Anderson, and others formed the Pioneer Square Association to prevent widespread demolition. The city government helped, too, enacting a preservation ordinance in 1970 aimed at barring wanton demolition. Recognizing that Seattle lacks conventional landmarks in its core area, its citizens have approved a broader type of preservation, stressing historical significance and continuity as well as neighborhood character. Pioneer Square proved an excellent model, and an economical one as well: Its buildings were renovated at three-fourths the cost of new construction; and the offices on the upper floors and the shops and restaurants on the street and lower levels have quadrupled in rents and property values. In 1971, following this example, voters approved a referendum to preserve a warehouse area used as a farmers' market since 1907, but now threatened with demolition to make way for highrise construction. Pike Place Market, featuring food stores, flea markets, crafts shops, cafés, and boarding houses, plans to remain less expensive and sophisticated than Pioneer Square.

In the cases of both Pioneer Square and Pike Place, the impetus for renovation was private—in fact, it came from local architects. Still, the city's commitment to preservation has attracted state and federal funds and guaranteed some urban amenities. By 1975 investment had totaled about $8 million in private property acquisition and renovation, $2 million in state and federal grants, and only about $300,000 in city funds used to plant trees and to develop two parks; one of them, Pioneer Square Park, displays a totem pole, a statue of Chief Sealth, and a restored iron pergola dating from 1909. The city, with the strong support of former mayor Wes Uhlmann, also established, in 1974, the Historic Seattle Preservation and Development Authority, with a revolving fund to buy endangered historic buildings and resell them for renovation. The agency, modeled on Historic Savannah, has had a hand in the renovation of several old firehouses, an institutional home, and one of Seattle's most storied and luxurious mansions, the Stimson-Green House, now a museum. Private projects include the recent conversion of an old garage into a shopping arcade. But it is Pioneer Square that remains Seattle's model renovation project—and that, in a signal honor, was chosen in 1975 as the site of a three-day conference of the National Trust for Historic Preservation.

During construction, Pioneer Building. Photo: Art Hupy.

OPPOSITE TOP: before, Corner Market Building, 1977. Photo: Theron Hooks, courtesy City of Seattle Department of Commercial Development.

OPPOSITE BOTTOM: before, exterior, Grand Central on the Park. Photo: Art Hupy.

ABOVE: after, exterior, Grand Central on the Park. Photo: Art Hupy.

LEFT: after, Grand Central on the Park. Photo: Art Hupy.

E. E. Cooley Building

From: cotton mill
To: university maintenance-department headquarters

As governor of Mississippi, John Marshall Stone played a key role in establishing the Textile School at the state's Agricultural and Mechanical College in Starkville. So it was appropriate that when a big new cotton mill was built from Stewart Cramer's design in 1902, two years after the governor's death, it was named the John M. Stone Cotton Mill in his honor. Rather than ship the state's primary cash crop to other parts of the country for processing, mills such as this generated employment at home and saved money for the cotton growers, into the bargain. Ties between the Textile School and the mill were close, though the school closed in 1914 and the mill continued to function until 1962, when it also was closed.

In 1965 the relationship was renewed when Mississippi State University (which evolved from the old Mississippi A & M) bought the Stone Cotton Mill for $125,688, renamed it the E. E. Cooley Building, and adapted it to house the school's Physical Plant Department.

The building is representative of an important era in the economic growth of a large portion of the southeast. Situated one mile west of the MSU main campus, the 384-foot-long, 75-foot-wide, two-story brick structure has been somewhat modified over the years. A 1913 photograph reveals that, since that time,

additions were made to either end of the rectangular building, and a smaller wing attached. The 45-bay facade is broken by a square four-story tower that once contained a stairway and the mill's water tank. Except for a bracketed cornice and corbeling, only the tower's top floor has external ornamentation, and that consists of paired corner pilasters on each facade and blind roundels in place of windows.

When renovation began in 1968, the tower's stairway was removed. Other interior renovations consisted mainly of repair work. Some 16-by-18-inch wood support beams were rotting and had to be spliced, while tongue-in-groove floor boards were repaired and covered to protect them from heavy maintenance equipment. Some walls, partitions, and false ceilings were installed.

The original brick exterior, painted often over the years, was sandblasted. Structural repairs were made, and new windows put in. Today the old mill houses offices, a conference room, sign-printing facilities, and storage space for everything from blueprint files to general supplies needed to keep mechanical systems operating on the nearby campus. The 107,558 square feet of floor space was purchased and converted into office and storage space at a total cost of $4.02 per square foot.

OPPOSITE: before, interior.

TOP: before, exterior.

MIDDLE: after, exterior.

BELOW: after, interior.

Photos: Don Mott/Mississippi State University Physical Plant Department.

McCabe/Elliott House

From: church
To: private residence, rental apartment

The old wooden Baptist church in the seaside town of Stonington underwent its first recycling when the congregation's treasurer absconded with the funds and the building had to be put up for sale. Editor Ann Fuller and her architect husband Charles were attracted by the ribbed barrel vault of the 45-foot-high nave separating the three-story choir loft from the four-story bell tower, and by the original stained-glass windows as well. They bought the church, which stands on the narrow end of a shady Stonington street, and with architectural writer Richard Pratt converted it into an ingenious, though improvisatory, summer house and art gallery. Pegboard walls were erected in the nave to screen the living and dining rooms. The bell tower became a master bedroom suite with a view over the town and harbor. The front portion of the church was demolished, and the remaining stone foundations were used to fence the garden and patio. A wide veranda was added, overlooking the garden.

In the late 1960s Inger McCabe, just back in New York after six years in the Far East, began looking for a summer place and was introduced to Stonington by a friend. With a population made up mostly of Portuguese fishermen and mill workers, the town is not primarily a resort, but it does have a number of summer families, mostly editors and writers. Inger McCabe, herself a photojournalist and businesswoman, bought the church in 1968 and, with her three children, began using it as a summer retreat.

When Mrs. McCabe married Osborn Elliott, former editor-in-chief of *Newsweek* magazine, a few years later, the church's layout had to be rearranged to suit a family that now included six children. The plumbing and wiring were redone. The Elliotts replaced the pegboard with a roofed interior pavilion, which defined the living and dining area within the nave. The wooden slats that form the ceiling of the pavilion permit a view of the nave's ceiling, which was turned from a dirty yellow-brown into cerulean blue with white crossbeams, in the style of Italian church interiors. The weathered brown facade was painted white with blue shutters, except for the east end, left in its original state to please a neighbor.

A fully equipped efficiency kitchen was installed. The long corridor below the choir loft became a row of four bedrooms for the younger children and for guests, each with a floor and ceiling painted a different primary color chosen by the children. The second story of the choir became an independent apartment with its own entrance and stairwell, to be rented off-season. The master bedroom remained in the bell-tower, with exposed studs, so that bookshelves could be installed between them, and with the old ladder stairs leading to the outdoor cupola where the church bell was once rung. The leftover interior space in the nave, surrounding the enclosed living/dining pavilion, is used as a theater or a neighborhood playground, as needed. The veranda has become the family's main congregating place.

Furnishings for the summer house were economically chosen—from the offerings of neighbors, hand-me-downs, and available bargains—producing a style that Inger Elliott calls "Early Salvation Army and Late Mother." Cushions for the sofas and rattan chairs are covered with fabrics that she discovered on her travels in Indonesia or imported for her firm, China Seas, Inc.

TOP LEFT: before, interior. Photo: Rapho Guillumette Pictures.

TOP RIGHT: after, exterior. Photo: courtesy Rollie McKenna.

BOTTOM: after, interior. Photo: courtesy Inger McCabe Elliot.

Tacoma Art Museum

From: bank
To: art museum

This Neoclassical bank building, designed by Tacoma architects Sutton, Whitney & Dugan and built in 1920, is typical in terms of style and current status of hundreds of bank buildings across the United States. As banks move to larger corporate headquarters or smaller drive-in branches, their older buildings present excellent opportunities for recycling. Their open interiors especially lend themselves to arts-oriented uses. This building, in fact, has been recycled as an art museum.

Before the National Bank of Washington moved into a new building by the architectural firm of Skidmore, Owings & Merrill, it had extensively renovated its old headquarters. The original character of the exterior was preserved, despite the installation of new window sashes, but the interior was completely modernized.

Since the historic interior was already gone, the usual difficult problem of incorporating a new use while remaining faithful to the existing design was not an issue. In the main gallery on the ground floor, architect Alan Liddle, whose own offices are in a recycled Tacoma building, installed new flexible museum lighting from the existing dropped ceiling, which contained the bank's now discarded fluorescent lighting and concealed air-conditioning ducts. He blocked the imposing arched windows along the side elevation. These closed windows, facing the plaza of the new office tower across the street, where the National Bank is now headquartered, retain the rhythm of the original fenestration and may be reopened in the future. Administrative offices and a 200-seat auditorium were installed upstairs and a children's gallery with a small theater in the former vault were built in the basement. Cost of renovation: $100,000.

OPPOSITE: before, interior. Photo: courtesy Alan Liddle, FAIA.

TOP: after, interior. Photo: Hugh N. Stratford.

LEFT: after, exterior. Photo: Hugh N. Stratford.

ABOVE: after, entrance to children's auditorium. Photo: Hugh N. Stratford.

Museum of African Art

From: private townhouse
To: art museum, school, boutique

The pacesetting Museum of African Art in Washington is designed to fulfill two functions: to dramatize Africa's growing role in the world; and to focus attention on the importance of traditional African art in the culture of man. According to Warren Robbins, who founded the museum in 1964 and continues to direct it with vigor and flair: "Just as it is vitally important for black Americans to have an opportunity to learn more about African culture, its legitimacy, its creative richness, it is equally important for the predominantly white population of America to have a better understanding of African culture and of the cultural antecedents of America's black population."

How appropriate, then, that the museum's initial quarters should have been the first Washington residence of Frederick Douglass, the brilliant black abolitionist orator and publisher. In 1871, Douglass and his family moved into a charming three-story "bookend house" with a bay window and mansard roof in the Capitol Hill area. From the Douglass home, the museum expanded until it now occupies no fewer than nine contiguous townhouses from No. 316 to No. 332 on A Street. Anchored by the Douglass place at one end and by a Neo-Colonial dwelling at the other, the townhouses fill a full block. None is more than three stories high, and the oldest dates back to 1840. Together, they form an appealing, human-scale complex, one well-designed to invite further examination.

As the museum gradually took over the townhouses, care was taken to preserve the facades and to renovate the interiors without doing violence to the spirit in which they were designed. Today the Douglass double house with a new wing added in the rear is used for public galleries and curatorial reserves. Though the museum possesses more than 7,000 objects of African art, ranging from sculpture to textiles, artifacts, musical instruments, and weaponry, only 500 or so are on view at any given time, in a dozen separate galleries in the A Street complex.

Next door to the gallery and storage area is Boutique Africa, where contemporary African jewelry, clothing, fabrics, and craft objects are sold. Also in these two townhouses are a gallery, a learning center for elementary and secondary schoolchildren, and education staff offices. The next two townhouses provide shelter for a variety of administrative functions and for a graphics department.

In the last three of the townhouses are a department of higher education, class and reading rooms, a library, and one of the gems of the museum's collections: the Eliot Elisofon Photo Archives. Elisofon, the late photographer for *Life* magazine, had assembled one of the world's great collections of photographs on Africa. He donated the collection to the museum to serve as the core of what is now a 150,000-photograph record of the continent.

The rear area of the townhouse complex provides an ideal space not only for parking but also for large gatherings, and the museum is turning this oversized patio into an indoor-outdoor auditorium with a seating capacity of 300 and a reception area that can accommodate 800 persons.

Statistics tell only part of any story, but in the museum's case, they are a pretty fair indicator of success. In less than a decade and a half, the Museum of African Art has attracted a million visitors to its galleries and programs, played host to around 12,000 groups for orientation in African culture, and today operates educational extension programs at many museums, colleges, schools, and conferences around the country. Legislation has been introduced in Congress to make the museum part of the Smithsonian Institution. This would mean not only a considerable easing of the museum's budgetary problems, but would give it the stability and resources to fully realize its potential as an institution of world stature.

TOP: before, exterior. Photo: courtesy Museum of African Art.

MIDDLE: after, exterior. Photo: courtesy Museum of African Art, Eliot Elisofon Archives.

BOTTOM: after, interior. Photo: courtesy Museum of African Art, Eliot Elisofon Archives.

National Collection of Fine Arts/
National Portrait Gallery

From: Patent Office Building
To: exhibition galleries

Monumental is the word for the old Patent Office Building in Washington, midway between Capitol Hill and the White House. With 36 exterior Doric columns, one measuring 18 feet in circumference, the Greek Revival building is 404 feet long and 275 feet wide, enclosing an imposing courtyard that itself is 270 feet long and 112 feet wide. Yet, were it not for the intervention of a president, the third-oldest building in Washington would have been torn down some 20 years ago.

The structure's brick bearing walls, inside and out, were faced and embellished with Maryland marble, granite from Maine, Connecticut, and Massachusetts, and sandstone from the Aquia Creek quarry in Virginia first operated by George Washington. Authorized by Congress in 1836, the four-wing building was completed in stages between 1840 and 1867 to the specifications of four noted American architects: William Parker Elliot, Robert Mills (who designed the Washington Monument), Ithiel Town, and Thomas U. Walter. Designed to be fire-resistant, the masonry piers and the vaults protecting the wooden roof trusses in the south and east wings withstood an 1877 blaze; the modern iron framing in the other two wings did not. Reconstruction was carried out according to contemporary Victorian taste, defying the austere aesthetic elsewhere in the structure.

Though the building served first the Patent Office and then the Civil Service Commission, its great vaulted halls were drafted during the Civil War for use as a hospital; Clara Barton was a nurse there and Walt Whitman consoled soldiers. In the breathtaking Model Hall on the third floor, 300 feet long with 28 marble columns, Abraham Lincoln's second inaugural ball was held, only five weeks before his assassination.

When demolition was proposed in the mid-1950s to make way for a parking lot, President Eisenhower (David Finley, head of the Commission of Fine Arts, brought the building's fate to his attention) urged that the building be rescued. Congress concurred and assigned it to the Smithsonian Institution. In 1965, a $6.2-million project was begun to adapt the structure for the National Collection of Fine Arts, the National Portrait Gallery, and the Archives of American Art. Waldron Faulkner of Faulkner, Stenhouse, Fryer & Faulkner was the designer, with Bayard Underwood as consulting architect to the National Collection and the late Victor Proetz to the National Gallery. While the exterior was simply cleaned and lightly restored, the interior was divided into 64 galleries. The three largest: the Granite Gallery in the basement, where massive pillars support low barrel vaults; the second-floor Sandstone Gallery; and the third-floor Lincoln Gallery with its marble columns. Though curatorial space and galleries occupy most of the building's 78,000 square feet, there are also a library, a conservation laboratory, lecture and assembly rooms, and a sculpture garden.

The much-admired renovation won an AIA Honor Award in 1970. As the jury put it, the building's preservation was "to the everlasting credit of the Smithsonian Institution."

TOP: before, 1865 rendering. Photo: courtesy National Collection of Fine Arts, Smithsonian Institution.

BOTTOM: after, exterior. Photo: National Collection of Fine Arts, Smithsonian Institution.

OPPOSITE TOP: before, east corridor, c. 1923. Photo: National Archives, courtesy National Collection of Fine Arts, Smithsonian Institution.

OPPOSITE BOTTOM: after, Lincoln Gallery. Photo: courtesy National Collection of Fine Arts, Smithsonian Institution.

LEFT: after, interior, 1968. Photo: Jack Boucher, courtesy H.A.B.S., Library of Congress.

BELOW: after, stair detail. Photo: courtesy Faulkner, Fryer, and Vanderpool, Architects.

The Renwick Gallery

From: art gallery, federal offices, U.S. Court of Claims
To: art gallery

In the mid-19th century, the Corcoran Gallery must have seemed an outrageous intruder indeed amidst the Federalist and Neoclassical structures of the capital. It was an American mini-Louvre in the exuberant Second Empire style designed to house the paintings, bronzes, and plaster casts collected by banker-philanthropist William Wilson Corcoran. Both Corcoran and the brilliant James Renwick, Jr., who had designed the Norman castle on Washington's Mall for the infant Smithsonian Institution when he was only 27, had been inspired by Lefuel's additions to the Louvre. Their brick, sandstone, and zinc concoction featured three massed pavilions with individual crested mansard roofs, paired columns framing second-floor sculpture niches under segmental arches to accommodate seven-foot-high marble statues of such artists as Phidias, Leonardo, and Rubens. Instead of using traditional capitals of acanthus leaves, Corcoran chose to crown the gallery's columns with ears of Indian corn. The overall effect astonished American eyes; even the interior renovation architect, Hugh Jacobsen, concedes that it could be characterized as "nutty stuff."

Renwick planned an all-white marble entry hall and grand staircase to offset the colorful facade, but the Civil War intervened. In 1861 the Union Army turned the building into a warehouse for the quartermaster general's corps; three years later the quartermaster converted it into his offices. When Corcoran got his building back in 1869, he redecorated the interior in gaudier fashion than Renwick had stipulated. The stairhall was paved with marble, but the stair was finished in brownstone and carpeted in crimson. The dados were paneled in wood and the stairway walls were painted in imitation of colored marble. The galleries ringing the staircase core included the Octagon Room, designed for his prized sculpture by Hiram Powers, the naughty "Greek Slave," and culminated in the Main Painting Gallery at the top of the stairs, where the choicest pictures were hung in double and triple rows from a 24-foot cornice against plum walls and illuminated by a 34-foot-high skylight.

By 1897 the collection had outgrown the building and was moved to a new building two blocks away.

The second-floor statues were sold off. The government took over the old building for the U.S. Court of Claims, and there followed 67 years of insult and neglect. Iron crestings, for example, were melted down for scrap metal during World War II and replaced with wooden mockups of machine guns to forestall attack on the White House across the street. In 1956, when the building began to crumble and endanger passers-by, Senator Lyndon Johnson introduced a bill calling for its demolition. But in 1963 President John F. Kennedy stated a preference for its preservation, and in 1965 President Lyndon Johnson transferred the building to the Smithsonian Institution. The old structure owed its reprieve largely to San Francisco architect John Carl Warnecke, who convinced Kennedy (and later Johnson) to scrap a plan for an all-new Lafayette Square and to rededicate the old Corcoran to art.

Warnecke supervised the dismantling of the Court of Claims partitions, the installation of new mechanical systems, and structural repairs to the wrought-iron beams and brick walls. Universal Restoration, Inc., was responsible for the facade, much of which had been obliterated by weather and pollutants. With the help of archival photographic research, Italian master stonemason Renato Lucchetti carved models for latex molds from which lost ornament was recast. Masonry surfaces were rebuilt with chemically bonded compounds.

Restoration of the galleries was carried out by the firm of Hugh Jacobsen. Since Renwick's original design had never been executed, much of the work was interpretive rather than literal. The Grand Salon, minus its original ornate ceiling paintings, is now graced by many of the original paintings that hung there, borrowed from the relocated Corcoran; the dark red walls and wainscoting have been restored. The room is now used for receptions, film showings, lectures, and concerts.

Restoring this elegant showcase for the American decorative arts and crafts cost $2.8 million. As the director of the recycled Renwick Gallery, Lloyd Herman, puts it: "The building is our own biggest exhibit."

TOP: before, exterior, Corcoran Gallery of Art, 1880.

BOTTOM LEFT: before, Model Hall, 1880.

BOTTOM RIGHT: after, interior.

Photos: courtesy National Collection of Fine Arts, Smithsonian Institution.

Omnisphere/Earth-Space Center

From: public library
To: planetarium, museum

The Wichita City Library, designed by Anthony Allaire Crowley, was built in 1915 with a $75,000 grant from Andrew Carnegie. The city of Wichita supplied the site for the structure, which was decorated by Louise Murdock, the state's first interior decorator, who commissioned sunflower stained-glass windows from Elizabeth Stubblefield and murals from Arthur Sinclair Covey. In 1968, when the library moved across Main Street to its present location, the new municipal courts center took over the old Carnegie building. At the time of this transition the celebrated sunflower windows were removed. Most of them stayed in town, finding homes in the Wichita Historical Museum, the Wichita Art Association, the Soroptimist House, and the YWCA. Some of the windows, however, were shipped as far away as Washington, D.C., where they were installed in the chapel of the Daughters of the American Revolution.

When the city courts left the building in 1975, a city-sponsored restoration project began to turn the structure into a planetarium-museum named the Omnisphere/Earth-Space Center. The exterior was left as it originally appeared. Constructed of pressed Bedford stone in a Neoclassical style, its deep-set arched entry is elaborated by a keystone and paired pilasters on either side of the opening. At the roof level a much heavier bracketed cornice completes the facade decoration. Inside, the original marble columns and iron stair railings still exist. Forgotten stained-glass skylights upstairs were discovered behind a false ceiling. Interior balconies have been repaired and a 60-seat theater created. This is the planetarium's central projection area, crowned by Omnisphere's 30-foot domed screen.

Outside the theater, visitors can stop at the gift shop, called the Space Station, or view exhibits in related earth-space sciences such as astronomy, geology, meteorology, and paleontology. A mirrored vestibule forms the main entry and reception area.

The old library's physical setting may eventually be altered almost as considerably as its interior. In 1975 a project was planned to create a downtown Heritage Square joining the planetarium to the adjacent Historical Museum with a mall that would include gardens, a bandstand, and pedestrian walkways.

OPPOSITE: before, exterior, c. 1915. Photo: Local History Division, City of Wichita.

ABOVE: after, lobby.

LEFT: before, interior. Photo: Local History Division, City of Wichita.

From: hotel
To: offices, studios, restaurant, crafts center, radio station

Windsor House, a handsome Greek Revival structure completed in 1840, was once considered the finest hotel between Boston and Montreal. But neglect and changing travel patterns reduced its luster, and by the last third of the 20th century, it seemed fated to go the way of countless other old buildings. The Vermont National Bank was preparing to demolish it for a modern drive-in branch, and there seemed to be nothing standing in its way. Windsor, however, has a well-developed sense of history. It was in this Connecticut River town that the Vermont constitution was adopted in 1777. The American Precision Museum, a collection of machine tools rivaling that of the Smithsonian Institution, reflects Windsor's role in inventing interchangeable parts and thereby bringing about the Industrial Revolution.

To save Windsor House, a group of townspeople formed Historic Windsor, Inc., in 1971, and launched a campaign. Despite initial opposition, the town eventually voted to accept the group's proposal to buy the hotel from the bank, give it to the town so as to become eligible for a major grant from the Department of Housing and Urban Development, and then lease it back from the town at a rent of $2,500 a year in lieu of taxes. HUD subsequently came through with $92,500, a matching grant intended to equal half the purchase and restoration costs; with a challenge grant from the Eva Gebhard Gourgaud Foundation, other funds and volunteer labor came from foundations and from private individuals and firms that saw the rescue of Windsor House as a step toward refurbishing the downtown core and reviving business on Main Street.

When Historic Windsor moved into the old dining room to begin renovation, the house lacked heat, electricity, and functioning plumbing. The National Guard volunteered to landscape the grounds. Cone Machine Tool, the Red Cross, and a local antique store, among others, lent or donated furnishings. The highway department brought wood for the fireplace and the fire department supplied chairs and tables for receptions and porch lighting for Christmas festivities. Architect Robert Burley, who supervised the renovation, incorporated into his plans for the interior the great arched windows salvaged from the Ammi B. Young post office/courthouse across the street.

Historic Windsor now operates from offices in Windsor House, which also provides quarters for a wholesale/retail outlet of the Vermont State Crafts Center. The work of about 200 Vermont craftsmen is sold there, and in 1977 more than 600 students attended classes in ceramics, weaving, stained glass, drawing, and other crafts. The antique bathtubs from the old hotel are used as dyeing vats. Other tenants are a restaurant, a dentist's office, a Social Security office, the Windsor Area Chamber of Commerce, and Vermont's first noncommercial radio station, WVPA, which broadcasts from the top floor of the three-story building.

Windsor House is now listed in the National Register of Historic Places and has won a Department of Commerce award as a tourist attraction. It has, in fact, attracted interest from as far away as Switzerland. In the fall of 1977, the center exchanged craft exhibits with a counterpart in Geneva.

LEFT: after, front facade. Photo: Georgianna Fitzhugh.

OPPOSITE TOP: during construction, lobby interior looking through to craft center. Photo: Paul Atwood.

OPPOSITE BOTTOM: after, craft center interior. Photo: John Evarts.

Yuma Arts Center

From: railroad depot
To: arts center

Times change, and so do travel patterns, so it happened that in 1971 the Southern Pacific Railroad announced that it planned to demolish the lovely little depot in Yuma to make way for—guess what?—a parking lot. Completion of the $150,000 depot back in 1926 had meant the beginning of regular train service to Yuma. The arrival of the first train on April 7, 1926, was a truly festive occasion: the Yuma Indian Band played as the locomotive chugged to a halt, and each of the passengers was presented with a grapefruit from Yuma's "Frostless Mesa" and a copy of the local newspaper. For the next 45 years the depot served a necessary function, but the automobile and airplane finally doomed it.

Enter the Yuma Fine Arts Association. Organized in 1952, the association had prospered, acquiring a small permanent art collection, and it was fast outgrowing its quarters in the Century House and gardens, former residence of E. F. Sanguinetti, Sr. Seeing an opportunity, the association began bargaining to trade off some land it had acquired for the depot, so that the railroad could have its parking lot without destroying the old building. In 1972, the association purchased the depot and in 1975 gave it to the city of Yuma in exchange for a $1 per year lease.

The original building was quite elegant: a two-winged frame structure, with an exterior covering of buff stucco and a terra-cotta tile roof. Inside, the original marble, white tile, and all-oak woodwork provided an impressive backdrop for arriving and departing passengers. The front and rear facades, designed to match one another, both have five central arches containing windows and three main doors. To the back, facing the tracks, was added a platform half the height of the arches and nine bays long, with a roof supported by delicate spiral columns, the place where people once gathered to await trains.

Most of the interior surfaces were restored during the 1975 renovation. Major changes included installing new air conditioning, lighting, carpeting, and kitchen, removing the old ticket booths, and constructing offices. Liberty-Pogue Associates, responsible for the conversion, altered the depot's original 11-room plan to provide for 5 exhibition areas with adjoining offices, conference rooms, and storage facilities. To accomplish this, more than 8,000 square feet of drywall was put up. The trackside platform was transformed into open workshop space for local artists. It was discovered during renovation that the main entry doors, thought to be of painted oak, were actually made of Arizona copper. They were carefully restored, as was the tile roof. Future plans call for a small outdoor theater and a children's museum in a railroad car.

To finance the conversion, local leaders launched a fundraising drive that brought in more than $90,000. Construction materials were donated by Yuma businessmen.

OPPOSITE: after, exterior.

ABOVE: after, lobby.

LEFT: before, waiting room.

Photos: courtesy Yuma Art Center.

SELECTED BIBLIOGRAPHY

245

BOOKS AND REPORTS

Barnett, Jonathan. *Urban Design as Public Policy.* New York: McGraw-Hill, 1974.

Binns, Archie. *Northwest Gateway, The Story of the Port of Seattle.* Portland, Ore.: Binfords & Mort, 1941.

Blake, Peter. *The Master Builders.* New York: W. W. Norton & Company, 1976.

Boston Redevelopment Authority. *Recycled Boston.* Boston: Boston Redevelopment Authority, 1976.

Brown, Charles Bernard. *The Conversion of Old Buildings into New Homes for Occupation and Investment.* London: Batsford, 1955.

Burnham, Alan, ed. *New York Landmarks.* Middletown, Conn.: Wesleyan University Press, 1963.

Cantacuzino, Sherban. *New Uses for Old Buildings.* New York: Watson-Guptill, 1976.

Chesley, Gene. *The National List of Historic Theatre Buildings.* Prepared for League of Historic American Theatres.

Clay, Grady. *Close-Up: How to Read the American City.* New York: Praeger, 1973.

Custom House Institute. *Custom House Institute Planning Study.* New York: Custom House Institute, 1974.

Department of Development and Planning of the City of Chicago. *Historic City: The Settlement of Chicago.* Chicago: Department of Development and Planning, 1976.

Educational Facilities Laboratories and the National Endowment for the Arts. *The Arts in Found Places.* New York: Educational Facilities Laboratories, Inc., 1976.

———. Research and text by Hardy Holzman Pfeiffer Associates. *Reusing Railroad Stations.* New York: Educational Facilities Laboratories, Inc., 1974.

1886 Guide to New York City. New York: Schocken Books, 1975.

Fracchia, Charles A., and Bragstad, Jeremiah O. *Converted into Houses.* New York: The Viking Press, 1976.

Gayle, Margot, and Gillon, Edmund V., Jr. *Cast-Iron Architecture in New York: A Photographic Survey.* New York: Dover, 1974.

Goldstone, Harmon, and Dalrymple, Martha. *History Preserved: A Guide to New York City Landmarks and Historic Districts.* New York: Simon & Schuster, 1974.

Gould, William A., and Associates. *Cleveland Warehouse District Plan 1977.* Cleveland: Cleveland Landmarks Commission, 1977.

Greiff, Constance. *Lost America: From the Atlantic to the Mississippi.* New York: Weathervane Books, 1971.

———. *Lost America: From the Mississippi to the Pacific.* New York: Weathervane Books, 1972.

Harrison, Myra Fraser. *Adaptive Use of Historic Structures: A Series of Case Studies.* Unpublished. The National Trust for Historic Preservation, 1971.

Heckscher, August. *Open Spaces: The Life of American Cities.* New York: Harper & Row, 1977.

Hosmer, Charles B., Jr. *Presence of the Past.* New York: G. P. Putnam's Sons, 1965.

Jacobs, Jane. *The Death and Life of Great American Cities.* New York: Vantage Books, 1961.

Jacopetti, Roland, VanMeer, Ben, and McCall, Wayne. *Rescued Buildings.* Santa Barbara: Capra Press, 1977.

Kidney, Walter. *Working Places: The Adaptive Use of Industrial Buildings.* Pittsburgh: Ober Park Associates, Inc., 1976.

Kliment, Stephen A., ed. *Neighborhood Conservation: A Source Book.* New York: Watson-Guptill, 1975.

Los Angeles Community Design Center. *Recycling for Housing.* Los Angeles: The Los Angeles Community Design Center, 1977.

Lottman, Herbert R. *How Cities Are Saved.* New York: Universe Books, 1976.

Lowell Historic Canal District Commission. *Lowell, Massachusetts. A Report of the Lowell Historic Canal District Commission to the Ninety-Fifth Congress of the United States of America.* Washington, D.C.: U.S. Government Printing Office, 1977.

Lynch, Kevin. *What Time Is This Place?* Cambridge: M.I.T. Press, 1972.

Michels, Ellen. *The Old Federal Courts Building: A Landmark Reclaimed.* St. Paul: Minnesota Landmarks, 1977.

Mitchell, James R., ed. *Antique Metalware.* New York: Universe Books.

Mobile City Planning Commission and City of Mobile. *Nineteenth Century Mobile Architecture.* Mobile: Mobile City Planning Commission, 1974.

National Trust for Historic Preservation. *Economic Benefits of Preserving Old Buildings.* Washington, D.C.: Preservation Press, 1976.

National Trust for Historic Preservation and Colonial Williamsburg. *Historic Preservation Tomorrow.* Williamsburg: Second Workshop, 1967.

National Trust for Historic Preservation, Wrenn, Tony P., and Mulloy, Elizabeth D. *America's Forgotten Architecture.* New York: Pantheon, 1976.

New York City Planning Commission. *Neighborhood Preservation in New York City.* New York: City Planning Commission of New York City, 1973.

New York State Office of Parks and Recreation, Division of Historic Preservation. *The National Register of Historic Places in New York State.* New York: New York State Office of Parks and Recreation, 1976.

Old San Diego Planned District Review Board and the City of San Diego. *Old San Diego Architecture and Site Development Standards.* San Diego: City of San Diego, 1972.

Old Town Restorations, Inc. *Building the Future from Our Past. A Report on the St. Paul Historic District Planning Program.* St. Paul: Old Town Restorations, Inc., 1975.

Pevsner, Nikolaus. *A History of Building Types.* Bollingen Series XXXV. Princeton: Princeton University Press, 1976.

Polley, Robert L. *America's Historic Houses: The Living Past.* New York: G. P. Putnam's Sons, 1967.

Portland Historical Landmarks Commission and Portland City Planning Commission. *A Proposal for Historic Conservation Zoning.* Portland: City of Portland, 1977.

The Providence Partnership. *The Urban Design Plan-Historic Hill.* Newport: Newport Redevelopment Agency, 1971.

Rains, Albert, and Henderson, Laurance, et al. *With Heritage So Rich. A Report of a Special Committee on Historic Preservation.* New York: Random House, 1966.

Robinson, Neil, Bass and Associates. *Recycling Nashville's Waterfront.* National Endowment for the Arts, Architecture, and Environmental Arts, July 1975.

Rosebrock, Ellen Fletcher, and Gillon, Edmund V., Jr. *South Street: A Photographic Guide to New York's Historic Sea Port.* New York: Dover, 1974.

Sande, Theodore Anton. *Industrial Archeology.* Brattleboro, Vt.: Stephen Greene Press, 1976.

Santa Cruz City Planning Department. *Historic Preservation Plan.* Santa Cruz, New Mexico: City Planning Department, 1974.

Shopsin, William C. *Adapting Old Buildings to New Uses.* New York: New York State Council on Architecture, 1974.

Smith, Baird. *Adaptive Use: A Survey of Construction.*

Stanforth, Deirdre. *Restored America.* New York: Praeger, 1975.

Thompson, Elisabeth Kendall, ed. *Recycling Buildings.* New York: McGraw-Hill, 1977.

Ware, Merrill. *Federal Architecture: Adaptive Use Facilities.* Washington, D.C.: National Endowment for the Arts, 1975.

Weatherford, Regan. *Benefits of Recycling Buildings.* Washington, D.C.: Center for the Visual Environment, 1976.

Young, Toni. *The Grand Experience.* Watkins Glen, N.Y.: The American Life Foundation and Study Institute, 1976.

Abercrombie, Stanley. "Recycling." *Architecture Plus* 2 (March–April 1974): 36–87.

Burke, Padraic. "To Market, To Market." *Historic Preservation* 29 (January–March 1977): 32–38.

Candee, Richard M. "New Hampshire: Preservation Redefined." *Historic Preservation* 27 (July–September 1975): 20–25.

Cavaglieri, Giorgio. "Design in Adaptive Reuse." *Historic Preservation* 26 (January 1974): 12–17.

Dean, Andrea O. "Adaptive Use: Economic and Other Advantages." *A.I.A. Journal* 65 (June 1976): 26–38.

Edmunds, Frances R. "The Adaptive Use of Charleston Buildings in Historic Preservation." *Antiques* 97 (April 1970): 590–95.

Fisher, Tom. "A Look at Ourselves." *Historic Preservation* 28 (January–March 1976): 28–31.

"The Future of Our Past." *Progressive Architecture.* Complete issue devoted to preservation: 53 (November 1972).

Galbreath, Carol J. "Small Town Preservation—A Systemic View." *Historic Preservation* 27 (April–July 1975): 12–19.

Gueft, Olga. "D/R to the Rescue." *Interiors* 135 (April 1976): 62–69.

Harney, Andy Leon. "Adaptive Use: Saving Energy (and Money) as Well as Historic Buildings." *A.I.A. Journal* 62 (August 1974): 49–54.

Hieronymus, Bill. "Firms Renovate Buildings: Eye on History, Energy Crisis." *Preservation News* 14 (February 1974): 12.

Hollis, Jay S. "Gristmills: One Man's View." *Historic Preservation* 29 (January–March 1977): 10–13.

The Journal of the Society for Industrial Archeology. Complete issue: 1 (summer 1975).

Ketchum, Morris, Jr. "Recycling and Restoring Landmarks: An Architectural Challenge and Opportunity." *A.I.A. Journal* 64 (September 1975): 31–39.

Knight, Carleton, III. "Adaptive Use: Apartments from a Factory and a Store." *A.I.A. Journal* 62 (November 1974): 38–41.

———. "Ringing in the Old." *Architectural Forum* 138 (April 1973).

The Livable City. Complete issues: 2 (May 1975); 4 (August 1977); 4 (September 1977). New York: Municipal Art Society.

Muff, Jane. "Buildings Can Be Recycled Too." *Fortune* (May 1975): 192–200.

"New Life for Old Buildings." *Preservation News* 13 (April 1973).

"New Life for Old Buildings: The Architect's Renewed Commitment to Preservation." Building Types Study 429. Special Issue. *Architectural Record* 150 (December 1971): 81–88.

"Preserving the Recent Past." *Progressive Architecture* 55 (July 1974): 48–79; 96–103.

Progressive Architecture. Complete issue devoted to adaptive re-use: 58 (November 1977).

"Rehabilitation and Reuse." *Architectural Record* 158 (August 1975): 67–81.

Seiberling, Rep. John F. "The Urgency of Land Use Planning." *Historic Preservation* 26 (April–June 1977): 32–37.

Sisler, Carol U., and Phillips, Marion G. "The Foundation Game and How Historic Ithaca Won." *Historic Preservation* 27 (January–March 1975): 38–42.

"Six Architects' Offices in Recycled Buildings." *A.I.A. Journal* 64 (January 1975): 35–38.

Snow, Barbara. "Preservation for Use." *Antiques* 77 (April 1960): 370–77.

"The Tax Advantages in Restoring Buildings." *Business Week* (August 1975): 91–92.

Uhlman, Wes. "Preserving Pioneer Square in Seattle." *H.U.D. Challenge* (June 1973).

Acknowledgments

Concern for our built environment and for the need to preserve at least portions of that environment is, as yet, shared by too few Americans. But the number is growing, as is progress toward making our surroundings more livable without either destroying the past or denying the future.

This book was made possible by men and women who welcomed me into the buildings that they had helped to adapt, patiently discussed them with me, and offered both information and encouragement. To compile the list from which the final choice of projects was made, I was in touch with landmarks commissions, planning commissions, historical societies, state historical preservation officers, architectural society preservation officials, state and local arts councils, individual architects, politicians, preservation activists, and concerned citizens all over the United States, as well as groups like the National Trust for Historic Preservation and the Society for Industrial Archaeology. More than 7,000 inquiries went out. Many of those who responded to my request for materials know me through my work. Many responses came from people who did not know me at all but who felt strongly that the subject was sufficiently important for them to help me collect dates, anecdotes, and photographs.

These are men and women who have chosen to rescue and restore, to pour their time, energy, and money into the imaginative conversion of buildings that might otherwise have been lost to us and who have thereby added to the architectural flavor and vitality of countless communities. All deserve praise as environmental pioneers.

For that, as well as for their efforts on my behalf, I would like to thank: Katherine Fischer

June Abrams
W. Howard Adams
Ann H. Alexander
Charles C. Arensberg
Terrell L. Armistead
R. V. Asbury, Jr.
Calvert Audrain
Roger Bacon
Steve Badanes
William Baker
Susan Baldwin
Marie S. Ball
David Barcus
Edward Larrabee Barnes
Jonathan Barnett
Ann Bartley
Paul Beard
Linda F. Becher
Brenda Becker
Lynne A. Beebe
Richard Behr
Ann K. Bennett
Perry Benson
Miles Berger
Richard Bergman
Sandra Bergman
Mrs. J. J. W. Biggars, Jr.
Mayor Michael Bilandic
Gordon Binder
Stephen Bingler
Sergio Cantino Bird
Jerome M. Birdman
John Bitterman
John Blaine
Donald Blinken
Mary Boardman
John C. Boles
Peter Borelli

Sue Bolka
Allison Booker
Mary Boyette
T. Brooks Brademas
Lenore Bradley
Susan Braybrooke
Porter Briggs
Peter Brink
Mary Broaddus
Cherry Brown
J. Carter Brown
Jerome Brown
Jonathan Brown
Robert Bruegmann
Georgiana Brush
Richard Buford
James Wood Burch
Mary R. Burchak
Alan Burnham
Tonia Burnette
Jerome Butler
Tom Caine
John Carpenter
Frank Cartwright
Ellen Cash
Brooks Cavin
Patricia Cavin
Winthrop Chamberlain
Ruth Chapman
Melisande Charles
Peter Chermayeff
Lucius M. Cheshire, Jr.
Irving Choban
Stephanie D. Churchill
Diana Clark
Robin Clawson
Christopher W. Closs
Donna S. Cobb

Marion B. Cone
Dennis J. Connors
Gayle Cook
Sylvia L. Cook
William Cook
Susan Cosgrove
Wency E. Cox
Patricia Cristol
Jean Marie Croddock
Michael F. Crowe
Abbott Cummings
Maureen E. Daly
Edward Daniels
Nancy Davis
Mike V. DeKalb
Joel Deutsch
Ed Diehl
Jean Dillon
Emily C. DiMaggio
Linda Dubro
Charles Duell
Brian Dumaine
Jack Duncan
Robert R. Dykstra
Helen M. Eccles
Kathryn B. Eckert
Mrs. Donald B. Ehrlich
Mayor Frank Einswiler
Joseph M. Eisenhut
Coco Eisman
Kamran T. Elghanayan
Mike Ellis
Arvid Elness
Cynthia Emrick
Walter J. Engstrom
Lawrence Ericsson
Mrs. John Estes, Jr.
Robert Eulich

Margaret B. Evans
Mrs. Sandige Evans
Bea Evenson
Steven Facey
J. Everette Fauber, Jr.
Carolyn Feasey
William Ferris
John L. Field
Camille Fife
Mimi Findlay
Barbara Flanagan
Ronald Lee Flemming
Margaret H. Floyd
W. Warner Floyd
Nancy A. Fogel
Roy Forrey
George Fowler
Mary Franco
Clayton Fraser
Gregory B. Free
Lynda C. Friedman
Frederick L. Fryer
Robert Garvey
Ronald Gascoyne
Tim Geis
Nina Gibans
Brendan Gill
Huntley Gill
William Lampton Gill
John Gillis
Sherman Goldin
Robert Goldstine
Mercedes Gonzales
Peter S. Gordon
Dennis Gould
Thomas Graham
Edward Gray
Leslie B. Gray
Lois M. Gray
Ronald M. Greenberg
Beverly B. Griffin
Janet Grinnell
Beth Gosvenor
Bernard E. Gruenke, Jr.
Julia Guice
Tadescu Gusseck
Charles P. Hagenah
Carl Haglund
Sandy Hale
Charles L. Hall
Ellen Hall
Lee Hall
William A. Hall
R. Philip Hanes, Jr.
Carol V. Harford
Mrs. P. W. Harrington
William Marcus Haynes
John Heimann
Mr. and Mrs. Clarence T. Hellums, Jr.
Lloyd Herman
George W. Heston
Ronald J. Hewitt
Charles E. Hilburn
Carrol C. Hill

Lewis Hill
Maxine C. Hilton
Ann Hines
Ron Holliday
Mary Bryan Hood
Charlotte Hooker
Ruth M. Hornsby
Milo B. Howard
Barb Howe
Elbert W. Hubbard
Elizabeth Hult Huffman
Carolyn Humphries
Owen D. Hungerford
Anna Belle Illien
George M. Irwin
Mary Ison
A. Iudicello
Bob Jackson
Estelle Jackson
Peter Jessup
Herbert Johnson
Walker Johnson
Wallace Johnson
Harold Jones
Susan H. Jones
Mark Junge
Donald P. Kahn
Ann Kalberg
Ron Kauffman
Eleanor R. Kaufman
Don Kearns
Elbert Keith
Patricia E. Kelley
Anna Dean Kepper
Meg Kershaw
William Kessler
Gerald M. Kimball
Lee Kimche
Carleton Knight
Trudy Kramer
Henry W. Krotzer, Jr.
Merle Krummer
Clem Labine
Albert Landa
Thomas J. Lando
Helen Lane
Oscar E. Lanford
Roger Lang
Todd Lee
Dalia Leeds
Stephen Lepp
Saundra K. Levy
Barbara Lewis
Alan Liddle
Barnett Lieberman
Chester H. Liebs
Mayor Russell Lloyd
Joseph Pell Lombardi
William L. Long
Calder C. Loth
Harry Lowe
Weiming Lu
Elizabeth A. Lyon
Dawn Maddox
Paul J. Maney

248 Grania Bolton Marcus
Frederick Marks
Peggy Marks
Christopher Martin
Edward Maryon
Robert Mayer
Joan Maynard
Mary C. Means
Laurel Meinig
Dr. Knox Mellon
Elizabeth R. Menk
John Meritt
Louise M. Merritt
Hyman Meyers
Charles A. Miller
Mrs. J. Irwin Miller
Nancy Miller
Benjamin Minifie
Norman Mintz
Terry Morton
Don Mott
James Mowry
Maria F. Murray
Nat Murrow
William J. Murtagh
Marcia Myers
Joanne McCandless
William McDonald
Galen McFadyen
Michael McGuire
Barnabus McHenry
P. G. McHenry, Jr.
Diana McKowan
Herbert McLaughlin
Gene McNulty
William McQueen
William Nagle
Lance Necker
Kris Nelson
Larry Nelson
Mark Nesbitt

Louise Nevelson
Susan Newhouse
Betsy Newman
Michael Newton
Edward B. Norris
R. Kirk Noyes
William P. O'Brien
Mayor J. J. O'Keefe
Chris Owen
Jane Owen
Paulin Pace
Tom Page
James E. Palmer
Mara Palmer
Joseph Papp
James K. Paris
Joan Patota
Bradford Paul
I. M. Pei
Lian Pei
Judy Peiser
Brian Pelletier
Paul N. Perrot
Robert Peters
Nancy A. Peterson
Carolyn Pitts
Adolf Placzek
Jan Hird Pokorny
John Poppeliers
Jack C. Porter
William J. Porter
George O. Pratt
Dorothy Quinn
Laura Rae
Bridgid Rapp
Judy Rash
Neil St. John Raymond
Marcus Rector
Beth Reiter
Jay Reiter
Geraldine Remer

Ann Vines Reynolds
Audrey Rhangos
Donald Rieshe
Peter Rippe
Tommis Robbins
James Rogers
Jonathan Rogers
Barry Rosen
Didi and Fred Rubin
Robin Rubin
Alicia Rudolf
A. B. Ryan
Cindy Sanford
J. Harvey Saunders
Alice F. Schammel
Sally Schanbacher
Ray Schuhman
Nancy B. Schwartz
Ralph Schwarz
Carolyn J. Schwenker
William Scott
Janet K. Seapker
Virginia Seemann
Dr. Jerome Selinger
Martha Senger
Randall T. Shepard
Dorothy Sherry
Sally and Jack Simmons
Donald E. Simon
Jacqueline Simon
Anne C. Simpson
Sonny Sloan
Brian Smith

G. E. Kidder Smith
Herbert L. Smith III
Justine Smith
Neil G. Smith
Peter H. Smith
Sarah Izard Smith
K. Rita Souweine
Carl Spielvogel
Alfred Staehli
I. Elizabeth Stafford
Clare Stallings
Richard Stange
Dr. Richard M. Steidle
Joseph D. Steller
E. Frank Stephenson
Joanne Stern
Michael Stern
Vance Stevens
Jack R. Stokvis
James B. Stubbins
Donald G. Sullivan
Madelyn Summers
Jane C. Symmes
Kenneth Tatman
Christine Taylor
Fanie Taylor
James C. Thomas
Benjamin Thompson
Kathleen Thompson
William M. Thompson
Jenny Thurston
Mary Ann Tighe
Stephen Tindall

Susana Torre
Andrew Trivers
Robin Tryloff
S. J. Tuminello
George Turnbull
Richard L. Turner
Mayor Wes Uhlman
Beatrice Utley
Mai F. VanArsdall
Marian VanLandingham
Lorraine Veach
Pat Walker
Roger S. Webb
Marj Weber
Harry Weese
Judy Weisman
Barbara Welanetz
Ileana Welch
William A. Werner
Erin Wheeler
David A. Wicks
Donald Winter
Helen Winter
Beatrice Wolfe
Mimi Wolk
Evans Woollen
Virginia Bagley Wright
Dwight L. Young
Margaret Young
Toni Young
Louis Zelle
Joel Zenitz
Robert Zion

There were others, but space prevents me from thanking individually each of those who furnished photographs, information, and suggestions, and from singling out contributions by the staffs of preservation groups, historical agencies, and private firms. To them I extend my thanks, too: Without their invaluable assistance this book would not have been possible.

INDEX

(Page numbers of illustrations are in italic figures.)